Supercharging the AS/400:
A Guide to Performance Management

Recent Titles in the IBM McGraw-Hill Series

Open Systems and IBM
Integration and Convergence
Pamela Gray

Risk Management for Software Projects
Alex Down
Michael Coleman
Peter Absolon

The New Organization
Growing the Culture of Organizational
Networking
Colin Hastings

Investing in Information Technology
Managing the Decision-making Process
Geoff Hogbin
David Thomas

Commonsense Computer Security 2nd Edition
Your Practical Guide to Information Protection
Martin Smith

The Advanced Programmer's Guide to AIX 3.x
Phil Colledge

The CICS Programmer's Guide to FEPI
Robert Harris

Business Objects
Delivering Cooperative Objects for Client-Server
Oliver Sims

Reshaping I.T. for Business Flexibility
The I.T. Architecture as a Common Language
for Dealing with Change
Mark Behrsin
Geoff Mason
Trevor Sharpe

Practical Queueing Analysis
Mike Tanner

MVS Capacity Planning for a Balanced System
Brian MacFarlane

Supercharging the AS/400
A Guide to Performance Management
Ron Fielder
Carolyn Machell

Details of these titles in the series are available from:

The Product Manager, Professional Books
McGraw-Hill Book Company Europe
Shoppenhangers Road, Maidenhead, Berkshire SL6 2QL
Telephone: 01628 23432 Fax: 01628 770224

Ron Fielder
Carolyn Machell

Supercharging the AS/400:
A Guide to Performance
Management

McGraw-Hill Book Company

London · New York · St Louis · San Francisco · Auckland
Bogota · Caracas · Lisbon · Madrid · Mexico · Milan
Montreal · New Delhi · Panama · Paris · San Juan
São Paulo · Singapore · Sydney · Tokyo · Toronto

Published by
McGraw-Hill Book Company Europe
Shoppenhangers Road, Maidenhead, Berkshire SL6 2QL, England
Telephone 01628 23432
Facsimile 01628 770224

British Library Cataloguing in Publication Data
Fielder, Ron
  Supercharging the AS/400: Guide to
  Performance Management
  I. Title II. Machell, Carolyn
  004.165

  ISBN 0-07-707997-3

Library of Congress Cataloging-in-Publication Data
Fielder, Ron.
  Supercharging the AS/400: a guide to performance management/Ron
Fielder, Carolyn Machell.
      p.   cm.
  Includes bibliographical references and index.
  ISBN 0-07-707997-3
      1. IBM AS/400 (Computer)–Evaluation.   2. Computer capacity–
Management.   I. Machell, Carolyn.   II. Title.
QA76.8.I25919F53
004.2'545–dc20   95-5553
                                                                                           CIP

1 2 3 4   CUP   9 7 6 5

Typeset by Paston Press Ltd, Loddon, Norfolk
and printed and bound in Great Britain at the University Press, Cambridge
Printed on permanent paper in compliance with ISO Standard 9706

Contents

IBM Series Foreword   ix
Preface   xi
Acknowledgements   xii
Trademarks   xiv
Reading this Book   xvi

PART I   INTRODUCTION TO AS/400 PERFORMANCE   **1**

1   Basic principles   **3**
  1.1   Performance management in practice   3
  1.2   What we mean by performance   5
  1.3   What controls performance?   8
  1.4   Additional interactive performance factors   13
  1.5   Client/server performance   14
  1.6   Hardware feeds and speeds   16

2   The AS/400 performance resources   **17**
  2.1   The CPU performance resource   17
  2.2   The DASD performance resource   23
  2.3   The memory performance resource   28
  2.4   The communications performance resource   31
  2.5   Other possible bottlenecks   32

3   AS/400 work management and other essential concepts   **34**
  3.1   Introduction to work management   34
  3.2   What is a job?   35
  3.3   Role of the subsystem in job creation   37
  3.4   Use of main memory   45
  3.5   Job states and transitions   48
  3.6   Paging options and alternatives   54
  3.7   Group jobs   58
  3.8   Batch jobs   60
  3.9   Single-level storage and other features of the AS/400 architecture   62

PART II   AS/400 SIZING   67

4   **Introduction to sizing**   69
     4.1   Basic principles   69
     4.2   Workload characterization   69
     4.3   Queuing   72
     4.4   Sizing objectives   79
     4.5   Manual sizing   80
     4.6   Measured workloads   83
     4.7   Predefined workloads   83
     4.8   User-defined workloads   88
     4.9   Estimation of batch run times   88
     4.10   Disk space sizing   90

5   **AS/400 performance examples**   95
     5.1   AS/400—a system for business   95
     5.2   AS/400—a mid-range system?   96
     5.3   Benchmarks in general   97
     5.4   The RAMP-C benchmarks   98
     5.5   Performance with recovery options   101
     5.6   Performance in a communications environment   105
     5.7   Save/restore performance   106
     5.8   AS/400 in a client/server environment   110
     5.9   The real world   112

6   **Use of BEST/1 for sizing**   116
     6.1   Overview of the tools   117
     6.2   Obtaining the input   122
     6.3   Sizing example   124

7   **Service-level agreements**   149
     7.1   The need for service level agreements   149
     7.2   How to establish an SLA   151
     7.3   Maintaining the service day to day   154
     7.4   Maintaining the service into the future   155
     7.5   Sample SLA on system performance   155

PART III   AS/400 SYSTEM TUNING   159

8   **Preparations for system tuning**   161
     8.1   Introduction to system tuning   161
     8.2   Action list   162
     8.3   Performance evaluation and monitoring   163
     8.4   External performance   164
     8.5   Secondary performance indicators   186

9   **Improving system performance**   189
     9.1   Documentation of initial memory usage   189
     9.2   Effect of automatic performance adjustment support   189
     9.3   Use of the Performance Tools/400 Advisor   191
     9.4   Recommended changes to the performance system values   192
     9.5   Estimation of spool and interactive pools   199
     9.6   Making the tuning changes   200
     9.7   Reassessment of system performance   201

9.8   Reassessment of CPU and disk utilization   203
9.9   Assessment of time slice values   205
9.10   Assessment of PURGE values   206
9.11   Use of separate pools for batch   206
9.12   Use of multiple pools for interactive work   208
9.13   Use of Expert Cache   210
9.14   Additional tuning for System/36 Environment users   210
9.15   Operational procedures and practice   212
9.16   Communications considerations   217
9.17   Considerations for PCs attached to the AS/400   223
9.18   Tuning a newly installed AS/400   225

10   Discriminating between applications   227
10.1   Class distinction and other systems of privilege   227
10.2   Enhancing execution priority for selected jobs   228
10.3   Providing an exclusive pool for selected jobs   229
10.4   Providing exclusive disk units for selected jobs   229
10.5   Reducing physical I/Os for selected jobs   231
10.6   Special batch considerations   233
10.7   Printing considerations   234

11   Case notes   235
11.1   Situation 1—Divided we fall   236
11.2   Situation 2—Don't lose your memory   237
11.3   Situation 3—Don't lock up your files   239
11.4   Situation 4—Don't thrash about   241
11.5   Situation 5—Keep your brain active   243

PART IV   AS/400 CAPACITY PLANNING   245

12   Performance and workload monitoring   247
12.1   Introduction to capacity planning and workload monitoring   247
12.2   When to collect the data   248
12.3   Collecting the data for capacity planning   250
12.4   Trend analysis   253

13   Producing a capacity plan   255
13.1   Selection of input data   256
13.2   Estimation of future workload   257
13.3   Use of BEST/1 for capacity planning   260

14   Preparing a business case for additional hardware   284
14.1   The detailed business case   284
14.2   The management summary   288
14.3   The never-ending cycle   288

Bibliography   289

Appendices   291
1   Useful Forms   291
2   Glossary   297

Index   305

Foreword

The IBM McGraw-Hill Series

IBM UK and McGraw-Hill Europe have worked together to publish this series of books about information technology and its use in business, industry and the public sector.

The series provides an up-to-date and authoritative insight into the wide range of products and services available, and offers strategic business advice. Some of the books have a technical bias, others are written from a broader business perspective. What they have in common is that their authors—some from IBM, some independent consultants—are experts in their field.

Apart from assisting where possible with the accuracy of the writing, IBM UK has not sought to inhibit the editorial freedom of the series, and therefore the views expressed in the books are those of the authors, and not necessarily those of IBM.

Where IBM has lent its expertise is in assisting McGraw-Hill to identify potential titles whose publication would help advance knowledge and increase awareness of computing topics. Hopefully these titles will also serve to widen the debate about the important information technology issues of today and of the future—such as open systems, networking, and the use of technology to give companies a competitive edge in their market.

IBM UK is pleased to be associated with McGraw-Hill in this series.

J. Barrie Morgans
Chief Executive
IBM United Kingdom Limited

Preface

It's an honour and a privilege to write an introduction to this book and I want to thank the authors for the opportunity. Ron and Carolyn's considerable effort has provided a significant contribution to the area of understanding AS/400 performance and I welcome them as fellow authors on the topic. This book should be one of your primary sources for performance information specifically about the AS/400 as well as for some general performance concepts and topics.

A brief review of the table of contents shows the prospective reader something of interest in many of the specific performance specialties. There's both introduction and detail for capacity planning and performance prediction. The book provides specific information about how to deal with some of the more common performance pitfalls that application design, implementation, and operations tend to encounter. They have provided a roadmap and directions through some of the intricacies of using the performance tools reports, given their lack of usability (of which I must take much of the blame for having been involved in their design a number of years ago). Unfortunately the design of many of the performance reports was driven by our immediate use and requirements and, for some of them at least, the end user interface hasn't changed much over the years.

My acquaintance with Ron and our involvement in performance goes back to the very early releases of the System/38 in the early 1980s when we first worked together. Since then the need for comprehensive performance reference material has increased as the usage and complexity of the system and its successor, the AS/400, has grown. The intent of this book is to help you to understand performance analysis without getting into a lot of the complexity, and to lead you to an understanding of what needs to be done to get the most out of your AS/400.

Rick Turner
Rochester, Minnesota, USA
August 1994

Acknowledgements

No book of this sort can be written without making use whether consciously or otherwise of the experience of others (or if it could, would be the worse for it). The authors wish to acknowledge the contributions of numerous IBM colleagues and customers with whom they have worked in the course of solving performance problems over the years. The following list is bound to be incomplete, but includes systems engineers, developers, planners and support people from many parts of the world:

Ken Allsen, Jean Bourdiaud'Huy, Rod Cheese, Kurt Eggerling, Fritz Gaebler, Debbie Hatt, Ian Hutchison, Conny Nordstrom, Tamas Palfai, Trond Russ, John Schiff, Gottfried Schimunek, Chuck Stupca, Bruce Wassell, Peter Watkins, Franz Wettstein.

Particular thanks are due to:
Les Knutson, Rick Turner (who also wrote the Preface), Bruce Wassell, Mark Williamson and Peter Watkins who reviewed the material as it was being prepared, and provided valuable suggestions for improvements; and Peter Machell who helped with the PC-related material.

Nigel Adams, John Cross, Amit Dave and Malcolm Haines for giving us access to IBM people, documents, and machine facilities, and Wayne Goodin of Earls Court and Olympia Group for 'real world' information.

IBM United Kingdom Limited for permission to use material from various documents.

Editorial, production and marketing staff at McGraw-Hill who worked with us to ensure the quality and hopefully the success of this book.

Lastly to our spouses, who suffered a certain amount of neglect while the work was being done, but supported the project throughout.

Despite all this assistance the authors remain responsible for the form and content of the book as it stands. We have done our best to extract the essence of experience gained in AS/400 performance investigation, and to explain the work management and 'internals' information which is crucial to make sense of this work. We trust that it will be a significant support to the reader whose ambition is to make his or her AS/400 users delighted with the service provided.

Trademarks

The following terms, denoted on first usage in this book by an asterisk (*), are trademarks:

Advanced Function Printing, AFP, Application System/400, APPN, AS/400, AS/400 Business Graphics Utility, AS/400 Cryptographic Support, C/400, CICS/400, Client Access/400, COBOL/400, Communications Utilities/400, IBM, ILE, OfficeVision, Operating System/400, Operational Assistant, OS/2, OS/400, OptiConnect/400, Performance Tools/400, PS/2, Query/400, Risc System/6000, RPG/400, SAA, SQL/400, System/32, System/34, System/36, System/360, System/370, S/36, S/360, System/38, S/38, are trademarks of International Business Machines Corporation.
Apple, Apple Macintosh are trademarks of Apple Computer Inc.
BEST/1 is a trademark of BGS Systems Inc.
Ethernet is a trademark of Xerox Corporation.
TPC, TPC-C are trademarks of the Transaction Processing Performance Council.
UNIX is a trademark of UNIX Systems Laboratories, Inc.
Other terms used in the book may be trademarks, and are acknowledged.

Disclaimers

References in this publication to IBM(*) products, programs or services do not imply that IBM intends to make these available in all countries in which IBM operates. Any reference to an IBM product, program or service is not intended to imply that only IBM's product, program or services may be used. Any functionally equivalent product, program or service may be used instead.

Opinions expressed and statements made in this book should not be construed as deriving from IBM or any source other than the authors. The authors have a reputation for successful consultancy and education in the AS/400(*) performance field, and have worked hard to validate the information presented in this book. However, they do not claim to be infallible, and users of the book should perhaps bear in mind that the authors also have well-earned reputations as AS/400 bigots.

Conventions

The following conventions and abbreviations are used throughout this book:

KB	1024 bytes ($= 2^{10}$ bytes)
K	Kilobytes ($= 1000$ bytes)
MB	Megabytes ($= 1\ 048\ 576$ bytes $= 2^{20}$ bytes)
M	Million bytes ($= 1\ 000\ 000$ bytes)
G	Gigabytes ($= 1000$ M)
Mhz	Megahertz ($=$ millions of cycles per second)
ms	Milliseconds ($= 10^{-3}$ seconds)
ns	Nanoseconds ($= 10^{-9}$ seconds)
bps	Bits per second
bpi	Bits per inch
tr/h	Transactions per hour

Reading this book

The book is intended mainly for AS/400 operations and technical support people, but also for users of other equipment who are considering the AS/400 platform. Anyone with a responsibility for AS/400 systems administration will want to understand performance management, and some will also need to know how to do it. Both sorts of reader should be satisfied by the material provided here.

There are a relatively small number of fundamental questions about performance management that must be answered and are answered in this book. Some of them require a lot of detailed information and explanation and others do not. Take the following questions, for example:

1. What is performance?
2. What controls performance?

If a general understanding of these matters is all you are after, then you need not read beyond Chapter 1. Should you be browsing in a bookshop, you can complete this assignment before leaving and replace the book on the shelves.

3. How do I choose the right machine configuration for my new application?

This is a question of *sizing* which is answered by Part II of the book, and the background material in Chapters 2 and 3.

4. How do I measure performance?
5. How do I decide if the performance of my machine is good or bad?
6. How can I tune my system to ensure that I am getting the best possible performance for the given workload?

These important questions relate to *system tuning*, which is the subject of Part III.

The purpose of Part IV is to answer the essential *capacity planning* questions:

7. How do I find out when growing workloads will force me to upgrade?
8. How do I decide what and how much hardware to add to my machine?

In each part of the book, if you are responsible for the relevant activity but do not have to carry out the process personally, then certain chapters can be skipped. The main 'how to do it' chapters are numbers 6, 9, 10, 12 (apart from Sec. 12.1) and 13.

When you reach the point that you have answered questions 1 to 8 by following the recommendations in this book, you can be sure that application functions are getting the performance they deserve. That is, the response times and run times are appropriate to the complexity and other characteristics of the work being run.

Whether the same functions could have been implemented more efficiently to place less demand on system resources is another question, which is beyond the scope of this book. If performance is still not meeting the needs of your users then attention should next turn to the design and coding of the applications. We intend to deal with this subject in a separate companion volume that will be of primary interest to development staff.

Providing you have tuned the system as recommended and have ensured by good planning that the machine is not overloaded, you will have succeeded in making the most of your AS/400 performance resources.

The two appendices are outside the main body of the book because they will be useful to only a subset of readers or to most readers on rare occasions.

Appendix 1 contains forms that can be copied and used as described in the text to assist in documenting performance and capacity planning information.
Appendix 2 is a glossary. Unfamiliar terms not explained in the text may be defined there.

The basis for the performance data quoted and for the screen print and report illustrations is Version 2 Release 3 of the OS/400(*) operating system, current during the production of the book. Where Version 3 Release 1 data is available and significantly different, the latter information is also given. The hardware described covers both Advanced Series and traditional AS/400 machines.

Part I
Introduction to AS/400 performance

1
Basic principles

1.1   Performance management in practice

In an ideal world this book would not be needed. Machines would be sized correctly by the manufacturer or application provider; technical support staff would tune the machine to make optimum use of the performance resources; operations staff would train users not to abuse the systems provided, and would monitor workload and performance as input to their regular capacity plan reviews. Furthermore, applications would always be designed and implemented with performance in mind, so that the machine would be the smallest and cheapest necessary to support the functions genuinely required by users.

If you have any experience in the real world of information technology you will probably agree with us that this is just another way of saying that virtually all computer installations require performance investigation and tuning activities from time to time. In those parts of the world we have visited sizing is usually imprecise (inevitably so if the software is not yet written) and human failings ensure that in the other areas also most installations fall noticeably short of the ideal. The nightmare result can be a running battle on several fronts, with the IT service providers seemingly hemmed in by angry users, importunate hardware salespeople, self-satisfied software suppliers, and demanding executive managers (Fig. 1.1).

The IBM Application System/400(*) is extremely successful in terms of number of installed machines and level of customer satisfaction, and it is high time for it to be represented and supported equally strongly in the field of computer literature. One particular need which this book intends to satisfy is for an accessible source document to bring together all the information relevant to performance management, and present it as part of a clear and logical method.

While performance is critical to the success of any computer system there are reasons why performance management may be particularly relevant to AS/400(*) users:

- It is a very productive machine for application development, so the workload on an individual system commonly increases steeply and can quickly exceed

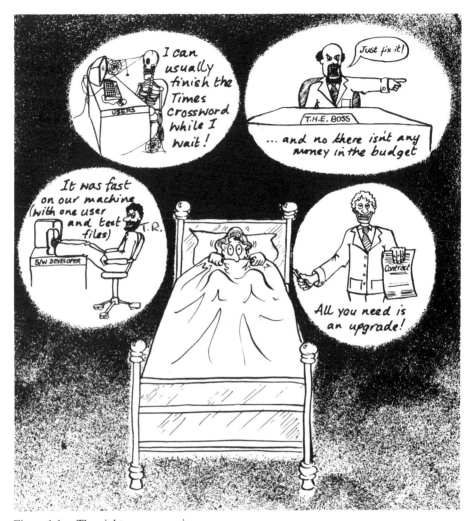

Figure 1.1.   The nightmare scenario.

the capacity of the installed model. The wide range of ready-made packages on offer multiplies this effect.

- Highly complex functions are available to application developers and end users. The correspondingly high price tags in terms of performance resource demands are often overlooked until too late.

- Many packages used on the AS/400 were developed originally for other machines with a different architecture, with the consequence that the migrated code may perform less well than native or converted applications.

- The architecture of the AS/400 system is unique and imposes its own particular constraints and preferred methods, which are different from those which apply to other machines.

We are fortunate that the available AS/400 models span a wide range of performance and throughput capabilities, and that there are effective performance management tools provided. Consequently deficiencies in performance can usually be put right without too much difficulty. All that is necessary to take control of this vital aspect of AS/400 operations is authoritative guidance. We expect that faithful followers of the methods described here who are not in the dream situation of paragraph one will avoid falling into the nightmare scenario of paragraph two.

1.2 What we mean by performance

As this book revolves around *performance* and ways to improve it we must be sure at the outset what we mean when we use the word. Normally it will refer to interactive performance, and will be measured by how long it takes for a response to be displayed on a user's terminal screen after an input key is pressed. This flow of data to the machine, the processing that goes on and the return of information to the display screen is seen as a unit by the end user. The user's experience of performance will be the corresponding response time, and the overall perception of performance will be based on a set of such responses judged against expectations.

1.2.1 Interactive transactions

If we add the end user activity (reading, thinking and keying) to the machine activity, we can visualize a continuous cycle of computer transactions arising from one end user which constitutes a dialogue with the system (Fig. 1.2). Of course, a business transaction such as entering an order can involve one or (more likely) several of these computer transactions, and it is always necessary to be clear which we are talking about when discussing transaction throughput. The performance measurement tools will deal in computer transactions but users will generally think in terms of business transactions. When the unqualified term *transaction* is used in this book, it will refer to computer transactions.

1.2.2 A user's workload

Each transaction will have its own key/think period determined by end user activity and its own individual response time. The response time is influenced primarily by:

- The amount of data transmitted and received, and the speed of the link between the user's terminal and the computer (determines transmission time)
- The processing needed to perform the function of the transaction and the speed of the central processing unit (determines CPU time)

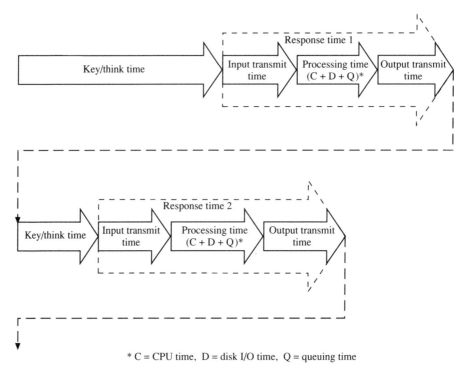

Figure 1.2.   The interactive cycle.

- The number of disk access arm (actuator) movements required to access any objects residing on the computer disk and the speed and number of disk actuators available (determines disk input/output time)
- The concurrent activity of other users competing for the same computer resources (determines queuing time).

When assessing a user's overall workload it is not generally practicable to consider individually all the different transactions the user performs. It is useful and normally sufficient to summarize this data over a period of time, in the form of averages. For example, we might find that a particular order entry clerk during a sample measurement period of half an hour had generated 90 transactions with an average response time of 1.1 seconds and an average key/think time of 18.9 seconds. This gives a useful overall picture of the activity, though we should always be aware that an acceptable looking average like this could easily hide some unacceptably long individual responses.

1.2.3   Overall system workload

The picture can be broadened by extending the averages to cover all active users. In this case we can see that the total interactive throughput in transactions per hour is a simple function of:

- The number of interactive users (N) and
- The average time taken to complete one transaction, consisting of
  average key/think time (K) plus
  average response time (R).

If K and R are measured in seconds, the average interactive cycle time will be $K + R$ seconds, and the average throughput per user is:

$$3600/(K + R) \text{ tr/h}$$

The total system throughput is then:

$$N \times 3600/(K + R) \text{ tr/h}$$

This relationship shows that if we know the number of users and the average response time, then the throughput is determined by the key/think time, and vice versa. When it comes to sizing in Part II of the book, we only have to specify one of these related items to establish the other.

1.2.4   Batch processing

While interactive performance is often of prime concern, it is also significant and sometimes critical how long a batch job or stream of batch jobs takes to complete. For example, some applications have extensive update, back-up and reporting requirements that can only start when the interactive business is closed for the day. Depending on the nature and design of the application and the size of the files involved, these activities can run for many hours.

Usually there is a natural deadline such as the end of the operator's shift, or the need for reports or files to start the next day, which must be met if severe problems are to be avoided. End-of-month processing can be particularly complex and time consuming, and may have to complete in an overnight window. Increasingly we also support PC clients who may periodically download file extracts and need to wait for this batch process to complete before they can get on with their work.

A batch job normally runs in parallel with and independently of the interactive jobs. It is used when a significant amount of processing is required which needs no interaction with the end user. Since it usually runs at lower priority than all the interactive jobs, it has only a small impact on any concurrent interactive users from the point of view of resource contention (see Sec. 3.8). However, the corollary of this is that batch jobs will be delayed if they need the CPU while any higher-priority job such as an interactive user session is using it.

1.2.5   Measuring batch performance

The performance of a batch job, which we will measure by the time from start to end, is highly dependent on the activity of any concurrent higher-priority jobs. It will also be dependent on the activity of any concurrent equal-priority batch jobs, but in a far less predictable way. For a fair measure of batch performance the job needs to be run dedicated, i.e. as the only job on the system. The essential performance characteristics of the job can then be described by:

- The elapsed time taken to complete the job, plus
- The amount of CPU time used during the run.

These figures can then be used to predict the performance of the job in other envir-onments. We will discuss in Part III of the book circumstances in which overall batch throughput can be increased by running multiple concurrent batch job streams.

1.3   What controls performance?

When exploring the subject of computer performance it is simpler to start by considering batch jobs. Interactive jobs consist of a series of transactions which in some ways can be thought of as a stream of tiny batch jobs. It is helpful to examine the case of a dedicated batch job initially and then apply the understanding gained to the more complex interactive environment.

If a batch job is running dedicated there is no possibility of contention for application objects such as database records, and no queuing for performance resources such as memory, disk actuators or the CPU. The total run time can be divided into two parts:

- The sum of all those periods during which it is using the CPU
- The sum of all those intervening periods when it is waiting for disk input or output operations (*I/Os*) to complete.

1.3.1   *Physical and logical I/Os*

There is a vital distinction to be made between physical I/Os, which are actual data transfers between disk and memory, and logical I/Os, which are program requests for data movement. No simple correlation between the two is possible.

Two examples of logical I/Os might be a direct read record by key instruction followed by an update instruction. The number of resulting physical I/Os could be zero, several or many, depending on the circumstances; and it is *physical* I/Os that matter when it comes to performance.

The read might result in two or three physical I/Os to locate the index sector containing the correct index entry (depends on the number of records in the file and the key length) followed by one further physical I/O to bring the record. On the other hand, if the index sectors and the record happen to be in memory already due to recent use (by any job in any memory partition) then zero physical I/Os will result.

The update could cause a single physical I/O to rewrite the changed record to disk. However, if the changed field(s) are part of the key of any logical files, then depending on the number of such related files, and the number of affected access paths that need to be maintained, many additional physical I/Os will be needed to make all the changes arising from the single record update.

Physical I/Os will also be required to bring into memory sections of system and user program code and program-defined variables that are not there already when needed. These are examples of *non-database* I/Os. Database I/Os involve the movement of database records or database index segments.

More reasons will be explained later, but it should already be obvious why we cannot expect to quantify the physical I/Os that will arise from a set of logical I/Os in a program. It is the physical I/Os that place a significant resource demand on the system and which count in determining performance and peak throughput. An important objective of our work will therefore be to reduce the number of physical I/Os generated by the workload. Whenever the unqualified term I/O is used in this book, physical I/O is implied.

1.3.2   Synchronous and asynchronous I/Os

A physical I/O may delay the job for which it is being performed (synchronous I/O) or may happen in parallel while the job continues processing (asynchronous I/O). An example of a synchronous I/O would occur when a program branches to an instruction that is not in memory. The job cannot continue execution until the system has brought the appropriate block of code from disk.

An asynchronous I/O can occur in advance, as when the system fetches a record or block of records before the job gets to the corresponding read instruction. It can also happen after the event, as when a job passes a block of output records to the database manager and continues executing. The records get written to disk at some later time when higher-priority jobs are not using the CPU.

The total I/O load on the system can be measured in I/Os per second. Whether they are synchronous or asynchronous from some particular job's point of view is irrelevant to the system. However, changing some I/Os from synchronous to asynchronous can clearly shorten the run time of a particular job. This will tend to increase the overall I/O rate, because the system must handle the same number of I/Os in a shorter period. Another objective of our work must be to minimize the number of synchronous I/Os arising from the workload.

1.3.3   Improving batch performance

We can imagine a commercial batch job that takes 1 hour to complete, running as the only active job on an AS/400 Model F50. The division into CPU time and disk I/O time is dependent on many factors, but let us say that the file processing is such that the job spends 18 minutes executing CPU instructions and 42 minutes waiting

CPU time	Disk I/O time

0   10   20   30   40   50   60

Minutes

Figure 1.3.   Batch run-time components (consolidated).

for disk I/Os to complete using 9332 drives (Fig. 1.3). How might we set about reducing the run time to 30 minutes or less?

1.3.4   Increasing the speed of the CPU

Since this is a hypothetical question we can assume what we like, for example that money is no object; and consider first the effect of upgrading the CPU to a Model F60, which is roughly twice as fast as the F50. This will reduce the CPU component of the run-time by 50 per cent—i.e. 9 minutes—leaving us with a run-time of 51 minutes; only a 15 per cent improvement overall. The CPU utilization, which was $18/60 = 30$ per cent on the F50 has become $9/50 = 18$ per cent on the F60, giving us some extra capacity, which we didn't really need (Fig. 1.4).

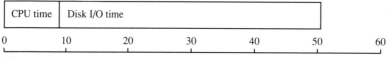

CPU time	Disk I/O time

0   10   20   30   40   50   60

Minutes

Figure 1.4.   Effect of doubling the CPU speed.

   Relative CPU speeds of current and older AS/400 models are presented and discussed in Chapter 2 (see Fig. 2.2).

1.3.5   Increasing the speed of the disks

Perhaps it would be more productive to start by attacking the larger part of the run time due to disk activity. Thinking first of the hardware approach (at least disks are relatively cheap compared to CPUs) it is now true that the various attachable disks cover a significant performance range. For example, in round numbers the average service time for one physical disk I/O is about 30 ms for a 9332 and about 20 ms for a 9336 disk. Swapping disks could therefore reduce our dedicated run-time by about $42/3 = 14$ minutes (Fig. 1.5).

CPU time	Disk I/O time

Minutes

Figure 1.5. Effect of swapping from 9332 to 9336 disks.

We will see from the comparative performance figures in Table 2.2 in the next chapter that use of 9337 DASD could reduce the run time by an even more significant margin.

1.3.6 *Improving CPU and disk utilization*

Before investing in any hardware upgrades it is worth pondering the fact that our expensive CPU and our disk access arms are currently spending most of their time doing nothing. Is there some way of making use of this spare capacity to fix the problem? The answer is yes (or we would not have asked) and it is called multiprogramming.

If our job can be replicated into four separate jobs each dealing with a quarter of the input transaction file then these jobs might run happily side by side. There would probably be some contention but it is quite conceivable that overlapping the I/Os of these four concurrent jobs could push the CPU utilization up to around 90 per cent so that the four jobs complete in about 20 minutes (Fig. 1.6). The rate at

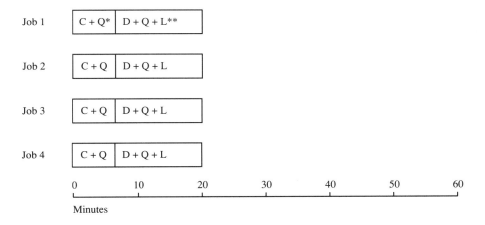

* C + Q = one quarter of original CPU time, plus some CPU queuing time

** D + Q + L = one quarter of original disk I/O time, plus some actuator queuing time plus record lock contention time

Figure 1.6. Effect of multi-programming.

which I/O requests are passed to the system would thereby be raised to three times the rate for the original dedicated job.

1.3.7   Reducing the requirement for disk I/Os

Another way to reduce the disk component of the run time would be to reduce the number of disk I/Os required to do the job. This is frequently possible and is a very effective as well as minimum cost way to reduce the overall run time. Remember that only disk I/Os for which the job has to wait count towards the run time. These are the synchronous I/Os. If we can organize our data and programs in such a way that fewer disk I/Os are required for the same function, or can make some of the

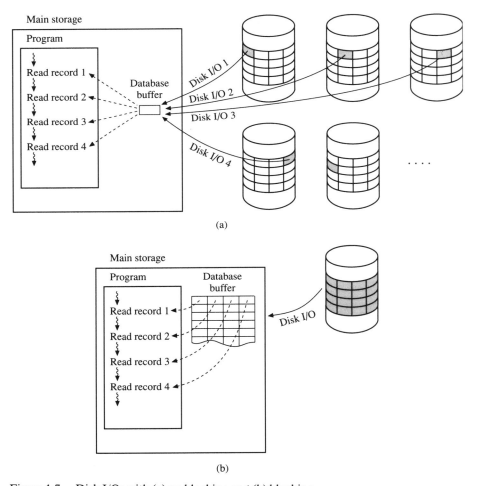

Figure 1.7.   Disk I/Os with (a) no blocking and (b) blocking.

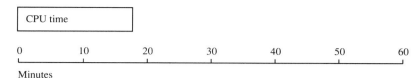

Figure 1.8.   The ultimate objective: no disk I/O delays.

synchronous I/Os asynchronous, the I/O component of the run time can be dramatically reduced.

A simple example would be to ensure that a physical input operation brings a block of pre-sequenced records into memory (see Fig. 1.7). The following series of perhaps 50 logical read instructions from the program are then satisfied without any further physical arm movements. The part of the run time due to this activity would be reduced by a large factor.

A number of practical ways to achieve this sort of reduction in I/O time are described in Part III. In an ideal situation synchronous disk I/Os can be avoided altogether, the CPU is 100 per cent utilized and the run time is just the CPU time required by the job. Any further improvement would require development effort to simplify the processing or improve the efficiency of the program design or coding (Fig. 1.8).

1.4   Additional interactive performance factors

1.4.1   Resource utilization and queuing time

When it comes to interactive performance, the basic determinant of performance is as for batch: the CPU processor time and the number of synchronous disk I/Os required to perform the function of the transaction. Because there are normally many concurrent interactive jobs competing for resources we will have to add some queuing time which transactions will usually spend waiting for the CPU or the required disk actuator to become available. They may also spend some time waiting to become active because other transactions are occupying all the available memory. See Chapter 3 for a thorough discussion of these factors.

The queuing time will depend on how busy the required resource is, which in turn will be controlled by the total level of activity on the system. How busy a resource is can be described by the average percentage utilization of the resource over a specified interval.

The average utilization resulting from a given level of activity will be reduced by increasing the speed of the resource but also by increasing the number of units of that resource on the system, e.g. the number of disk actuators or the number of main processors. This is a significant difference between interactive and batch performance. The number of disk actuators and the number of main processors is crucial in sizing for an interactive workload because of the concurrent CPU and disk I/O demands that arise. Beyond a basic small number of access arms, they are irrelevant to the performance of a dedicated batch job.

1.4.2   Transmission time

The other distinguishing feature of interactive performance is the necessity for data transmission between main memory and the terminal—an input and an output transmission for each transaction. For locally attached screens working through a workstation controller or LAN adapter the additional component of response time will be small, of the order of 0.1 to 0.2 seconds per transaction. Where the link medium is a communications line, the speed of the line may be relatively low and can become a significant factor. At 9600 bits per second the basic line time can easily add more than a second to the response, even with low utilization of the line.

1.4.3   Access conflicts

The final main factor controlling the performance of interactive jobs, and of batch jobs running in a multi-job environment, is potential conflict between concurrent jobs wishing to access the same application objects. The system will manage this activity to maintain data integrity, with the result that some jobs may be delayed while other jobs are allocated use of an object or part of an object through a system of locks.

These lock conflicts will generally be small and should contribute very little to the response time of the average transaction. They can be significant in some environments; for example where commitment control is used in the application, and multiple users are allowed to lock large numbers of records for extended periods. If lock conflicts are responsible for more than about 20 per cent of the average response time, then examination of the applications with a view to redesign or scheduling is probably worth while.

1.5   Client/server performance

The term client/server means different things to different people, but always involves a programmable workstation such as a PC (the client), cooperating to some degree with another computer (the server) to carry out an application function. The two machines will be connected through a LAN, and some additional performance considerations may apply depending on how the application function is shared.

The commonest and simplest arrangement is for the PCs to be used as dependent terminals by the AS/400. The PCs run workstation emulation software so that AS/400 applications written for 'dumb' terminals work unchanged with the client machines. The 'screen scraper' programs running on the PCs can optionally add a graphical user interface quite independent of the AS/400 application. Either way this gives the user access to PC-based and AS/400-based applications and printers through a single terminal. No new response time components are introduced.

Another common arrangement is for the client to download copies, extracts or summaries of AS/400 database files at the beginning of a session. These local disk file copies are then used by applications running on the client. From the AS/400 point of view the file downloads are batch functions. They differ from the batch jobs described earlier because, in addition to queuing for and using the CPU and disk actuators, they also queue for and use the LAN to transport data to the client.

The speed and utilization of the LAN are factors which affect the performance of the download functions. From the AS/400 viewpoint, the introduction of a relatively slow communications element in what is otherwise a file search reduces the potential for intensive I/O activity within the job. On the other hand, if a large number of users tend to download data at the same time, we will have that number of parallel batch jobs competing for resources. The system tuning must control the resulting demands (see Chapter 9).

Access to the AS/400 database is not limited to this batch copy mode. An application running on the client (which could be a PC or another machine such as an AS/400) can view, update and insert records directly using either distributed data management (DDM) or Remote SQL. Here the AS/400 is working simply as a file server, and is not involved in the processing or end-user interaction. The service time for the I/O request(s) will contribute to the user response time, but control of the other components is with the client.

Because remote I/Os involve communications time, interactive performance at the client is very dependent on the number of such I/Os per transaction and the speed of the communications link. This kind of remote data access generates additional utilization of the AS/400 disks, LAN I/O processor and CPU.

Other approaches to client/server application design are perfectly feasible in which not only the database but also the processing logic are distributed between the cooperating machines. User programs on the client and the server AS/400 communicate with each other as necessary and otherwise run in parallel. The number of such applications available today is growing, but still relatively small.

The principles involved in tuning and sizing the component machines involved in client/server activities are unchanged. However, capacity planning, which implies prediction and control of end-user performance, becomes more complex. So too do other systems management jobs (e.g. problem management, access control and availability) as well as application development. Why then choose complexity and possibly reduced performance, when simplicity and good performance are available?

One possible answer is cheapness, and if this benefit is demonstrable and significant it could justify the approach. Another reason might be to integrate applications already running on disparate platforms. We choose to remain somewhat reactionary and slow to follow this trend, preferring the simplicity and consequent lower costs of managing a single system rather than a network.

1.6   Hardware feeds and speeds

We have previously quoted some examples of hardware performance figures. A typical system configuration will contain an assortment of connected hardware devices with widely disparate operating speeds, which must be coordinated to satisfy various information processing requirements. These might include line printers, workstation printers, tape drives, communications lines and keyboard entry devices as well as disk drives and the CPU.

One of the obstacles to getting a feel for the relative speeds of these devices is that their performance figures are stated in incompatible units. Taking a few examples at random we have:

- A communications line at 9600 bps
- A 3816 laser printer at 24 pages per minute
- A 4245 line printer at 2000 lines per minute
- A 9336 disk unit data transfer rate at up to 5.7 M per second
- A 9336 disk unit I/O service time at about 19 milliseconds
- A 9348 tape drive instantaneous device rate at 763 K per second
- A processor effective instruction execution time at 10 nanoseconds

As most of us have difficulty relating to nanoseconds, it is instructive to scale up the last figure to something more meaningful in a human environment, and see how other activities around the system measure up relative to this unit. Table 1.1 shows the results of such an exercise with the figures rounded for clarity.

Table 1.1.   Relative timings

Activity	Scaled time
Processor executes 50 HLIC[a] instructions	1 second
Disk transfers 250 bytes to memory	90 seconds
Tape transfers 250 bytes to memory	10 minutes
Disk completes one I/O including actuator movement	10 hours
4245 printer prints one line	18 hours
Communications line transfers 250 bytes	6 days
3816 printer prints one page	8 weeks
User enters short response	10 months

[a]HLIC = Horizontal Licensed Internal Code

It is easy to understand from these comparisons why lots of concurrent end users, printers and disk actuators are usually needed to keep the main processor occupied, why spooling is used to make printing asynchronous, and why reducing the number of synchronous disk I/Os is so desirable.

2
The AS/400 performance resources

The prime performance resources are CPU power, disk actuators, main memory and communication lines. These AS/400 hardware items are described and evaluated in the following sections.

Given the rate at which technology advances are incorporated into the AS/400, it is inevitable that by the time this information appears in print, additional hardware options will be available. For example, processors based on RISC technology will probably have been announced. These will substantially extend the performance range of the system. However, the principles are unchanged.

We therefore invite you to add information to the performance data in this book, as IBM refreshes its AS/400 hardware offerings. IBM's own online systems are the only reliable source of current information, and the data provided here is a snapshot of this information, taken at the end of 1994.

2.1   The CPU performance resource

Here we need to compare CPU speeds. The classic measure of CPU performance is MIPS (millions of instructions per second) but this is not a useful way to compare processors unless they are executing the same instruction set. It is rather like measuring the speed of your car in rpm (engine revolutions per minute) and ignoring what gear you are in.

Depending on the gear selected, rpm translate into widely different miles per hour figures, and it is road speed that really interests drivers. Analogously, MIPS are internal measures which cannot be used to compare the effective speeds of different hardware implementations of the AS/400; and are quite useless when comparing the AS/400 with machines of different architecture (Fig. 2.1).

Other hardware measures such as cycle time or clock rate are often encountered. Cycle times are usually quoted in nanoseconds (10^{-9} seconds) and clock rates are usually quoted in megahertz (millions of cycles per second). Obviously, the time for one cycle varies inversely with the cycle speed. A clock rate of 100 Mhz is equivalent to a 10 ns cycle time and 1000 Mhz (when possible) will equate to a cycle time of 1 ns.

Figure 2.1.   Performance versus engine speed.

Such measures of CPU speed are even further removed from comparability, because different processor designs do widely different amounts of work in one cycle. Features used in AS/400 processors such as pipelining, multiprocessors, intelligent main storage, memory interleaving, store-through cache and wide data paths profoundly influence CPU performance. They provide further gearing and are not represented in any way by a cycle time or clock rate figure.

2.1.1   *Relative CPU speeds*

What is needed is a measure related to the rate at which external work is performed, i.e. some sort of standard benchmark. The most appropriate benchmark would be an interactive commercial workload, because this is most commonly the arena in which AS/400's are expected to perform. For many years IBM have used a standard workload of this type called RAMP-C (Repeatable Approach to Measuring Performance—COBOL).

The RAMP-C benchmark is outlined in Sec. 4.7 (Predefined workloads) and illustrated in Chapter 5. For our present purpose it might be criticized because the peak throughput capacity of a system derives not just from the CPU speed but from the combined primary performance resources brought to bear. However, we will see that in the RAMP-C environment, systems are generally configured with sufficient disk actuators and memory so that they will not cause a bottleneck. In these circumstances the CPU is the limiting factor, and the measured throughput is a good guide to the power of the CPU.

Table 2.1. Peak relative throughput of AS/400 models with RAMP-C workload

Models[a]	B Range	C Range	D Range	E Range	F Range	.... Advanced series		
						Model	CPU feature	Throughput capacity
X02			1.3	1.5	1.9			
X04		1.1	1.5	1.9	2.5			
X06		1.3	1.9	2.6	3.3			
X10	1.0	1.3	1.9	2.6	3.4	200	2030	2.5
X20	1.7	1.8	2.4	3.5	4.2	200	2031	4.0
X25		2.2	3.4	4.2	4.8	200	2032	6.2
X30	1.4							
X35	1.6		2.6	3.4	4.8	300	2040	4.2
X40	2.0					300	2041	6.0
X45	2.3		3.7	4.8	6.0	300	2042	7.5
X50	3.2		4.8	6.4	10.2			
X60	5.2		8.3	10.2	14.7	310	2043	12.0
X70	7.0		11.2	14.2	21.0	310	2044	20.2
X80			19.8	25.2	36.5			
X90				34.4	50.5	320	2050	25.7
X95				42.1	59.0	320	2051	45.8
X97					71.5	320	2052	71.5

[a] In these model numbers X stands for B, C, D, E or F.
Note: 16M Model B10 with maximum disk configuration = 1.0.
Results with other workloads could vary.

A benefit of an external measure like this is that it can be applied to assess the performance of any machine of whatever architecture, in terms of its ability to do useful commercial work. Also the figures are widely published in manuals, reports and technical brochures. In Table 2.1 relative CPU performance data are derived from RAMP-C benchmarks and stated relative to the power of an AS/400 model B10.

It is likely that relative power results derived from other workloads would vary slightly from these results. Although RAMP-C is 'commercial' in nature, i.e. includes a fair amount of I/O activity, it cannot be claimed to be representative of any particular installation workload.

As a further refinement of this approach, when comparing the performance of AS/400 models in the IBM performance evaluation laboratory environment, it is possible to isolate and measure the effective CPU speed directly. While still based on the instruction streams generated by the RAMP-C workload, the relative speeds deviate slightly from the tabulated comparisons based on peak interactive throughput. The direct CPU speed figures are referred to as relative internal processor performance and are presented in Fig. 2.2.

Note: The back row of Fig. 2.2 shows the eleven Advanced Series non-server models in the following sequence: 200/2030/2031/2032, 300/2040/2041/2042, 310/ 2043/2044, 320/2050/2051/2052. This does not conform to the axis labels, but it is useful to consolidate the information into one figure.

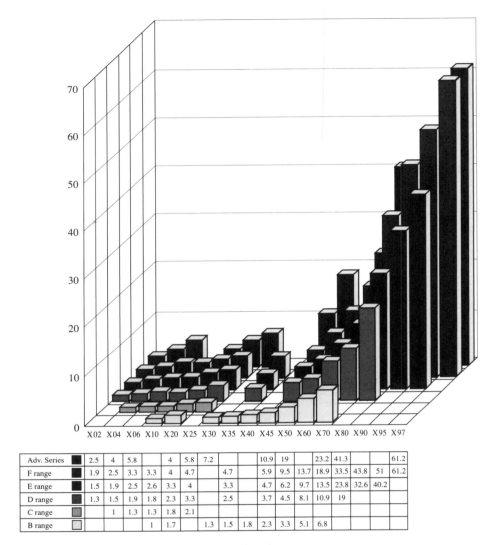

		X02	X04	X06	X10	X20	X25	X30	X35	X40	X45	X50	X60	X70	X80	X90	X95	X97
Adv. Series	■	2.5	4	5.8		4	5.8	7.2			10.9	19		23.2	41.3			61.2
F range	■	1.9	2.5	3.3	3.3	4	4.7		4.7		5.9	9.5	13.7	18.9	33.5	43.8	51	61.2
E range	■	1.5	1.9	2.5	2.6	3.3	4		3.3		4.7	6.2	9.7	13.5	23.8	32.6	40.2	
D range	■	1.3	1.5	1.9	1.8	2.3	3.3		2.5		3.7	4.5	8.1	10.9	19			
C range	▩		1	1.3	1.3	1.8	2.1											
B range	☐				1	1.7		1.3	1.5	1.8	2.3	3.3	5.1	6.8				

B C D E or F model number

Figure 2.2.   Relative internal processor performance.
16 MB B10 with maximum disks = 1.0; RAMP-C workload.

Figure 2.3 presents similar information for the server models, both traditional and Advanced Series. The servers exhibit two distinct performance ratings concurrently, depending on the type of work. They execute batch and server functions roughly three to six times faster than interactive functions.

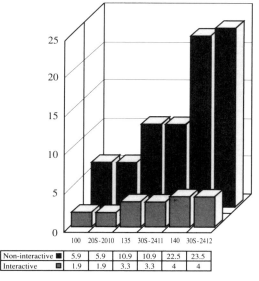

		100	20S-2010	135	30S-2411	140	30S-2412
Non-interactive	■	5.9	5.9	10.9	10.9	22.5	23.5
Interactive	▣	1.9	1.9	3.3	3.3	4	4

Model number

Figure 2.3.   Relative internal processor performance (server models).
16 MB B10 with maximum disks = 1.0.

2.1.2   Effect of CPU speed on transaction character

The figures allow us to adjust a measured transaction characteristic to see what it would look like on a different machine. Suppose a sample measured workload includes a transaction which needs 1.0 CPU seconds on a B10. On a more powerful machine the CPU demand is reduced by the ratio of the two relative performance figures. If we were considering upgrading to an F10 the CPU demand per transaction would become $1.0 \times 1/3.3 = 0.30$ seconds.

At the top end of the range the n-way processor design may also have to be taken into account, if very few jobs are running concurrently. All traditional non-server models up to and including the X70 models have a single main processor. The X80s have two X70 processors, the X90s have three X70 processors and the X95s have four. The overhead of coordinating the activities of multiprocessors means that the net performance (shown in Table 2.1) diverges progressively further from the ideals of twice, three times and four times the X70 performance as extra processors are added. The server model 140 has a two-way processor.

The F97 is a four-way processor, like the X95s, but the component processors are significantly faster than the F70. All the processor features in the Advanced Series are single processors except as follows.

Two-way processors:	310/2044 30S/2412	320/2051
Four-way processors:	320/2052.	

One effect of this design is that a single dedicated job with no opportunities for parallel processing will run no faster on, say, an F95 than on an F70. To take advantage of the additional processing power we must have concurrent activities; either a normal interactive workload or multiple batch streams.

A useful feature of the multiprocessor machines is that a top-priority job is prevented from monopolizing the whole system. We could have a batch job stream running at higher than interactive priority to perform urgent batch functions, and still ensure that one or more processors are available for interactive work. The disk I/Os generated by the batch job could, however, have an additional impact on performance (see Sec. 3.8).

2.1.3   CPU packaging

The CPU models are managed by the same operating system, so that identical function is provided throughout the range, and applications can be moved between different models without change. The hardware is packaged in different ways for flexible growth at the medium- and high-performance end, plus low-cost entry-level performance.

The larger models are identified by the machine type number 9406. AS/400 traditional models X30 and upwards are 9406 machines, mounted in 1.6 metre high racks which are extended laterally by connecting as many secondary racks as are needed to house the selected hardware. The Advanced Series 9406 machines are packaged into much smaller modular towers. Rack-mounted peripherals formerly used with a traditional model can be connected to the new towers (with some exceptions).

Engineers may wish to know that the racks conform to the EIA (Electronic Industries Association) RS-310-C standard and provide 32 EIA units of vertical mounting space (one EIA unit equals 1.75 inches). The racks provide sequenced power on and off supplies, overcurrent protection, operator panels and acoustic noise reduction for the mounted units.

The traditional 9402 and 9404 machines are designed to operate in a quiet office environment and are supplied as compact boxes which will fit unobtrusively under a desk (Fig. 2.4). AS/400 models X02, X04 and X06 come in the 9402 system unit and models X10, X20 and X25 come in the somewhat wider 9404 unit. The Advanced Series 9402 machines are again packaged in a new compact tower. Traditional 9404 machine types can be upgraded to either Model 200 or Model 3XX processors and hence can be mounted in either of the towers.

Hardware upgrades occur only within machine type, e.g. a change from F10 to F25 is a simple field upgrade, whereas a change from F25 to F35 requires complete replacement of the hardware. Similar considerations apply to upgrades from 200 to 3XX models.

In performance terms the Advanced Series covers much the same range as the FXX models with a smaller number of intermediate processor options. As usual,

Traditional models ————————————————→   Advanced Series – – – – – – – –→

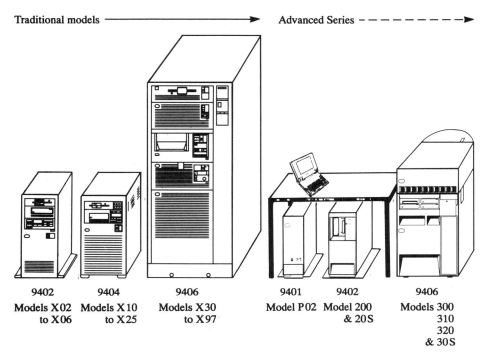

9402	9404	9406	9401	9402	9406
Models X02	Models X10	Models X30	Model P02	Model 200	Models 300
to X06	to X25	to X97		& 20S	310
					320
					& 30S

Figure 2.4.   Traditional and Advanced Series AS/400 machines.

the latest hardware offers significant price–performance improvements. There is
also a large overlap in performance between the 200 and 300 models. Presumably,
increased absolute performance at the top end of the range will also be delivered to
Advanced Series users, by installing expected new processor technology in the
current boxes.

2.2   The DASD performance resource

A variety of DASD (direct access storage devices) are provided by IBM and other
vendors to complement the AS/400 range. Each device has its own characteristic
performance and storage attributes. From our viewpoint it is primarily the disk
I/O service time and the number of actuators which are relevant.

As terminology can become a little confusing when describing disk devices,
especially when multiple generations of hardware technology exist side by side, we
will explain our usage at the outset:

• The rotating magnetizable disk used to store information is a *disk*. Other terms
  used elsewhere for this item include *file*, *hard disk*, *drive* and *HDA* (head and
  disk assembly).

- The moveable arm with its read/write head used to retrieve and store information on the disk is an *actuator*. Another term for this is *access arm*.
- The combination of the above two functional parts is a *DASD*. A DASD contains one disk plus one or more actuators.
- Where multiple DASD plus disk controllers can be bundled into a single package we need another term in the hierarchy to describe the result. We will use *disk subsystem* to refer to these items, and bear in mind that the term *disk unit* is sometimes also applied.

2.2.1   Sample disk configuration

Figure 2.5 shows a possible mixed DASD configuration attached to an AS/400 model F45, as an illustration of some of the options documented in the following tables. There is a hierarchy which starts from two buses and fans out through five IOPs (I/O processors), 14 disk controllers, 28 DASD and ends with 40 actuators.

Service times range from 10.7 ms to 29.4 ms. In general, the I/O service time will be the sum of actuator seek time for moving the access arm to the required track, rotational delay (latency) waiting for the required disk sector to arrive at the read/write head, plus relatively small increments to transfer the data through the disk controller, IOP and bus. Note that when we quote I/O service times in this book they include all the above components and are based on the following assumptions:

- No queuing for the actuator.
- 80 per cent 1/3 seek and 20 per cent 0 seek.
- 70 per cent read and 30 per cent write.
- 3.5 K transfer size.
- 70 I/Os per second or less through the I/O processor.

No attempt is made to estimate the potential performance enhancement provided by read cache buffering on the 9336 and 9337 devices, nor the possible degradation resulting from write overheads with some 9337 HA (high availability) models. See notes (b), (d) and (e) to Table 2.2 for further information on these points.

Like all 9406 D, E and F models, the F45 has two integrated disk devices forming part of the base system and attached through the base multi-function IOP. Other disk devices are optional, and depending on the device type may be aggregated into a set of up to eight devices within a single rack-mounted subsystem.

Disk subsystems or units usually contain their own integral controller(s) whereas in the case of 9335 DASD, controllers are separate rack-mounted items. Each 9336 subsystem consists of up to four DASD and a disk controller, integrated into a single rack-mountable drawer. The disk subsystem is connected to one of the system buses through an IOP interface.

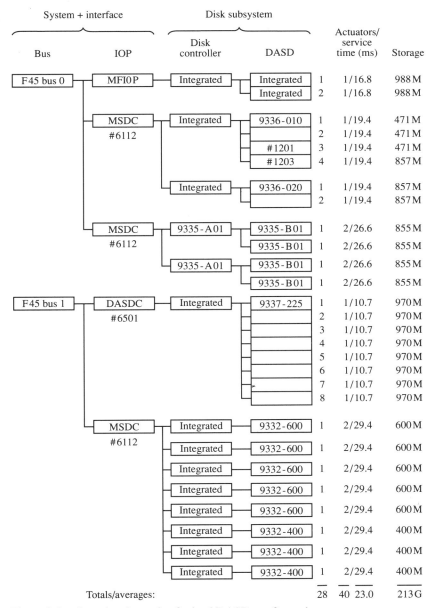

Figure 2.5. Sample schematic of mixed DASD configuration.

The particular I/O processor used here is called an MSDC (magnetic storage device controller) which is an optional feature (#6112) of the system and supports up to two 9336 subsystems. The MSDC will alternatively support up to four 9335 controllers (eight DASD) or one rack of 9332s (eight DASD). Device types cannot be mixed on the same MSDC.

There may be configuration limitations at each level in the DASD → controller → IOP → bus hierarchy depending on the particular devices and AS/400 models we are considering. Useful reference information about the AS/400 disks supplied by IBM is presented next in a series of tables. Equivalent performance information for disks supplied by other manufacturers should be sought from the vendor.

2.2.2   DASD characteristics

The DASD and disk subsystems portrayed in Table 2.2 are attachable to AS/400 9406 traditional models and, except as noted in note (c), to Advanced Series 3XX models, when an appropriate IOP is provided.

Table 2.2.   DASD for Model 3XX and 9406 traditional AS/400 systems

Machine or feature #	Models	Number of DASD min/max[a]	Capacity per disk	I/O service time (ms) Ver 2 h/w[b]
9332[c]	200/400/600	1/1	200M/400M/600M	29.4
9335[c]	B01	1/1	855M	25.1
9336	010/020	2/4	471M/857M	19.4
	025	4/4	857M	16.7
9337	010/020/110/120[d]	2/7	542M/970M	19.0
	040/140[d]	4/7	1.97G	17.1
	015/115[d]	2/7	542M	15.0
	025/125[d]	2/7	970M	16.6
	210/220[e]	2/8	542M/970M	12.1
	240[e]	4/8	1.96G	11.0
	225[e]	2/8	970M	10.7
	215[e]	2/8	542M	9.5
	420[e]	4/8	970M	N/A
	440[e]	4/8	1.96G	N/A
	480[e]	4/8	4.19G	N/A
#2800[f]		4/4	320M	19.5
#2801[f]		2/4	988M	16.8
#2802[f]		2/4	1.03G	13.5
#4606[g]		N/A	1.96G	N/A
#4607[g]		N/A	4.19G	N/A

[a] Each DASD has one actuator except in the cases of 9335 and 9332 models 400 and 600 which have two actuators per disk.

[b] Disk service times are based on the assumptions listed in Topic 2.2.1. Additional performance considerations may apply and are not factored into the figures. For example, 9337 DASD controllers have read ahead buffers which store data from recent I/Os for each actuator. Depending on the pattern of data access, this can significantly improve on the quoted average service time.

[c] 9332 and 9335 DASD cannot be connected to Advanced Series machines.

[d] The 1XX models are high-availability models which implement RAID-5 architecture, to protect against a single drive failure per subsystem. A minimum of four drives is required in these models. The effective storage capacity is reduced by the equivalent of one drive per subsystem. Each write operation to a 9337 model 1XX results in four I/Os of which three *may* be carried out asynchronously by the device. The quoted service time can be significantly exceeded for these models if many concurrent write operations are issued to the device, causing high utilization of the write assist disk (WAD).

[e] These 'high-performance' models can be switched between normal and high availability (HA) mode. In HA mode the RAID-5 protection is similar to that described under note (d), but the potential write overhead is virtually eliminated by use of a write cache supported by a back-up non-volatile write cache. Only in extreme cases, for example when there are sequences of hundreds of writes to a single IOP in a short time, will HA mode result in performance degradation.

[f] These internal DASD are available with 9406 D, E and F models.

[g] These integrated DASD are available with Advanced Series models.

Table 2.3. DASD for Advanced Series and traditional 9402/9404 systems

Disk capacity		315M	320M	400M	988M	1.96G	1.03G	4.19G
Number of actuators		1	1	1	1	1	1	1
Attachable	Advanced series		Y	Y	Y	Y	Y	Y
to these	E and F	Y	Y	Y	Y	Y	Y	
AS/400	D	Y	Y	Y				
models	B and C (9404)	Y	Y					
	C (9402)		Y					
I/O service times (ms)[a,b]			17.7	16.6	15.6	10.5	10.1	N/A
[c]			17.7	16.6	15.6	14.0	13.5	
[d]		32.0	18.9	17.8	16.8	14,2	13.5	
[e]		35.1	24.4	23.2	N/A	N/A	N/A	
Device buffer space[f]		None	64K	128K	256/512K	512K	512K	N/A

[a] These service times are based on the assumptions listed in Sec. 2.2.1.
[b] These numbers apply when the disk is connected to the #6502 I/O processor, which can attach to any Advanced Series box. This IOP combines the functions of an IOP and a DASD I/O controller. It also has a write cache which is used only for the 1.96G and 1.03G DASD. Note that 1.03G and 1.96G disks attached to the #6502 IOP can be RAID-5 protected, giving an inexpensive high-availability option for the smaller Advanced Series machines otherwise only available to 9406 machines.
[c] These numbers apply when the disk is connected to the #6530 I/O processor, which can attach to any Advanced Series box. This IOP combines the functions of an IOP and a DASD I/O controller.
[d] These numbers apply when the disk is connected to the following I/O processors: #2624 SDC, E or F Models MFIOP, D02 or D25 Models MFIOP, #9152 or #9153 MFIOP.
[e] These numbers apply when the disk is connected to the following I/O processors: #2600 MFIOP, Models D04, D06, D10 or D20 MFIOP, Ver 1 B or C Models IOPs.
[f] Depending on the pattern of I/O requests, the device buffer space can significantly reduce the need for physical actuator movements. In the four largest devices the buffers are divided into multiple logical areas that are managed by the DASD controller.

Similar information is given in Table 2.3 for the various DASD attachable to the AS/400 9402 and 9404 Model 200 systems. These disks are not identified by separate machine numbers, but are ordered as features of the base system (e.g. feature #6109 is a 400M disk drive on an F20).

Table 2.4. Maximum capacity of one rack

Machine	Model	Number of disk units per rack	Number of actuators per unit/rack	Rack storage capacity
9332	600	8	2/16	4.8G
9335	B01	4	2/8	3.4G
9336	020	6	4/24	20.2G
9337	110/115	6	7/42	19.5G
	010/015	6	7/42	22.7G
	120/125	6	7/42	34.9G
	020/025	6	7/42	40.7G
	140	6	7/42	70.8G
	040	6	7/42	82.6G
	210/215	6	8/48	25.9G
	220/225	6	8/48	46.5G
	240	6	8/48	94.5G
	420	6	8/48	46.5G
	440	6	8/48	94.5G
	480	6	8/48	201.1G

In the case of rack-mounted disks it is informative to consider the rack space needed to hold the selected DASD. Table 2.4 shows how much you can pack into one standard 1.6m rack using a selection of the available disk types.

The rate and direction of technology advance is well illustrated by these tables. A rack of 9337s can now offer 201G of storage. Five years ago we would have had to buy 60 racks of 9335s to equal this. Assuming our AS/400 could support the number of devices (and our floor could support the weight) we would have had 480 actuators to seek over our data compared to only 48 (much faster ones) today.

It is clear that the maximum number of actuators and the maximum storage capacity for a given AS/400 model cannot normally be achieved together. The process of sizing should be based first on the number and speed of actuators required to give satisfactory performance. The precise choice of disk subsystems is then concluded from the storage capacity required, and the approach to be taken over availability (whether disk mirroring or RAID technology will be employed).

2.2.3   DASD configuration limits

An IOP requires a card slot in one of the buses. The number of buses and associated I/O card slots is model and feature dependent, and they are used for all sorts of I/O interfaces including workstation controllers and communications controllers. Potentially therefore the need for other devices could limit the disk configuration, or more likely vice versa.

In practice, there are generally plenty of slots for configuration requirements. For example, on the F35 there is a maximum of 55 I/O slots on the buses and bus extensions, while on an F95 or F97 fully configured with additional buses and extensions there are 195 slots. The maximum number of disk IOPs allowed is a much smaller number in each case, but allows for a large disk configuration. See Table 2.5 for details.

2.3   The memory performance resource

Jobs cannot use the primary performance resources (CPU and disk actuators) until they are partially resident in memory. Sufficient main storage to accommodate the essential working parts (working sets) of all jobs ready to become concurrently active is therefore desirable. We will see in Sec. 3.4.4 how access to a memory pool is controlled at an appropriate concurrency (activity) level, and how excess jobs are queued by the system.

Memory utilization is clearly very different from CPU or disk actuator utilization in that it takes place in parallel with these other activities and adds nothing to the response time or batch run time. Only queuing for memory will directly impact performance. Nevertheless, memory is equally important and for a number of reasons system performance is very sensitive to memory availability:

Table 2.5. DASD configuration limits for AS/400 models

Traditional 9402/9404 and smaller Advanced Series models	Maximum buses/I/O adapter slots	Maximum DASD IOPs	Maximum actuators/storage	Traditional 9406 and larger Advanced Series models	Maximum buses/I/O adapter slots	Maximum DASD IOPs	Maximum actuators/storage
100	2/6	1	8/8.20G	135	2/6	2	16/27.5G
20S	1/5	1	12/23.60G	140	3/11	3	26/47.2G
				30S	5/64	3	26/86.5G
200	1/6	1	12/23.60G	310	5/115	16	68/149.5G
300	2/45	6	28/55.10G	320	7/151	28	128/259.6G
D02	1/1	0	3/1.20G	B30/B35	1/14	2	32/13.7G
E02	1/1	0	2/1.97G	B40/B45	1/24	2	32/13.7G
F02	1/1	0	2/2.06G	B50	2/39	5	64/27.4G
C04/C06	1/3	0	4/1.28G	D35/D45	2/55	6	68/65.7G
D04/D06	1/3	0	4/1.60G	E35/F35	2/55	6	68/67.2G
E04	1/3	0	4/3.95G	E45/F45	2/55	6	68/67.2G
F04	1/3	0	4/4.12G	B60/B70	3/71	8	132/54.8G
B10/C10	1/4	1	6/1.92G	D50	3/84	9	132/97.0G
E06	1/7	2	8/7.90G	E50	3/84	9	116/98.3G
F06	2/7	2	8/8.24G	F50	5/140	16	116/114.3G
B20	2/7	2	12/3.84G	D60/D70	5/140	16	180/144.4G
C20/C25	2/9	2	12/3.84G	E60/F60	5/140	16	180/145.8G
D10/D20	2/9	2	12/4.80G	E70	5/140	16	180/145.7G
D25	2/9	2	16/6.40G	F70	7/195	28	180/255.8G
E10/E20	2/9	2	12/11.85G	D80	7/196	28	254/254.5G
F10/F20	2/9	2	12/20.60G	E80/90/95	7/196	28	254/255.8G
E25	2/9	2	12/19.67G	F80/90/95	7/195	28	254/255.8G
F25	2/9	2	12/20.60G	F97	7/195	28	254/255.8G

Notes:
A variety of DASD IOPs are attachable, and the choice is controlled by the model of AS/400 and the type of disk units selected. The maximum number tabulated assumes 9337 model 2XX disk subsystems are chosen where available. The base multi-function IOP (MFIOP) is not included.
The 9406 D and E models have internal storage of 1.28G associated with 4 × 320M DASD as part of the base system. The 9406 F models have internal storage of 2.06G associated with two of the 1.03G DASD. An optional 2 × 1.03G disks can be added to the internal storage of the F models. The totals quoted above include the internal DASD.
The maximum storage figures quoted for the traditional models does not take account of the option to attach 9337 model 480 subsystems, announced as this book went to press.

1. As with any serving arrangement, if the utilization becomes very high the queuing time escalates beyond acceptable bounds.
2. The working set size of the average transaction must be accommodated, multiplied by the required activity level. The more complex the transaction, the greater generally is the working set size.
3. More complex transactions also spend longer in memory using the CPU and disks, and therefore increase the level of concurrency required for a given transaction throughput. Increasing complexity therefore has a double effect on memory demand.
4. Any attempt to reduce queuing by increasing the activity level *without adding memory* will simply introduce extra non-productive paging as the concurrent jobs steal each other's active pages. This particular cure is always worse than

Table 2.6. Main storage sizes for AS/400 models

Traditional 9402 and smaller Advanced Series models	Memory sizes: min/max (MB)	Traditional 994 and medium Advanced Series models	Memory sizes: min/max (MB)	Traditional 9406 and larger Advanced series models	Memory sizes: min/max (MB)
200 #2030	8/24	300 #2040	8/72	310 #2043	64/832
200 #2031	8/56	300 #2041	16/80	310 #2044	64/832
200 #2032	16/128	300 #2042	32/160	320 #2050/1/2	128/1536
100	16/56	135	32/384	140	64/512
20S #2010	16/128	30S #2411	32/384	30S #2412	64/832
C04	8/12	B10	4/16	B30	4/36
D02/D04/C06	8/16	C10	8/20	B35/B40/B45	8/40
D06	8/20	B20	4/28	B50	16/48
E/F02/E/F04	8/24	D10/C20	8/32	D35/E35	8/72
E06/F06	8/40	E10/D20/C25	8/40	F35/D/E/F45	16/80
		D25	16/64	B60	32/96
		F10/E20	8/72	D50/E50	32/128
		F20/F25/E25	16/80	B70	32/192
				F50/D60/E60	64/192
				D70/E70	64/256
				D80	64/384
				F60	128/384
				E80	64/512
				F70	128/512
				F80	128/768
				E90	64/1024
				F90	128/1024
				E95	64/1152
				F95	128/1280
				F97	128/1536

the original disease. The additional I/Os increase the apparent complexity of the workload, and performance deteriorates.

5. Main storage is also required for system tables and functions, transient routines and other concurrent activities such as spool writers and batch jobs. Guidance on estimating for this is given in Chapter 9.

In Chapter 3 we will describe a range of system facilities and work management options which modify the way memory is used. These include subdivision of main memory into partitions, to isolate different types of work; sharing of memory between jobs and across partition boundaries; and methods to optimize the occupancy of memory by database and non-database objects.

Each AS/400 model has a range of permissible main storage sizes. The limits are listed in the Table 2.6. There is also a quantity of high speed control storage accessible only to system microcode. Each model will have its own type and quantity of control storage which is fixed by the designers, and is not shown in the table. The crucial effect of memory availability in controlling performance is explained through a quantitative example in Chapter 4.

2.4 The communications performance resource

Workstations can be attached locally or remotely through a variety of transmission media to AS/400 communications adapters and I/O controllers. The number and speed of the communications facilities available will influence the data transmission time between workstation user and main storage which we identified in Chapter 1 as a component of interactive response times.

Local connections are often via twin-axial cable into AS/400 local workstation controllers. These are I/O processors that occupy an I/O card slot on a system bus

Table 2.7. Workstation attachment facilities on the AS/400 models

Traditional 9402/9404 and Advanced Series server models	Maximum local 5250 W/Ss	Maximum LAN adapters	Maximum communication lines	Traditional 9406 and Advanced Series models	Maximum local 5250 W/Ss	Maximum LAN adapters	Maximum communication lines
D02/E02	14	1	3	B30/B35	160	4	16
C04	14	1	5	D35	240	4	16
F02/D04	28	1	8	B40/B45	240	4	32
B10/C10	40	1	8	E35	360	4	20
E04	42	1	8	D45/B50	400	4	32
C06	54	1	5	F35	480	4	20
D06	54	1	8	E45	480	4	33
F04	68	1	8	D50/B60	600	4	32
E06	68	2	14	F45/E50	720	4	33
B20/C20/C25	80	2	14	D60/B70	800	4	48
D10/D20	80	2	14	F50/E60	1,000	4	33
F06	108	2	14	D70	1,200	4	48
E10/D25	160	2	14	F60/E70	1,400	4	49
E20	160	2	20	D80	2,000	4	64
E25	240	3	26	E80/90/95	2,400	6	64
F10	360	2	14	F70/80/90/95	2,400	6	64
F20	360	4	20	F97	4,800	8	96
F25	360	4	26	200	280	2	20
100/20S	7	2	8/20	300	1,000	4	33
135	7	4	14	310	2,400	6	64
140/30S	7	6	20/33	320	4,800	8	96

Notes:
5250 workstations are attached to local workstation controller ports through twin-axial cable. The workstation cable-through facility allows up to seven devices to be 'daisy-chained' into one port. Alternative workstation controllers permit local attachment of a smaller number of ASCII devices. Another workstation controller (not possible on B and C models) allows direct attachment of LocalTalk terminals. Each LocalTalk adapter connects up to 31 devices, and the number of adapters supported ranges from one on the F02 and 20S models up to 120 on the F97 and 320 models. Each LAN adapter can be either an IBM token ring or an Ethernet adapter. The IBM token ring adapters attach to one 16M bps or 4M bps token ring network. A subset of the maximum number of LAN adapters may be FDDI adapters which connect to a 100M bps LAN. A dual purpose File Server IOP counts as two LANs and provides high-performance PC access to AS/400 files plus normal token ring or Ethernet connection facilities.
A wireless LAN can be used to provide IBM token ring or Ethernet connectivity over radio links for PC users who are mobile, or where normal cabling is impossible or expensive.
Each line can support multiple remote control units, and each control unit (depending on the model) can support up to 28 non-programmable workstations or up to 40 programmable workstations, or a mixture. The line can be operated at up to 19.2K bps using a V.24 interface, or up to 64K bps using an X.21 or an ISDN interface. Maximum speeds through a V.35 interface are protocol dependent.
The communications line maxima are subject to the limitation that the aggregate speeds of all concurrently active lines going through one IOP should not exceed the capacity of the IOP. They are also subject to system limits on high-speed lines. A high-speed line is a communications line operating at a rated speed of 48 000 bps or greater.

and the most common ones can each support up to forty 5250 type displays or printers. Intelligent workstations may alternatively be connected via IBM token ring or Ethernet(*) LAN (local area network) adapters. In either case the hardware speeds are such that data transmission time is likely to add only a few tens of milliseconds to the response time.

It is quite different when the transmission link is a communications line running at a typical speed of 9600 bps. If we round this to 10 000 bps and make a rough adjustment for protocol overheads by assuming each byte transmitted contains 10 bits, the net transfer rate is about 1000 bytes per second, assuming no queuing.

A full-screen format can easily require 1000 bytes (equivalent to one second of dedicated line time) or more to be sent. The return traffic is generally much smaller, but can also be large in some situations, e.g. when use of help or group jobs facilities causes the current screen format to be saved.

Modem turnaround time and polling delay will add a further 0.1 second or so to the transmission time, which is already a significant part of remote interactive response times. Use of slower lines will multiply the transmission component, and a 2400 bps link could easily result in 4 seconds or more being added to response times relative to the experience of local users.

The workstation attachment facilities provided by the different AS/400 models are summarized in the Table 2.7.

2.5 Other possible bottlenecks

We have seen how devices such as disks and communication lines attach to the system through IOPs, with multiple devices funnelling into one IOP. A variety of IOPs may be used and each has a limited throughput capability. In general, the IOPs are designed to be fast enough for the number and speed of attachable devices, but it is possible in some configurations for the IOP speed to limit the performance of devices.

Table 2.8. AS/400 disk IOP service times

IOP feature #	Service time (ms)	Maximum DASD attachable	IOP feature #	Service time (ms)	Maximum DASD attachable
2507/2600	3.7	4	6501	0.3	16
2611	1.4	7	6502	1.7	16
2615	1.4	4	B502	1.7	8
2624	1.4	6	6522/6523	N/A	N/A
2642/2643	3.7	4	6530	0.5	16
2651	1.4	4	B530	0.5	8
6110	2.7	8	9143/9144	1.4	4
6111/6112	1.4	8	9145/9146	1.4	3
6500	1.4	7	9152/9153	2.0	4
			9171/2/3	2.0	4

It does make sense therefore to configure your machine with the devices spread over the available IOPs to even out the IOP utilizations. Similar considerations apply to multiple disk units attached to one disk controller and multiple workstations attached to one remote control unit. Table 2.8 lists the AS/400 disk and multifunction IOPs and estimates their contributions to overall I/O service times. The figures are those used by the capacity planning tool (see Chapter 6) and incorporate assumptions about the effects of features such as write cache where appropriate.

3
AS/400 work management and other essential concepts

3.1 Introduction to work management

The AS/400 has a unique architecture, and its own way of doing things. It was designed to manage multiple concurrent jobs of different types, including, of course, batch and interactive, with the emphasis on promoting good performance for interactive commercial workloads. To do this well the system must have flexible and efficient methods for sharing out its performance resources.

The methods used to share resources are known as *work management*. If we wish to tune the system to optimize some aspect of performance, then we will do so by intervening in the work management processes. It follows that a good understanding of work management and some of the underlying structures is desirable if changes to the default arrangements are to be beneficial.

The purpose of this chapter is to provide the necessary background information, in preparation for the system tuning tips presented in Chapters 8–10, and life with the AS/400 in general. Where material in this chapter relates directly to tuning advice given in later chapters, the words 'tuning point' are inserted in parentheses.

Illustrations of system display panels assume that the standard system interface is used. This is obtained by having the value 'ASTLVL(*INTERMED)' in your user profile when you sign on. A profile value of 'ASTLVL(*SYSVAL)' will also suffice if the QASTLVL system value is set to '*INTERMED'.

3.1.1 The purpose of subsystems

Some system resources like disk drives, CPU(s), and printers are managed centrally and made available to any job on a system-wide basis. Other resources such as memory pools and the potential sources of work such as workstations and job queues are split into groups, and each group is managed by a different *subsystem*.

A subsystem is an environment for running jobs, and each subsystem has its own system management job called a *subsystem monitor*. The monitor is responsible within its own subsystem for job initiation and termination, and for some other job-related functions.

The subsystem environment includes a subset of the system memory and of the various potential sources of work. It also has facilities for initiating and running jobs. Jobs are partially isolated within their different subsystems, but still receive many services direct from central system-wide resources. The obvious analogy in politics is a system where central government has ultimate control and deals directly with individuals (e.g. when collecting taxes), but delegates responsibility for some services (rubbish collection, perhaps) to semi-autonomous local authorities, financed by a share of central funds.

By running different sorts of work and possibly different groups of users in different subsystems it becomes easier to control their use of the system independently. We will be looking at some details of how the subsystem monitors do their work in a moment, after we have examined an even more fundamental concept which we have used so far without explanation: the *job*.

3.2   What is a job?

A job is a uniquely identified temporary entity which consumes resources and performs work for a user. It is a bundle of related items (storage for variables, control blocks, file buffers and the like) through which processing requests are mediated, and is seen as an independent unit of work by the system. Any user activity and some of the system activity on the machine belongs to one or other particular job out of the set of jobs in the system.

3.2.1   Tracking jobs

At any moment there may be tens, hundreds or even thousands of jobs running concurrently, new jobs may be starting, and others may be terminating. A user job is created through one of a set of possible mechanisms described shortly. The job then remains known to the system throughout the following phases:

1. During the time it may spend waiting to get started
2. While it is active
3. After termination until all job related items are cleared.

A batch job may wait on a job queue for any length of time before becoming active. For instance, it may be in 'HELD' status, or the job queue may be held, or the job queue may not be associated with an active subsystem. If these obstacles are not in place, the job gets initiated after it reaches the front of its queue. Controlling factors include the job's scheduling priority, the sequence number of the job queue entry in the subsystem, and activity level settings for the queue.

Any job which produces a spool file will remain in the system list indefinitely if the spool file is not printed or deleted. The way jobs are tracked is that each job known to the system has an entry in the WCBT (work control block table). The WCBT entry contains some information about the job plus pointers to other job-related structures used to control the job. Depending on the rate at which new jobs are created, and the system management procedures for clearing old jobs from the system, the WCBT can become quite large (*tuning point*).

The current number of entries in the WCBT is seen on the WRKSYSSTS display against the prompt 'Number of jobs in system'. The initial number of entry slots allocated in the table is controlled by the system value QTOTJOB and this is extended as necessary by the value in QADLTOTJ (*tuning point*).

In general, jobs are only performing useful work and actively consuming system resources during a part of their life cycle within the system. A separate much smaller table containing entries for currently active jobs is maintained by the system in addition to the WCBT. The current number of entries in the active jobs table is seen at the top of the WRKACTJOB display. The initial and incremental sizes of this table are controlled by the system values QACTJOB and QADLACTJ (*tuning point*).

3.2.2   *Job attributes*

The temporary job structure created by the subsystem monitor for a new job contains a large number of parameters or attributes whose values influence how the job is allowed to do its work. Examples are execution priority number, output spool queue name, and accounting code. The job gains its initial attributes from a set of three permanent system objects referenced during job creation. Each job must be associated with one specific *user profile*, one nominated *job description*, and one selected *class*.

These three object types and the way they are selected and combined during the creation of a job are described in the next section. In the case of some attributes, the object which could supply a value to the job may decline to do so, and direct that a system-wide 'system value' is used instead. System values are therefore a fourth source of job attributes (Fig. 3.1).

Note that, unlike the job description, and the class and system values which influence the job only at job-creation time, the user profile remains actively associated with the job during its life cycle. It includes parameters other than those which become part of the job structure at job-creation time. For example, it contains authorizations which specify access rights to objects, and any change to these takes effect immediately on all existing jobs associated with the user profile without having to change the jobs.

To help understand how the work management facilities operate we will now follow the life cycle of a particular job belonging to an interactive application user. New terms will normally be explained as they arise, but the Glossary (Appendix 2) can also be consulted in case of need.

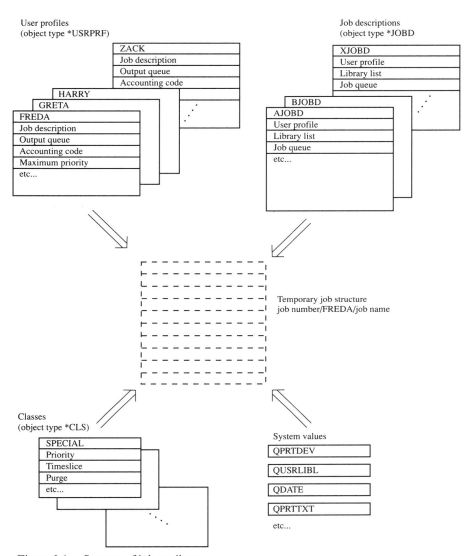

Figure 3.1.   Sources of job attributes.

3.3   Role of the subsystem in job creation

The subsystems are normally started automatically following system start-up, sometimes called IPL (initial program load) or IMPL (initial micro-program load). They can also be started and stopped by command (STRSBS and ENDSBS). Our typical interactive user might be an order entry clerk, a manager wanting to look at business results, or indeed a system operator. Their first action could well be to sit down at a terminal and switch it on. What happens next, depends on how the active subsystems were set up.

3.3.1   *Workstation entries*

However a subsystem is started, the monitor's first action is to examine its work entries. These include the names of potential sources of work, grouped by type. For example, the subsystem may have job queue entries naming the queues currently allocated to the subsystem. It may also have workstation entries naming the terminals belonging to the subsystem (by individual device name or by type).

The subsystem will take ownership of all the nominated workstations which are switched on, by allocating (taking a lock on) the corresponding device descriptions, and will display a sign-on prompt at each screen. Figure 3.2 shows a possible sign-on screen that our user could be faced with. Notice the subsystem name among the three fields in the top right-hand corner: QINTER is one of the standard subsystems shipped with OS/400(*) and is designed to be used for interactive work.

The three fields mentioned above, plus the underscored input fields and their prompts, are part of the supplied sign-on display file. Tailored logos such as the extra material in the example screen can be easily added. The user's interactive job has not yet started; it begins at workstation sign-on and ends its active phase at sign-off. Before job creation can begin the user must enter a user profile name (and normally a password also) into the sign-on screen. This is the first of the three essential job reference objects.

Beware of the confusion that arises if a workstation name or type is mentioned in more than one active subsystem. The user is then liable to start a job in different subsystems on different occasions, depending on the sequence in which subsystems

```
     AA                           Sign On
    AAAA                                  System  . . . . . :    NBS400A
   AA  AA                                 Subsystem . . . . :    QINTER
  AAAAAAAA                                Display . . . . . :    PSTRNF05J
  AA    AA
  AA    AA           User  . . . . . . . . . . . .    _____
                     Password  . . . . . . . . . .    _____
                     Program/procedure . . . . . . .  _____
                     Menu  . . . . . . . . . . .      _____
                     Current library . . . . . . . .  _____
                     ..............................................................
 III  BBBBB   MM   MM :                                                          :
  I   B   B   MM MM   : IBM assets, including this computer system, should be :
  I   BBBB    M M M   :    used only for IBM Management Approved Purposes.    :
  I   B   B   M   M   : You should be aware that it may be a criminal offence :
 III  BBBBB   MM   MM : to secure unauthorised access to any program or data  :
                      :        in the system or to make any unauthorised       :
    E D U C A T I O N :             modification to its contents.              :
                      :                                                        :
     S E R V I C E S  : If you are not authorised by IBM Management to access :
                      :          this system, please SIGNOFF now.              :
       C E N T R E    :..............................................................:
                              (C) COPYRIGHT IBM CORP. 1980, 1993.
```

Figure 3.2.   Example of sign-on screen.

are started and the timing of the sign-on event. When a subsystem starts it will take over control of any workstation nominated in its workstation entries if a user has not already signed on to the previous 'owning' subsystem. This unpredictable resolution of conflicting specifications seems a fair enough result if you are not sure yourself where you want the terminal to run.

Once started in a subsystem, a job can transfer itself into another subsystem through use of the TFRJOB (transfer job) command. It is much more common, however, for routing into subsystems to be controlled by the work entries alone, and for jobs to continue executing in the subsystem in which they start. In the example we will look at shortly our user is one of a privileged group who remain in a common subsystem with other users, but are given enhanced private facilities.

Each workstation entry in the subsystem has a job description value specified for use with the corresponding workstation job. This can be an explicit job description name, giving a direct link to the second object required for job creation. The value in the delivered QINTER subsystem (and in our example subsystem) is '*USRPRF'. This is a way of 'passing the buck', that is, declining to provide the information and referring the system to the user profile for the job description name.

In this way all the job attributes which come from the job description can be tailored to the user rather than to the device they happen to be using. If it makes more sense in a particular environment to match the job attributes to the device then, of course, the workstation entry can be changed accordingly. This is just one example of the flexibility provided by part of AS/400 work management, but it is representative of the whole.

In general there are several ways to achieve a given requirement and multiple potential sources of controlling parameters. For this reason work management can appear complex and unnecessarily indirect on first acquaintance. The benefit is the flexibility which allows almost any work management needs to be satisfied. At the same time, the delivered defaults are such that the system works well for most users with the minimum of tailoring.

3.3.2   Routing entries

Referring to Fig. 3.1 you can see that one of the attributes that will be provided by a job description is called routing data. This is the vital link that is used to connect our job to the third essential reference object. Just as workstation entries are used to link the initiating user profile with a job description, routing entries in the subsystem are used to link the emerging job with a specific class object. The class contains important performance-related attributes.

The routing data is a string of characters that is used to search through a table of compare values that form one element of the routing entries. When a match is found, a corresponding character string is selected from another table. Each entry in the second table contains a number of values that are used to complete the routing process. Not only is the class name identified, but also the subsystem pool to be used and the program to be given control.

The whole process is illustrated by example in Sec. 3.3.4 but first a couple of items of background information will be useful.

3.3.3   Program and pool references in the routing entries

The interactive job has now started, but how do we determine what the user sees immediately after signing on? Although the program named in the routing table can be a user application program, the default arrangement is more indirect. The system command processor program QCMD is usually given control. This invokes the initial application program as explained in the next section, and remains in control at the top of the job's program stack.

Each subsystem can define or refer to up to ten memory pools, identified by numbers 1, 2, 3 up to 10. These numbers are internal to the subsystem and should not be confused with the system pool numbers which are assigned sequentially as new pools are allocated from available system memory.

Thus several subsystems can have pool 1 defined internally. These are allocated space or associated with a shared pool at the time the subsystems are started. They may end up as system pools 2, 3, and 5, for example. The correspondence between subsystem and system pools at any moment is revealed by the WRKSBS command output. See Fig. 3.3 for an example. It is unfortunate the OS/400 developers did not label the subsystem pools A, B, C, etc. to make the distinction clearer.

```
                        Work with Subsystems
                                                    System:    NBS400B
       Type options, press Enter.
         4=End subsystem   5=Display subsystem description
         8=Work with subsystem jobs

                          Total    -----------Subsystem Pools-----------
       Opt  Subsystem   Storage (K)   1   2   3   4   5   6   7   8   9   10
            QBATCH          0         2
            QCMN            0         2
            QCTL            0         2
            QINTER          0         2   4
            QPGMR           0         2   2
            QSNADS          0         2
            QSPL            0         2   3
            QSYSWRK         0         2
            QXFPCS          0         2

                                                                Bottom
       Parameters or command
       ===>
       F3=Exit    F5=Refresh   F11=Display system data    F12=Cancel
       F14=Work with system status
```

Figure 3.3.   WRKSBS display: pools information.

At the end of the IPL process the system has at least two pools allocated. Pool 1 is the machine pool, used exclusively for system tables and activities, and pool 2 is *BASE, containing the rest of the system memory. *BASE (pronounced not 'asterisk-base' but '*star-base*' which sounds pleasantly futuristic) is a shared pool which can be named as the destination for any subsystem pool.

Even if user jobs are not routed into this pool, certain system activities take place here; for example, all file open and close routines run in *BASE. As subsystems are started with privately defined pools, these become separate system pools which are given space at the expense of the *BASE pool. *BASE cannot be reduced below the size specified in the QBASPOOL system value (*tuning point*).

3.3.4   Job-creation example

Figure 3.4 and the associated notes describe the job-creation process outlined above, in a user-created subsystem. It is worth reviewing this until it starts to become familiar. Then come back another day and try to commit it to memory. Although it illustrates what was said earlier about apparent complexity and indirectness it also demonstrates the flexibility that can be exploited by users who are prepared to change default workstation and routing entries.

The following notes apply to Fig. 3.4.

(a)   The subsystem is started by command. The command could be part of the program run by the QSTRUPJD job which is started automatically by the controlling subsystem.

(b)   Three pools are defined in the subsystem description. Pools 1 and 2 will direct jobs into the shared system pools *BASE and *INTERACT. Pool 3 is private to the XYZ subsystem and requires 8 MB of memory to be allocated. The value 5 is the activity level for the pool which will be further explained in a following section.

(c)   The subsystem monitor sends a sign on screen to device WS2 because it is mentioned in a WSE (workstation entry) and is switched on but not signed on to any other subsystem. The second part of the entry means that the job description is to be specified in the user profile. The entry for WS3 shows that the job description can be supplied directly. Other work entries are indicated under the headings AJE (autostart job entries) and JOBQE (job queue entries), but are not used in this example.

(d)   The end user signs on under the profile 'FREDA', created for this particular individual.

(e)   In the user profile the job description value has been set to point to 'SPECIAL'. For the purpose of this example, we assume that the referenced job description has been created for the benefit of a select group of users who will run in their own private pool (pool 3) with higher than normal priority.

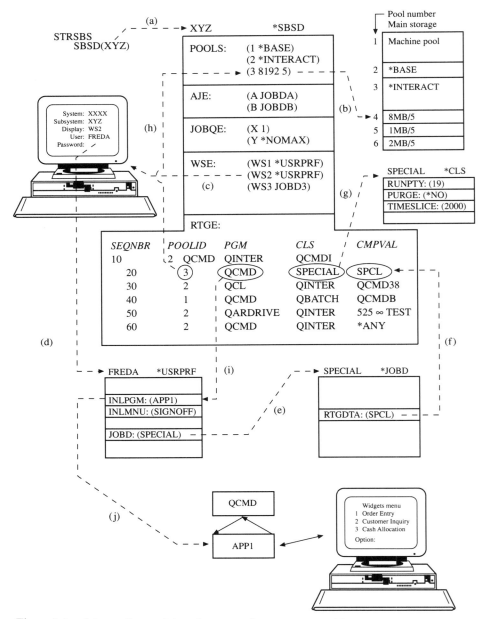

Figure 3.4.   Job creation and the relevant work management objects.

(f)   To this end the routing data ('SPCL') is set to match a compare value which
       has been placed in the subsystem routing tables using the ADDRTGE (add
       routing entry) command.

(g)   The selected routing entry is sequence number 20 and the corresponding class is called 'SPECIAL'. This class provides a higher priority than QINTER class, and ensures use of the PURGE(*NO) paging algorithm (discussed in Secs 3.6.1 and 3.6.2).

(h) The corresponding pool identifier is '3', the pool which is private to XYZ subsystem. Only users with the special job description in their profile will be routed into this pool and receive the privileged run-time attributes.

(i) The program given control is the normal OS/400 command interpreter QCMD. One of this program's functions is to check the user profile for an initial program and/or initial menu parameter. These are alternative ways of ensuring that the next screen the user sees after sign-on is a menu they know and love.

(j) In this case we assume the application program 'APP1' starts the user processing, and is specified as the initial program. QCMD therefore calls this program which then controls the progress of our job.

(k) Once a job has been routed the system knows all it needs to about how to run the job. It is possible for a job to repeat the routing process at some point by executing the RRTJOB (reroute job) command. This is rarely necessary and hardly ever done in practice, so that a job usually consists of just one routing step. When this ends, the job ends. As we have discussed, it does not necessarily leave the system at that time.

(l) APP1 will probably execute the SIGNOFF command when it is signalled to finish, but if it returns control QCMD will inspect the user profile for an initial menu value. This parameter would also be inspected if the initial program value was '*NONE'. In this instance we have used the initial program approach and the menu is set to the special value '*SIGNOFF' which results in job termination and the redisplay of the sign-on screen.

3.3.5   *Creation of other job types*

Although we have described only the creation of an interactive job, all jobs go through a similar process. Subsystems normally contain job queue entries and the monitor will initiate jobs which are placed on the queues named in these entries. Such jobs are called batch jobs and they originate through use of the SBMJOB (submit job) command in other jobs, or more rarely from diskette or database readers processing input batch command streams.

Autostart jobs are similar to batch jobs but do not require a job queue. They are associated with a subsystem by being explicitly listed in work entries of another type, called autostart job entries. The autostart jobs are initiated immediately after the subsystem is started. Both batch and autostart jobs arrive complete with user profile and job description, ready for the routing process already described. Batch job attributes can be further influenced by parameters of the SBMJOB command, as described in Sec. 3.8.

3.3.6   Subsystems shipped with OS/400

The operating system is shipped with a set of subsystems, complete with work entries and routing entries, plus sample user profiles, default job descriptions, matching classes and job queues, and system value settings so that all types of work can be run in default mode when the machine is first powered up. A standard work management set-up is in fact widely used for production work, with minor variations being introduced as special needs are recognized. There are two standard subsystem arrangements which are selected by choosing one of two alternative *controlling subsystems*.

The controlling subsystem is the one which is started automatically as the last step in the IPL process. Whatever subsystem is named in the QCTLSBSD system value is taken to be the controlling subsystem. It should contain a workstation entry for the system console (the first workstation on port 0 of the first workstation controller), and an autostart job entry to start the remaining subsystems.

As delivered, the controlling subsystem is QBASE. This starts the QSPL subsystem designed to run spool writers and readers, and runs all other kinds of work itself. In the majority of cases we recommend that QBASE is not used, and QCTLSBSD is changed to point to the alternative controlling subsystem (QCTL), because this gives better opportunities to control system operations. QCTL then starts the following subsystems:

- QINTER for interactive work
- QBATCH for batch work
- QSPL for spool writers and readers
- QCMN for communications jobs.

Figure 3.5 shows the partitioning of main memory and the usage of the resulting

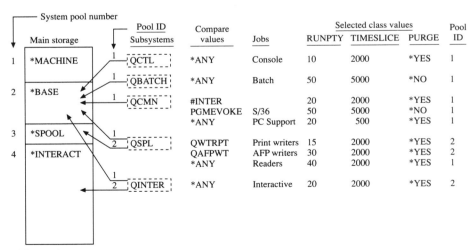

Figure 3.5.   Memory partitioning and usage by delivered subsystems.

pools by these subsystems; also the default run-time attributes which accrue to jobs created through the normal routing entries. Note that no jobs are routed into *BASE pool from the QINTER subsystem. The pool is defined there so that the QINTER subsystem monitor will run in *BASE. All subsystem monitors run in whatever is the first defined pool within their subsystem.

A number of other subsystems are provided and may be started in particular circumstances. These include QPGMR, QSNADS, QSYSWRK, QDSNX and QSYSSBSD.

3.4   Use of main memory

We pointed out in Sec. 2.3 that before a job can make use of the CPU and disk resources it must be partially resident in main memory. What exactly is needed in memory for a job to run? Executable instructions first spring to mind, and it is true that to start running our initial program the first 4 KB of executable code must be loaded (if not already resident due to use by another job). This remarkably modest requirement hardly justifies a machine which may have many hundreds of megabytes at its disposal, and indeed the main demand for memory arises from the need to accommodate a large amount of supporting data, as described shortly.

3.4.1   Page faulting and the LRU algorithm

Of course, when the program branches to a piece of code outside the initial 4 KB block, a further block will be provided. If this is brought from disk the resulting physical disk I/O is counted as a *page fault* and contributes to the non-database page fault rate which you can observe, for example, on the WRKSYSSTS display. A page is 512 bytes of main memory and this is the unit in which transfers to and from disk are measured. Application programs are handled in blocks of eight pages. Other items are transferred a page at a time, and yet others in larger blocks—up to 64 pages (32 KB) at a time. In future releases of the operating system the page size and the maximum block size are likely to be increased.

When program code or other material is brought into memory it is placed in those pages which have been least recently referenced. If the previous contents of those pages have been modified they must first be written out to disk. The operation of this standard 'least recently used' paging algorithm treats the whole of main memory as a kind of dynamic cache for active application objects. Depending on the pattern of activity over a period of time, memory can become filled with the most active parts of the various jobs.

3.4.2   Partitioning

Access to the CPU is determined by execution priority, hence the highest-priority jobs will normally be the most active. In Chapter 9 we will explain how this may push us towards extending the partitioning of main memory into separate pools. The isolation of jobs within memory partitions can either improve or detract from overall system performance (*tuning point*).

One very useful feature of main storage management is the automatic sharing of pages across partitions. The purpose of partitioning is to force jobs to use their own allocated memory pools when referenced items are brought from disk, thereby reducing interference with other jobs. However, if the referenced material is already somewhere in main storage, access is automatically given regardless of partition boundaries.

In this way the system ensures that multiple copies of database records, program code and other application items are not required in main storage. Note that all the AS/400 compilers generate re-entrant code, so that any number of jobs can use the same program pages concurrently. This somewhat reduces the demand for memory, but, most importantly, also reduces the need for physical disk I/Os when multiple users are performing the same application functions.

3.4.3   The PAG

The demand for memory made by our job arises largely from the need to store the active parts of its PAG (process access group). Every active job has one of these, that is private to the job, inaccessible to all other jobs, and can be very large. The PAG is a temporary object containing the following items that must be maintained on an individual job basis while the job executes:

1. Storage space for all the program-defined variables in all the currently active programs in the job. Depending on the languages used and the data definitions, space may be allocated in the program static storage area (PSSA) or program automatic storage area (PASA). Included in this space will be any tables or arrays used by the programs.
2. Space for open data paths (ODPs) for each file opened in the job. When a file is opened for use in a program an ODP is added to the PAG to hold the following:
   - Buffers for one or a block of database or device records. Note that data in these buffers is private to the job and not available for sharing with other jobs. Data is moved here from system data management buffers which *are* sharable.
   - Extensive feedback information about the current status of the file.
   - Select/omit logic in the case of database logical files.

   Appropriate programming may allow multiple programs using the same file to share a single ODP. It is beyond the scope of this book to consider the implications of sharing ODPs any further, but there is a significant performance benefit.
3. File override information. Override and open entries are added each time a file

is opened to hold information about temporary changes to file attributes or temporary redirection of files.
4. Subfile work areas. Subfiles are a programming facility which eases the handling of variable-length lists of records on a display screen. For display files that contain subfile records, work areas equal to the subfile size attribute multiplied by the record length may be placed in the PAG.
5. Process control space contains work areas required to control the execution of programs within the job. Among a variety of items it includes an invocation work area where entries are added whenever a subprogram is called. When microcode routines are called the variables used are also stored here.

It is apparent from the above that the size of the PAG is dynamic. It grows as new programs are invoked with defined variables and files, and may shrink as programs are terminated and files are closed. The current PAG size in use for any job can be displayed by entering the DSPACCGRP command. With appropriate keyword values the same command can produce output for all active jobs and dump it into a database file. The ANZACCGRP command will then produce summary reports based on this data. Both commands are part of the IBM Performance Tools/400(*) product.

PAG sizes are obviously dependent on the nature of the workload. The extremes in normal commercial workloads we have observed are around 100 KB at the low end and 1 MB at the high end, although even larger ones are encountered occasionally. Whenever a job is active (i.e. ready and waiting for its turn with the CPU) its PAG must be partly in memory. If the PAG has to be brought from disk the maximum block size is 32 KB and to load 0.5 MB of PAG would require about 15 synchronous physical disk I/Os. This could represent half a second on the response time before the transaction is ready to start running.

The reason PAGs are used is to simplify the handling of the many items contained. They are all needed more or less together and it is much simpler for the system to manage a single composite object rather than a large number of small items. A single auxiliary storage directory entry points to the PAG and a second entry points to the PAG table of contents which locates each component item within the PAG. This very much reduces the overhead of scanning the directory, and once found the PAG can be loaded in large chunks without regard to its internal structure.

Because of the size of the object it would clearly be much better for performance if we had enough memory to keep the bulk of the active PAGs in main memory (*tuning point*).

3.4.4   Activity levels

With such large objects needed in memory it is crucial to control the amount of concurrent activity within each pool. If too many jobs are allowed to become active, then loading a new PAG will overwrite the active PAG pages of another job. The latter will not be able to use the CPU until it has itself overwritten other active pages. The net result is a lot of unproductive paging activity and very little useful work going on. Performance suffers badly.

The mechanism provided to prevent this hyperactivity (often called 'thrashing') is an activity level setting associated with each pool. The activity level prevents more than the specified number of jobs from competing for the CPU (and thereby entering the pool) at one time. The activity level number must reflect the relationship between the size of the pool, the average working set size of the jobs, and the transaction rate (*tuning point*).

Pool sizes and activity levels can be set manually by using the CHGSBSD command or by keying over fields in the WRKSYSSTS or WRKSHRPOOL displays. In the case of shared pools we have the option to let the system manage sizes and activity levels dynamically. If we select automatic performance adjustment by setting the QPFRADJ system value to '2' or '3', page fault rates and job state changes (see next section) are monitored and used as a basis for periodic adjustments.

Excess jobs may run concurrently but will be queued on the ineligible queue for the pool when they are ready to become active. As jobs leave the activity levels, ineligible jobs are allowed in. A heavy workload, i.e. a high throughput of long transactions, will create a demand for more activity levels and hence more memory to avoid excessive queuing. We are now in a position to understand the way our job is treated by the system.

3.5   Job states and transitions

When you display the system status (WRKSYSSTS command) and look at the transition data after a short period (F11 key followed by F5) you see something similar to Fig. 3.6. The three right-hand columns in the body of the display reveal that the system is counting the number per minute of certain transitions.

These transitions are just a selection of those which will happen to our job. The performance tools allow us to trace these and other transitions and events while jobs are going about their business. The information can help us to make the best use of the resources available if we understand what it is telling us. This section explains the significance of the transitions, Chapter 8 covers interpretation of the performance reports and Chapter 9 tells us how to correct any anomalies.

The following steps are a sequence of events which we can imagine happening to our interactive job after signing on. Figure 3.7 can be used to trace the transitions, and visualization may be easier if different-coloured pins or paper clips are placed on the diagram to represent multiple jobs.

```
                    Work with System Status                NBS400B
                                               13/07/94   10:17:41
% CPU used . . . . . . . :      37.0   Auxiliary storage:
Elapsed time . . . . . . :   00:06:06     System ASP . . . . . . :      1712 M
Jobs in system . . . . . :       187     % system ASP used  . . :   56.6144
% addresses used:                         Total  . . . . . . . . :      1712 M
  Permanent  . . . . . . :     1.617     Current unprotect used :       463 M
  Temporary  . . . . . . :      .108     Maximum unprotect  . . :       464 M

Type changes (if allowed), press Enter.

System     Pool    Reserved    Max   Active->  Wait->  Active->
 Pool    Size (K)  Size (K)  Active    Wait     Inel     Inel
   1       6303      4058      +++     8.8       .0       .0
   2       3572        0        6      1.9       .0       .0
   3        700        0        2       .0       .0       .0
   4      22193        0       15     62.1       .0       .0

                                                            Bottom
Command
===>
F3=Exit    F4=Prompt     F5=Refresh    F9=Retrieve   F10=Restart
F11=Display pool data   F12=Cancel    F14=Work with subsystems   F24=More keys
```

Figure 3.6. WRKSYSSTS display: transition data.

3.5.1   *Exchange of control within the activity level*

At the end of the sign-on process we imagine the initial program passing from the start symbol through the decision diamond into one of the five activity level slots in the pool. The activity level was set by the POOLS attribute in the subsystem description, as must be done for all private pools. The pool is not in fact partitioned internally and any job can use as much memory as it needs within the pool.

Suppose that there are four other jobs already in the pool and there is only one main processor. Only one of the jobs can be actively executing instructions in the CPU. The active job will retain the CPU until it voluntarily gives up control (perhaps to wait for a database record to arrive) or is interrupted by a higher-priority job, or consumes a fixed amount of CPU time (dependent on the AS/400 model) without completing its transaction.

Once a job is in an activity level, access to the CPU is controlled strictly by the job's execution priority. This can have a value ranging from 1 (highest) to 99 (lowest). Every job on the system that has not terminated has a representative 1 KB control block called a task despatching element (TDE) in the machine pool. When the job is in an activity level *and is ready to execute* the TDE is linked into a queue of similar items.

The task despatcher is a central system component which processes this queue in priority sequence and gives control of the CPU to the top job. System tasks are also represented on this queue and may have priorities higher than the highest possible user job priority.

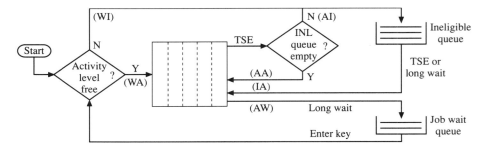

The following abbreviations are used in this diagram:

WA = wait-to-active transition   WI = wait-to-ineligible transition
TSE = timeslice end condition   AI = active-to-ineligible transition
AA = active-to-active transition   IA = ineligible-to-active transition
AW = active-to-wait transition   INL = ineligible

Figure 3.7.   Job state transitions.

Thinking back to the job-creation stage, our five jobs were routed into the pool via the same routing entry, which gave the jobs a priority of 19 by associating them with a class called 'SPECIAL'. This value is higher than that given to interactive jobs by default in the QINTER subsystem. If ready to execute, our jobs will therefore be ahead of other interactive users in the task despatching queue (TDQ).

Jobs of equal priority are queued in FIFO (first in, first out) sequence. Assuming the console job (priority 10) is not active, and ignoring the activity of higher-priority system tasks, control of the CPU will pass between the priority 19 jobs when the one using the CPU has to wait for a synchronous disk I/O. When all priority 19 jobs are waiting, control filters down to the priority 20 interactive users and eventually to the priority 50 batch jobs.

Assuming our job is placed in the TDQ when a batch job has control, the despatcher interrupts the batch job and gives control to our job. The other priority 19 jobs are waiting for disk I/Os to complete and their TDEs have been switched to I/O pending queues while various I/O manager tasks service their requests. They still occupy an activity level.

As the I/Os complete, the priority 19 TDEs are re-inserted in the TDQ ahead of any existing priority 19 entries, i.e. 'first among equals'. Control is thereby circulated around the five jobs as they attempt to perform the processing for their transactions. Despite the effective priority promotion following an I/O, this method of sharing out the CPU still tends to favour CPU-intensive transactions with few I/Os.

For this reason, transactions are also interrupted after each 500 ms of CPU usage (or less for faster CPUs) and enqueued behind any other equal priority TDEs. This fixed value is referred to as the job's *internal time slice* and is separate from the user-controlled time slice mechanism described in Sec. 3.5.3. The effect is to inhibit CPU-intensive transactions from monopolizing the CPU.

I/O-bound transactions are given further opportunities to gain control by having their priorities temporarily adjusted upwards. The adjustment is automatic, not visible to users other than through the performance effect, and increments never reach the next integral priority number (18 in our case).

3.5.2 Transitions caused by long waits

Assume that our job now completes its transaction by displaying a menu, issuing a READ to the screen and waiting for input. This wait is distinct from the short waits experienced earlier. The system categorizes workstation input as a long wait and makes our job vacate the activity level. In Fig. 3.7 the job moves to the job wait queue, having experienced an active-to-wait transition.

Our job stays here while the end user thinks, keys a menu selection number, and finally responds by pressing an input key. Following the clockwise arrow we reach the decision diamond again. Normally there will be a vacant activity level and the job will start its next transaction by entering the memory pool and rejoining the TDQ behind any priority 19 entries (a wait-to-active transition).

This time assume that five jobs are already in memory. We join the pool's ineligible queue (wait-to-ineligible transition) to wait for a slot to become available. The ineligible queue is kept in priority sequence, but for our pool this is irrelevant. In a fraction of a second one or more jobs clear their activity levels by passing into a long wait state, and our job reaches the front of the ineligible queue and then takes over a memory slot (ineligible-to-active transition).

3.5.3 Transitions due to exceeding the time slice

The new transaction continues like the first one described above, taking its share of the CPU broken up by short waits and a little queuing on the TDQ. Assume that this transaction is very complex and is still running when 2 seconds of CPU time have been used up. At this point the external time slice mechanism comes into play.

Reviewing the job-creation routing process in Fig. 3.4 we see that one of the class attributes picked up was a time slice value of 2000 ms. The job is said to reach a TSE (time slice end) condition which causes it to be interrupted. Following the arrow labelled TSE in Fig. 3.7 we see that the system checks the ineligible queue.

If any equal or higher-priority job is waiting, it will take over the activity level (ineligible-to-active transition) and our job will be banished to the ineligible queue (active-to-ineligible transition) behind any equal-priority jobs. Remember, this is happening in mid-transaction, so the response time would be extended by this wait. It is a mechanism for penalizing transactions which are exceptionally heavy on CPU, and prevents them from hogging an activity level at the expense of equal-priority jobs (*tuning point*).

When the transaction returns to the activity level it joins the TDQ behind equal-priority TDEs and can use up to 2 seconds more of CPU time before risking expulsion again. In our example we will assume there was no job on the ineligible queue. The heavy transaction therefore retains its activity level (an active-to-active transition) and rejoins the TDQ behind equal-priority TDEs. In this case the effect is identical to the internal time slice which passes control on after 500 ms or less of execution.

An additional work management facility which we could have selected to deal with the TSE condition is to change the QTSEPOOL system value from '*NONE' to '*BASE'. The effect would be that any interactive job reaching TSE would be moved into the *BASE pool until it reached a long wait. It could get placed on the *BASE ineligible queue at this point or at a subsequent TSE. The aim would be to avoid complex transactions disrupting our special pool (*tuning point*).

Nevertheless, there remain a few opportunities for a job to evade the internal and external time slice measures, and to end up monopolizing an activity level. Some functions performed by system tasks as a result of job activity are counted as system overhead, rather than against the individual job. With Version 3 Release 1 of the operating system, database parallel processing will come in this category.

3.5.4   Short waits and long waits

We have now explored all the possible transitions which a job can experience during its 'active' period. The time is made up of short periods of genuine activity interspersed with waits. Waits are classified as either short or long depending on their *expected* duration, and the system responds appropriately to each type.

The waits experienced by a job when synchronous disk I/O operations occur or when a higher-priority job takes control of the CPU are generally of short duration. This is normal processing activity, and the job will never be thrown out of the activity level as a result. The following other events are specifically identified as *short waits*, and are counted as such by the performance measurement functions of the operating system. The system treats them rather like disk I/O waits to start with, leaving the job in the activity level because it expects control to be regained relatively quickly.

1. The job has to wait for acknowledgement of a successful output operation to a workstation screen or communications device
2. The job waits for input to arrive on a data queue.

Some of these short waits and some disk I/O waits may turn out in practice to occupy a significant amount of time. An update operation to a record which causes the system to maintain a large number of logical file access paths could take multiple seconds to complete. For remote screens the display file attributes and the handling of record formats are critical factors affecting wait times.

Although line speeds are relevant to the second example, they are both really application design factors and therefore excluded from further consideration in this book. Except to say that the system does not let short waits go on for ever:

after 2 seconds in cases 1 and 2 above, it loses patience and redefines the event as a long wait (identified as *short wait extended* on performance reports discussed in later chapters).

In addition to the converts from short wait status, the following events are treated as long waits. The system immediately makes the job's activity level available to the next job that is ready to execute (on the ineligible queue):

• The job executes a read operation to a workstation screen.
• The job cannot immediately obtain a lock that it needs on an application item such as a database record, because it is in conflict with the activity of another job. Note that if the job holding the lock is of lower priority, the system promotes the lock holder to the priority of the waiter, until the lock is released. If this were not done, there would be a danger of an extended delay: on a busy system the lower-priority job might not get control again for some time.
• The job reaches time slice end and is moved to the ineligible queue.
• The job (e.g. a print writer) sends a block of records to a printer device.
• The job waits for input to arrive on a message queue.

When the job finishes its long wait and is ready to become active again, it will be given a vacant activity level. If all the activity levels are occupied, of course the job moves to the ineligible queue. In the case of a job returning from a lock wait or a short wait extended, it is enqueued 'first of equals' to encourage completion of partly processed transactions before new transactions are started. This is a significant benefit on an overloaded system.

3.5.5   *Job state transitions and the WRKSYSSTS display*

Referring back to Fig. 3.6, we might wonder why only three of the six possible transitions are counted. Part of the answer is that these are the ones we may wish to react to when considering system tuning (see Chapter 9). It is also true that two of the others are derivable.

Looking at Fig. 3.7, if we ignore the AA transition which is not really a change of state, we have five possible transitions (AW, WA, WI, AI and IA). In a steady-state condition with constant length queues the transition rates into and out of each queue must balance. Hence:

$$\underline{AW} = \underline{WI} + WA \quad \text{and} \quad IA = \underline{WI} + \underline{AI}$$

The underlined transition rates are provided by WRKSYSSTS and the other two are therefore implied.

3.5.6   *Breakdown of external response time*

Given our knowledge of what constitutes activity we can now understand a more detailed picture of transaction response time components than was presented in

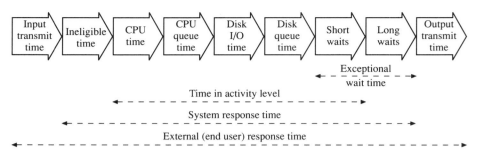

Figure 3.8.   Interactive response time components.

Chapter 1. In particular cases the relative size of the different components will vary widely, and our tuning response must react accordingly (Fig. 3.8).

3.6   Paging options and alternatives

Our interactive job enters and leaves pool activity levels in a continuous cycle corresponding to the sequence of transactions required by the user. For a concurrent job to make effective use of the activity level we vacate it must get its working set (the PAG principally) into memory and perhaps overwrite the pages we were using.

Some of the work management options we may want to change for tuning reasons control the way the system performs paging on our behalf. Two alternative paging algorithms are selected via the PURGE attribute which the job picks up initially from the class object. Consulting Fig. 3.4, we see that our job has PURGE(*NO) specified.

*3.6.1   Effect of PURGE(*NO)*

This means that the job's pages are left in the pool and managed individually according to the LRU (least recently used) criterion described earlier in Sec. 3.4.1. A new job entering the pool will overwrite some of these pages and other jobs' not recently referenced pages if it needs to. This is described as 'demand paging' and is a good way to manage a relatively stable pool where the contents do not change dramatically (Fig. 3.9) (*tuning point*).

It is ideal if we have a large enough pool to accommodate the working sets of all the jobs running in the pool. When a wait-to-active transition occurs at the start of a new transaction our job should find most of its pages in the pool, just as they were left at the end of the previous transaction. As it runs, a few additional pages will be brought in when needed. Because the PAG is largely resident it does not have to be brought from disk at the start of each transaction, and response times are minimized.

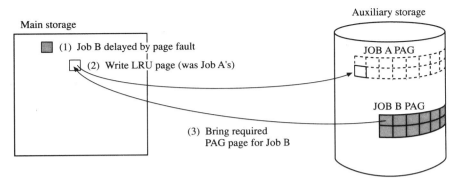

Figure 3.9.   Demand paging of PAG with PURGE(*NO).

It is easy to imagine a less well-endowed pool (perhaps on the same system) where there is not enough memory for all the jobs. At the start of every transaction space must be found for a PAG to be loaded because its pages will have been overwritten. With PURGE(*NO) in effect the system would have to identify a large number of target pages based on the LRU algorithm, and write changed pages back to disk. The contents of these overwritten pages will belong to a number of jobs and some will be brought back into memory again almost immediately.

3.6.2   Effect of PURGE(*YES)

A more efficient way of managing the memory in this over-committed pool is invoked by running jobs with the PURGE(*YES) attribute. This is the recommended and default delivered value for interactive jobs. When such a job goes into a long wait state the system may (depending on the demand for memory) immediately write its changed PAG segments to disk and mark all the job's pages as available for overwriting.

Fewer disk I/Os will be needed for this PAG swapping approach than for demand paging, when working in a memory-constrained environment. When a page fault occurs in a PURGE(*YES) environment, disk transfers occur in four-page blocks rather than individually. Depending on the relationship between key/ think time and response time the number of 'active' jobs using the pool may be several times the activity level number (Fig. 3.10).

Referring to Fig. 3.5, the delivered default for interactive and spool jobs is PURGE(*YES), and for batch it is PURGE(*NO). The attribute PURGE(*NO) is always obeyed even in memory-constrained interactive pools where it may cause excessive page faulting. However, the '*YES' value is treated as an initial mode which can be dynamically changed by the system if it determines that PAGs are being written out unnecessarily.

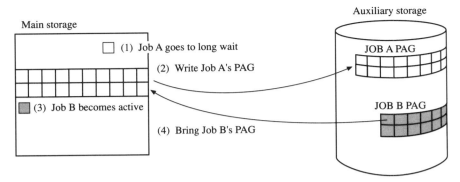

Figure 3.10.   PAG swapping with PURGE(*YES).

PURGE(*YES) is therefore the safe option, but when you are certain that '*NO' is correct a small CPU overhead can be avoided by specifying '*NO' explicitly (*tuning point*). Nowadays memory-constrained systems are less common and the change is frequently beneficial. For batch jobs the choice of purge value is unimportant, since they will normally experience no AW transitions.

3.6.3   Paging of non-PAG items

What we have said about purging options affects only the handling of PAGs, because these are private to individual jobs and will never be referenced by other jobs. When it comes to handling database and program pages the purge value does not apply. Effectively PURGE(*NO) is always used, and overwriting of these pages may occur on demand as a result of the LRU algorithm.

We have already said that program transfers into memory are blocked to 4 KB. The default for database transfers in some circumstances is also 4 KB. We next describe several ways we can modify the standard paging arrangements, both into and out of memory. These may well allow us to use our knowledge of how particular applications run to improve their performance (*tuning point*).

3.6.4   The SETOBJACC command

This command directs the system to load a named file or program into a pool. The complete object is loaded (assuming the pool is large enough) using large, overlapped block transfers from disk. Multiple objects can be placed into the same pool in this way. Subsequently the same command can clear named objects from the pool.

We can imagine some highly active programs and small files used by our job, and by many other jobs on the system. Rather than leave it to the automatic workings of demand paging to optimize memory usage we will put the objects into a private pool of adequate size and leave them there. If no jobs run in this pool, no paging occurs, and all references to program code and database indexes and records held here take place without the need for physical I/Os (*tuning point*).

The extent to which we can exploit the pre-loading of objects in memory will be limited by the system memory size. Ideally we need more memory than is required for the active jobs' working sets, plus many users performing the same functions and making repeated references to the same small files. In other circumstances we may do better by leaving the memory in the interactive pool and letting the system adaptively determine what it will contain.

For files with sizes running into tens of megabytes the density of record references will be small, and this approach is unlikely to be an efficient use of space.

3.6.5   *Expert Cache*

For large files we need to fetch parts of the file, perhaps as little as one record at a time, on demand. In Sec. 1.3.7 we explained how blocking transfers from disk can greatly reduce the synchronous physical I/Os needed to access records, providing the processing sequence matches the physical storage sequence on disk. Default blocking into a 4 KB buffer may be provided automatically where sequential file processing is used.

It is a function of the OVRDBF (override with database file) command to specify a blocking factor, which can take the block size to a maximum of 32 K. This allows us to block data transfers selectively on a job-by-job basis for each file which is processed sequentially and has its data conveniently sorted. The problem here is that we have to intervene in a very granular way, and understand the application processing going on and the state of the physical data.

Also, how do we estimate the optimum transfer size? If too much data is brought in we may overwrite active pages in the pool and cause disruptive page faulting. This is where Expert Cache comes in.

Expert Cache is a dormant facility of the operating system which can be switched on for selected shared pools by setting the paging option to '*CALC'. It can be turned on and off using the CHGSHRPOOL command. When enabled, the system monitors disk I/O activity and adjusts the transfer sizes to make optimum use of memory.

Providing memory and CPU are not over-committed, and the workload includes sequential processing of sorted data, the effect should be to reduce the overall I/O activity in the pool. Synchronous I/Os are particularly targeted. This means that batch run times and interactive response times can be significantly improved in favourable circumstances, without involving the user in detailed consideration of the applications, and insertion of appropriate overrides.

In the case of our pool, we might experiment with Expert Cache enabled and measure the performance impact. Additional memory in the pool will usually allow Expert Cache to deliver further benefits. Dynamic performance adjustment should be disabled (set QPFRADJ system value to '0') while experimenting, to get a fair measure of the effects. However, there is no problem in presenting Expert Cache with a moving target: once you have decided to use it, it can run concurrently with performance adjustment.

If the processing of non-resident files is mainly direct by key with little locality of reference we could find that the effect is negligible, or slightly negative because of the monitoring overhead, in which case we switch it off again. In many cases, though, particularly if we keep our data organized in a sensible physical sequence, and particularly in batch pools, Expert Cache gives us optimum performance managed and adjusted dynamically by the operating system, with no user intervention required.

This really neat facility should not be left idle unless it has been tried and found ineffective in each pool. It can potentially reduce CPU utilization also, due to the reduced activity of I/O functions in the operating system.

3.6.6   *Job termination*

The job continues to process transactions as described until finally the user signs off. The subsystem monitor comes to life in *BASE pool (but does not use any of the activity levels) and terminates the job. This process deletes all the temporary objects used by the job, e.g. the PAG and the temporary library (QTEMP). It releases all locks held, closes all files remaining open, and writes a job log if the job's LOG attribute so specifies or a SIGNOFF *LIST command was used.

The entry in the active jobs table is removed. The entry in the WCBT may also go, but if there is a job log or other spool file remaining the WCBTE is left.

3.7   Group jobs

3.7.1   *The need for group jobs*

In our short biography of an interactive job, we assumed for simplicity that one workstation entry resulted in only one job. In many instances this may be so, and the job will provide all the functions that the user requires during the session. A common problem in developing applications subject to this restriction is that users may require access to multiple diverse functions. A hierarchy of menus can satisfy the need, but when the user has to invoke many different functions in an unpredictable sequence this approach is often cumbersome and slow.

A more flexible and natural way to link varied functions is suggested by the AS/400 system request function. Use of this special key allows the user to sign-on a second time at the workstation, thus creating two jobs between which the user can jump at will. Many physical workstations are able to act as multiple devices, thus multiplying the number of jobs accessible from one workstation.

AS/400 group job support is somewhat similar to this but does not require multiple sign-on, and allows up to 15 extra jobs to be created from the initial main session. The first job for the workstation is started in exactly the same way as our job was started. This job can then transform itself into a group job via the CHGGRPA command and initiate new jobs via the TFRGRPJOB command.

Only one of the up to 16 group jobs can be active at a time. The rest are suspended, but ready to continue from the point at which they were previously interrupted. The attention key can be enabled in each group job, and can be handled by a simple CL program which allows switching directly between the members of the group.

This application design technique suits users who need to work in a spontaneous and unstructured way. An example might be an order entry clerk who handles telephone queries. While in the middle of an order the user can jump directly to an open enquiry application, perform the enquiry and then jump back to the order with all data still on the screen as it was before the interruption.

3.7.2 *Performance considerations with group jobs*

Compared to system request, group jobs extends the number of different functions which can be linked in this flexible way. Another advantage is that the application programmer can control the enabling of the attention key and prevent the user from leaving a job at a dangerous point; e.g. with records locked for update and uncommitted to the database. The system request key is always enabled and the user therefore has access to any authorized functions on the system request menu, including transfer to a secondary job, at any point in their application.

From a work management viewpoint the system handles each group job as a separate job. The group jobs each have their own PAG, local data area, QTEMP library and entries in the active jobs table and the WCBT. What was potentially a single monster job has been divided into a number of slim agile ones. Although the two control tables are extended the slim-line PAGs more than compensate, and group jobs qualify as one of the very few high-function facilities which also promise performance advantages.

Of course, the initial invocation of a new group job does carry an overhead, as the system must create the supporting structures for the additional job; but this will consume less resources than signing on again. It is possible to program so that all the user's group jobs are started when they sign-on, and subsequent transfers of control to all functions then involve minimum overhead.

3.7.3 *Group jobs and activation groups*

If you have software developed using the new Integrated Language Environment (ILE(*)) programming model, this may employ multiple 'activation groups' within a job. The purpose is to give logical separation of functions and increased control over resources used within the job, so to some extent it appears analogous to group jobs. However, as transfer of control between activation groups is effected through the normal call/return interface rather than a 'hot key' switching function the analogy is not close.

Unlike group jobs, a job using activation groups has a single shared PAG. From our point of view, although ILE may offer developers new ways to optimize performance (including much more significant items not mentioned here) there are no special operational or system tuning considerations. Note that group jobs and activation groups may co-exist to give full functionality.

3.8   Batch jobs

As outlined earlier, batch jobs go through the same creation and initiation steps as an interactive job and require three reference objects to help establish their attributes. What identifies them as batch type is that they are initiated from job queues. Job queues are associated with subsystems by adding job queue entries to the subsystem description (ADDJOBQE command).

Jobs normally arrive on a job queue through use of the SBMJOB command. The command has many parameters, and the defaults are such that many of the resulting jobs' attributes are inherited from the job which issues this command.

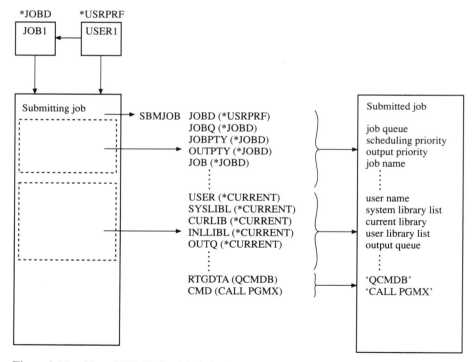

Figure 3.11.   Use of SBMJOB with default values.

Figure 3.11 illustrates the point. The job description to be used can be named directly but the default is to take it from the submitting job's user profile.

If the submitting job is interactive and was itself created using normal defaults the same job description (JOB1) will get used for both jobs. Some job attributes such as user, library list and output queue are copied by default from the current values of the submitting job. They may well differ from the values established initially by the job description. Others such as routing data and request data are normally specified directly as SBMJOB parameter values.

Figure 3.12 shows a common alternative way to submit a batch job. The job description XYZ has been tailored to the specific requirements of the batch job. It contains any attributes which differ from those of the submitting job plus the necessary routing and request data.

In either case the routing data is used in the normal way to select the class, pool and controlling program for the job. The program selected from the matching routing entry is normally the OS/400 command processor, QCMD. For batch jobs QCMD passes control to the command specified as request data in the RQSDTA or CMD parameters of the SBMJOB command.

The characteristic difference between batch and interactive jobs is that batch jobs do not normally need to interact with a human user, and therefore do not

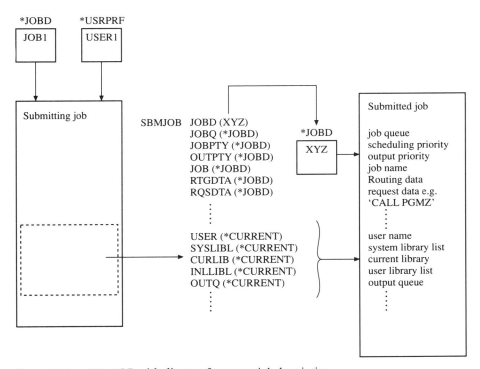

Figure 3.12.   SBMJOB with direct reference to job description.

move frequently from active to long wait state due to workstation I/O. By default, they run at run priority 50, and only get CPU access when all interactive and other higher priority jobs and system tasks are waiting voluntarily.

This 'background' processing mode prevents batch work from hogging system resource, which it would tend to do if run at interactive priority because of its more continuous demand characteristics. Because the higher-priority work is highly I/O bound (remember the relative timings in Table 1.1) sufficient CPU cycles usually filter through for batch jobs to make progress even at periods of peak interactive throughput.

When batch jobs do run they often generate lots of database I/O requests. I/O queues for disk actuators are not serviced in priority sequence. Therefore batch activity will have a secondary effect on interactive performance by increasing the queuing time for interactive disk I/Os.

3.9   Single-level storage and other features of the AS/400 architecture

We started this chapter by saying that the AS/400 has a unique architecture. The features which particularly characterize the system are:

1. *Layered machine architecture.*   A high-level instruction set is employed by the main software components including OS/400. These are currently implemented by two layers of licensed internal code. As has been demonstrated repeatedly by IBM this enables the rapid introduction of new hardware technology, because the software (including user applications) is not affected. Certain performance-critical supervisory functions are written in HLIC (horizontal licensed internal code) running in high-speed control storage. This allows the developers to optimize system performance for selected workload characteristics.

2. *Object orientation.*   We have tried to avoid using the word 'object' in its general sense (replacing it with 'item' or some such) because object has a special meaning on the AS/400. Most things we deal with on the system are objects, belonging to one of the list of defined object types. Examples of object types are programs, files, job descriptions, user profiles, classes, output queues, commands, panel groups and search indexes. The internal structure of objects is determined by the type but is not accessible directly to programmers working above the high-level machine interface. Objects can only be manipulated by certain type-dependent high-level instructions. This makes programs independent of the internal structure of objects and facilitates change without risk to system and data integrity. It also enables efficient object-level functions and run-time checks, and provides a platform for advanced application areas such as artificial intelligence.

3. *Hierarchy of microprocessors.*   We saw in Chapter 2 that DASD and workstations connect to a system bus through specialized independent processors. The same applies to other device types. On a fully configured large system there

could be over 200 processors. This allows control of vast amounts of I/O in parallel with main processor activity.

4. *Integrated operating system.*   OS/400 incorporates all the system services and facilities required in most commercial environments into a fully integrated entity. These include the DB2/400 relational database, communications and networking services, system availability and recovery functions, online information and education, and extensive security (access control) facilities. The AS/400 offers the same sophisticated and easy to use operating system across the range of models. Language-dependent items such as messages and display panels are packaged so that a single system can operate concurrently in multiple national languages.

5. *Single-level storage.*   Disk and main storage are managed by the system. Location of objects on disk and movement of objects into memory are handled by the machine without any need for users or programs to take account of specific hardware details. The number and mix of DASD types attached can be changed without any impact, other than performance, on operations.

Much though we would like to enlarge on all the above features, the one most relevant to this book is single-level storage, and we will confine ourselves to this topic in concluding the chapter. Some of what was covered earlier relates to single-level storage, but we have yet to explain the essential ideas behind it. The rest of this section will be easier to follow if you refer to Figs 3.13 and 3.14.

Every object created on or restored to the system is assigned a unique virtual address by the storage management component. The address is called virtual because there is no real location corresponding to this address: it is like the number of an imaginary house on a very, very long imaginary street. It is used as an internal identifier.

The virtual address is associated with the external name and stored in a directory system which we recognize as a library. The combination of library name, object name and object type must be unique for every object on a system. Objects can be renamed but this does not affect their virtual address, which is given for life.

The current AS/400 implementation uses a 6-byte (48-bit) virtual address which matches the hardware registers. The internal pointer objects used to hold addresses actually have space for 96-bit addresses as well as other necessary information, so the architecture is well placed to use more expansive hardware when it becomes available. The impact on applications, other than more performance at less cost, should be zero.

How constrained are we at present by the 48-bit address? It can represent a range of integral values from 0 up to $2^{48} - 1$. If we think of this as a number of bytes making up a logical address space, we get:

$$281, 474, 976, 710, 656 \text{ bytes or in excess of } 281\,000\text{G}$$

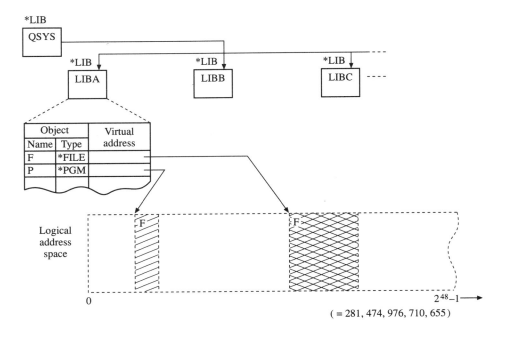

Figure 3.13.   Single-level storage.

A figure that may have lodged in your mind from Chapter 2 (Table 2.5) is the maximum DASD storage attachable to the system—about 260G. This is the current limit for storing objects online at real locations, still less than one thousandth of the virtual address space. As objects are always referenced through their

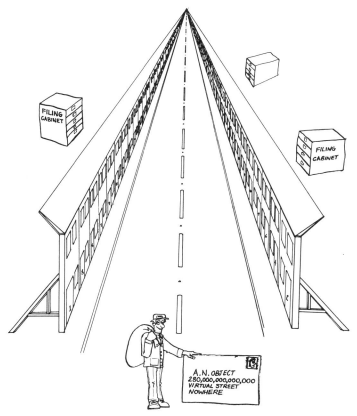

Figure 3.14.   Virtual addressing and real storage.

virtual address, the operating system and application programs see the various stored objects as though they are all located and directly accessible without I/Os in this huge address space with no effective limitation on object sizes.

The physical nature and extent of the real attached auxiliary storage and main memory is irrelevant at this level. Virtual address translator (VAT) hardware supports the translation of virtual addresses into main storage addresses. The responsibility for placing objects on auxiliary storage, keeping track of the extents occupied, allocating additional space as necessary, and paging objects into main storage when needed belongs to the auxiliary storage management (ASM) function of the system.

These system components bridge the gap between current reality and the simple-minded view which makes life so much easier above the machine interface. The details need not concern us too much. Clearly, ASM has to maintain auxiliary storage directories with entries to map virtual addresses to multiple DASD extents. It must also keep track of free space. At the front end a (resident) directory of pages currently in memory, called the primary directory in the diagram, must be maintained.

The simple 'black box' appearance of storage is breached in one or two areas only, where users are allowed optionally to influence aspects of the management process. We described some of these earlier in the section and others will be covered in Chapter 10.

Part II
AS/400 sizing

4
Introduction to sizing

4.1   Basic principles

Sizing is the process of choosing a machine configuration to support an estimated future workload. Doing this well is the first step towards achieving adequate performance and satisfied users. A naive newcomer to data processing (one of us) once asked a salesman about sizing. He said his method was to base it on the quality of cars in the prospective customer's car park. We think he *might* have been joking (Fig. 4.1).

An equally irrelevant but not uncommon approach is to discover the customer's budget and spend it on whatever kit is available in the warehouse. Neither of these techniques is guaranteed to generate satisfied and productive end users when the system goes live. The fact is that sizing is bound to involve estimation, but we can do a lot better than the salesman with just a little effort.

We will start by making the entirely reasonable assumption that an AS/400 is the best machine for the job. This could be because the software already chosen is written for the AS/400, or for any one of dozens of other convincing reasons. The required minimum configuration is then completely determined by the nature of the workload which it must run.

4.2   Workload characterization

This subject was introduced in Chapter 1. The crucial characteristics which we must know or estimate to size a machine for an interactive workload are the average transaction complexity and peak volume figures:

1. Average transaction complexity is the demand for performance resources of the 'average transaction', primarily:

    CPU seconds of a specified processor model
    Number of physical disk I/Os
    Space in memory to hold working set
    Amount of data transmitted to and from workstation.

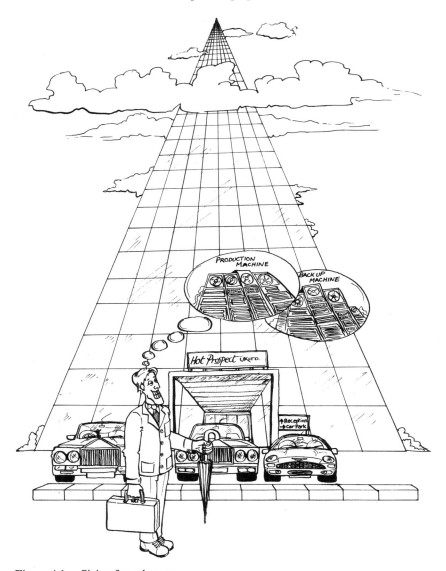

Figure 4.1.   Sizing for salesmen.

2. The peak volume figures are the transaction throughput and the number of active terminal users during peak activity periods.

4.2.1   *Real transactions*

Naturally, a real workload will consist of a mix of transactions with a wide range of characteristics. There will be some simple transactions, requiring a fraction of a second of CPU time plus less than 10 disk I/Os, and occupying just a couple of hundred K bytes of memory. There will be some complex transactions taking perhaps 1 second of CPU and causing 50 or more I/Os, while occupying a megabyte or so of memory.

Almost inevitably, there will also be a few ultra-complex (or 'rogue') transactions, consuming tens of seconds of CPU time and/or generating many hundreds or perhaps several thousands of I/Os. These might be database-scanning functions, and in a more perfect world would be running as low-priority batch jobs rather than interactively.

4.2.2 Average transactions

If we measure the total demand for resources of our real interactive workload during a peak period and divide this by the total number of transactions generating that demand, we get our 'average transaction' characteristics. This mythical transaction type is such that if we could present them to our machine at the measured throughput rate, they would make the same overall resource demands as the real workload.

For the purposes of sizing and capacity planning (dealt with later in Part IV) the homogeneous workload of imaginary transactions is much easier to deal with, and is equivalent to the real workload. We must simply bear in mind that any predicted response time will be only a weighted average of a wide range of expected response times. Actual responses will range from sub-second to multi-second, and there are likely to be few real transactions that conform closely to the predicted value. This is perfectly normal and does not negate the usefulness of the average figures.

4.2.3 A sample workload

Later we will describe how to obtain input data for sizing. For the moment just accept that we have somehow determined the overall characteristics of the workload as follows:

- Average transaction takes:
  1.0 second CPU time on a B10
  36 physical disk I/Os
  1 MB memory for working set
  800 bytes total data transmission on communications link.
- Required peak throughput:
  10 000 transactions per hour arising from 100 interactive users.

We will shortly show that it is a simple back-of-an-envelope job to derive the required machine configuration from the above information. Given an understanding of the range of AS/400 performance resources at our disposal, as documented in Chapter 2, we only need to establish how to allow for queuing in the otherwise commonsense arithmetic.

4.3   Queuing

Queues are a common feature of everyday life. Surely all of us have waited in line for a bus to arrive, or for a railway ticket office clerk to serve us. Generally these are managed by common consent in a first in, first out (FIFO) manner, but this is not always the case.

Quite apart from occasional sharp-elbowed queue jumpers there is sometimes a deliberate priority system imposed. In a hospital accident and emergency ward a newly arrived heart attack patient would expect to be given precedence over a queue of minor cuts and bruises. It is not so obvious that private fee-paying patients should get priority treatment, but in some situations this also happens.

In a computer system, when multiple jobs are running concurrently and making unscheduled demands on the performance resources, some of these demands may coincide. If at any time the number of units of the resource (e.g. main processors or activity level slots in memory) is less than the number of coincident requests, some queuing mechanism must be used to serialize the requests.

Delayed jobs are placed in queues, and we have already seen (Chapter 3) that these queues are kept in order by system software either on a FIFO basis (e.g. disk actuator queues) or prioritized (e.g. the task despatcher queue or the ineligible queues). Within a given priority FIFO applies, so in practice where most interactive work runs at the same priority, FIFO rules.

4.3.1   Single-server queues

An important distinction with queuing systems is the number of potential service points available to a queue. The simplest situation is one server per queue. An example of this is a system with a single main processor serving the task despatcher queue. A corresponding example in everyday life would be getting cash from an automatic teller machine (ATM) outside a bank. There is one machine which if you are lucky is free when you arrive, but at peak times you may have to wait behind other users.

This situation is illustrated in Fig. 4.2 and a simple formula is quoted to calculate the effect of queuing on the expected time to get served. To avoid confusion, from now on we will reserve the phrase 'service time' for the dedicated (no queuing) situation and use 'response time' to include any queuing. Therefore:

Response time = service time + queuing time

The assumptions underlying the formula are:

- normal distribution of arrival times to join the queue
- no prioritization within the queue
- distribution of service times about the mean is exponential.

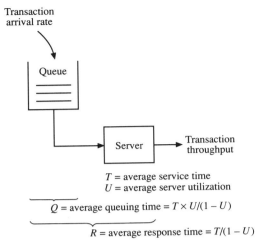

Transaction
arrival rate

Queue

Server → Transaction
throughput

T = average service time
U = average server utilization

Q = average queuing time = $T \times U/(1 - U)$

R = average response time = $T/(1 - U)$

Figure 4.2.   Single-server queuing.

If we assume a one-way processor which is 60 per cent busy (0.6 utilization) and a transaction which requires 0.2 second of dedicated CPU time, the response time of the transaction through the processor is:

Response time = $0.2/(1 - 0.6)$
$= 0.2/0.4$
$= 0.5$ second

The queuing multiplier $1/(1 - U)$ is the factor which multiplies the service time to give the response time in a queuing situation. Figure 4.3 shows the effect of increasing utilization on this factor.

Clearly the effect of increasing the utilization is small at first but accelerates and becomes very large at high utilizations. An increase from 0.8 to 0.9 doubles the response time whereas an increase from 0 to 0.1 only raises the response by 11 per cent. The 'elbow' of the curve is where the slope indicates a queuing multiplier increase of 1.0 for a utilization increase of 0.1. By eye we can see that this occurs at about 70 per cent utilization.

4.3.2   Multi-server queues

In general we may have any number of servers for a queue. This is akin to the situation where you join a queue inside the bank to get your cash and the front of the queue is served by the first clerk who is free. If they are not all out at lunch, there may be three or four people serving the queue and your wait time is reduced.

In computer terms the multi-server model applies to the ineligible queues (any activity level slot will do) and to n-way processors (any processor will do). Making

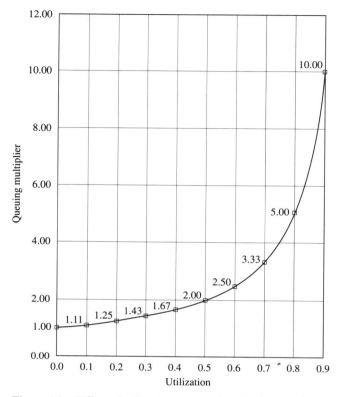

Figure 4.3.   Effect of utilization on queuing (single server).

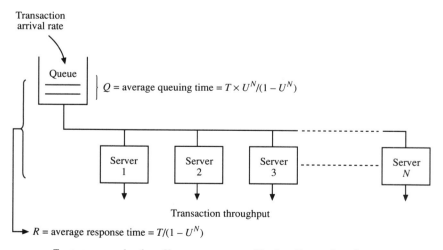

T = average service time, U = average server utilization, N = number of servers

Figure 4.4.   Multi-server queuing.

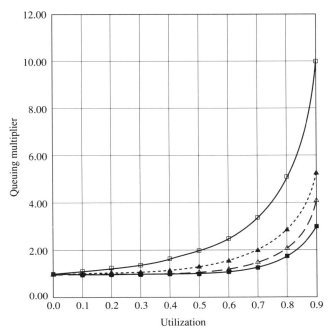

1 server	□	1.00	1.11	1.25	1.43	1.67	2.00	2.50	3.33	5.00	10.00
2 servers	▲	1.00	1.01	1.04	1.10	1.19	1.33	1.56	1.96	2.78	5.26
3 servers	△	1.00	1.00	1.01	1.03	1.07	1.14	1.28	1.52	2.05	3.69
4 servers	■	1.00	1.00	1.00	1.01	1.03	1.07	1.15	1.32	1.69	2.91

Figure 4.5.   Effect of multiple servers on queuing.

the same assumptions as before the general formula is shown in Fig. 4.4. If we apply it to the transaction in our previous example and assume again 60 per cent CPU utilization, of a 4-way processor this time:

$$\text{Response time} = 0.2/(1 - 0.6^4)$$
$$= 0.2/(1 - 0.13)$$
$$= 0.25 \text{ second}$$

The response time has been halved by the multi-processor although each of the component processors was just as busy as the single-processor machine.

You can see from Fig. 4.5 that adding servers still leaves us with a queuing multiplier effect of the same general shape, but with the elbow displaced towards higher utilization values. The response time collapse comes later but more dramatically.

4.3.3   Queuing for disk I/Os

When it comes to disk actuators, you might be misled because of the multiplicity of servers on the machine. A little thought shows that it is nevertheless the single-server model which must be used.

If a job issues an I/O request it will be to one specific actuator, because the item it needs to access is only in one place on disk (forget mirroring for the moment). The request cannot be satisfied by the first actuator to become free, but only by the one covering the required item. Each actuator must therefore have its own associated queue.

In a mirrored disk environment, the number of physical writes will be doubled compared to a non-mirrored situation, because objects are stored twice. On output operations, pairs of parallel requests will be generated to separate actuators. On input, the system's storage management function selects the device with the shortest request queue, giving a performance advantage over a non-mirrored environment for read operations.

4.3.4   Response time versus throughput

When you see the reponse time versus throughput graphs in Chapter 5 the general shape will be very familiar. This should be no surprise because transaction response time is the sum of the response times for the individual performance resources used during the transaction. Also the transaction throughput is what produces the (proportional) utilization of the resources.

In Fig. 4.6 the transaction response time/throughput curve which is the top line is just a composite derived from the underlying curves. What we are showing is the projected effect of the various resource utilizations on the response time for an average transaction. The base service time comprises 0.4 second of disk I/O time plus 0.15 second of CPU time. As the throughput increases, the utilization (not shown) of the CPU and the disk actuators also grows. The operation of the queuing multipliers (single server in each case) produces the response time patterns shown.

The CPU response reaches its elbow first in this example and overtakes the contribution of disk response at just over 80 000 transactions per hour. At about the same point the rapidly increasing memory residency time, due to CPU plus disk activity and queuing, causes queuing for memory to begin to make an impact. Because this is a multi-server facility with lots of activity levels, it has had a negligible effect on response until this point, but once it starts rising the ineligible (memory) queue time escalates rapidly.

4.3.5   Threshold-utilization values

When sizing we have to decide what is a sensible peak utilization figure to allow. The queuing and response time graphs show us that the machine must work below the elbow of these curves if we are to avoid gross performance degradation. As we approach the elbow the sensitivity of performance to small variations in throughput is more marked.

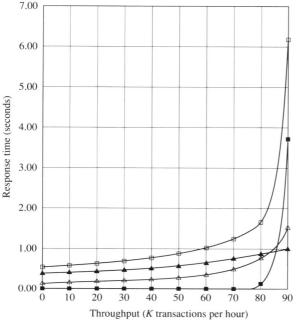

Tran rsp	□	0.55	0.59	0.65	0.71	0.79	0.89	1.03	1.23	1.67	6.16
Disk rsp	▲	0.40	0.43	0.46	0.50	0.54	0.59	0.65	0.73	0.82	0.95
CPU rsp	△	0.15	0.17	0.19	0.21	0.25	0.30	0.38	0.50	0.75	1.50
Mem Q time	■	0.00	0.00	0.00	0.00	0.00	0.00	0.00	0.00	0.10	3.71

Figure 4.6.   Response time versus throughput.

In general we can identify a *guideline* utilization value below which responses are stable, i.e. predictable and uniform for a given transaction complexity. A second (higher) *threshold* utilization marks the point beyond which the resource is overloaded and provides excessive or very variable response times. Between these values we will experience variable responses which may be tolerable for short periods or in exceptional circumstances.

The aim is to base our sizing on the guideline value and use the threshold as a buffer to protect us against unanticipated increases in transaction throughput and complexity while we justify and install an upgrade. The sizing estimates must include an allowance for anticipated growth and for estimation uncertainties.

The precise guideline and threshold values we choose are partly a question of judgement and experience. There is no magic formula, but there are some general considerations which guide the choice. First, we have seen that multi-server resources can perform well up to higher utilizations than equivalent speed single-server resources. Second, and this is the key point, the speed of the resource is crucial. A faster resource like a CPU which probably contributes a small amount of the transaction response time can be allowed to multiply its contribution by a larger factor, i.e. work at a higher utilization. A slower device like a disk actuator

Table 4.1. Maximum permissible utilizations for AS/400 hardware

Device	Sizing guideline	'No-go area' threshold
CPU (single processor)[a]	0.70	0.80
CPU (2-way processor)[a]	0.76	0.83
CPU (3-way processor)[a]	0.79	0.85
CPU (4-way processor)[a]	0.81	0.86
Disk actuator (9332/9335)	0.40	0.50
Disk actuator (9336/9337)	0.50	0.60
Traditional series disk IOP or MFIOP	0.45	0.50
Advanced series disk IOP	0.70	0.80
Local workstation IOP[b]	0.35	0.40
LAN IOP	0.40	0.50
Communication line	0.35	0.40
Communications IOP[b]	0.45	0.50
Remote workstation control unit	0.40	0.50

[a] The CPU figures are for the interactive and higher-priority components of the workload only. Lower-priority work (e.g. batch jobs) can use the remaining CPU without significant impact.
[b] Measured IOP utilizations include low-priority polling activity which does not impact performance. The tabulated figures refer to the utilization caused by application data transfer alone.

which usually contributes a large part of the transaction response should be restricted to lower queuing multipliers by keeping the utilization down. Table 4.1 summarizes the currently accepted values.

Figure 4.7 illustrates the concept of guideline and threshold values for the case of CPU utilization. Each curve in the figure represents one chosen CPU utilization figure, and we could plot any number of similar curves.

Taking the 50 per cent middle line as an example we see that a throughput of 6 K tr/h and a CPU service time of 0.3 second gives a point on the curve. We could get other points on the 50 per cent curve by using a lower throughput of more complex (higher CPU service time) transactions, or a higher throughput of simpler transactions. Examples are 3 K tr/h at 0.6 second CPU service time, and 18 K tr/h at 0.1 second CPU service time.

If we increase CPU per transaction or throughput without a corresponding decrease in the other factor, we increase the CPU utilization, i.e. move onto a higher curve in the series. The figure has been annotated to show the three important areas. If our particular combination of throughput and CPU service time puts us anywhere below the 70 per cent guideline curve then we can expect stable performance appropriate to the transaction complexity.

If our workload complexity and throughput combined are high enough to take us above the 80 per cent curve, then we will get poor performance with extended and unstable response times. Between these limits there is a region where response times will be unpredictable. It may be acceptable for the machine to enter this area during exceptional peaks, but the margin before crossing into the 'no-go' zone is dangerously small.

Table 4.1 points out that different threshold values apply to multiprocessor machines, but the general argument is identical. The same sort of utilization curves

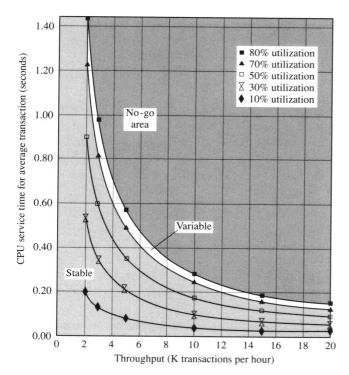

Figure 4.7.   Equal utilization curves.

can also be drawn for other performance resources, and the figures in Table 4.1 identify the boundaries of the three performance regions.

4.4   Sizing objectives

4.4.1   Balanced systems

The aim of sizing is to provide a system which is the right size for its workload. Certainly it has to be big enough, and should cater for some growth, but we also need to avoid extravagant over-provision. This means that the machine should reach its maximum throughput capacity during peak periods of activity. A balanced system is simply one where the same requirement applies to each of the main performance resources.

At peak periods all performance resources should be operating close to their limits. If this is not the case one or more resources are being under-used, perhaps because of deficiencies elsewhere. For example, a powerful CPU can be constrained to operate well below its limits if insufficient DASD and/or memory are attached: an expensive economy.

4.4.2   *Achieving response time aims*

It is perfectly possible to provide a machine which copes with the proposed workload without becoming overloaded, but fails to satisfy the performance expectations of users. This could be because expectations are unrealistic or have been wrongly set, for example by training on local screens with a lightly loaded system before going live at a remote location.

A poor perception of performance is not necessarily significant, though it should be avoided by conforming to agreed service levels (see Chapter 7). Long response times may, however, have a direct negative effect on the end users' ability to do their job. A system where users have to enter orders and make enquiries while dealing with customers on the telephone is an example where this can become a sensitive issue.

In such cases, if the complexity of the workload results in unacceptable performance, it may be necessary to provide a more powerful machine than is strictly justified by the utilization criteria. What we are describing is not normal, but neither is it very unusual. A machine can be lightly loaded, but a complex transaction can still take a significant amount of time to execute. If it is critical that this time is reduced and we cannot easily redesign the complex transaction, we may choose to over-size the machine.

To (say) halve a response time by using more and faster hardware would be an expensive course to take, and the resulting machine would be greatly under-utilized. Such action is normally a last resort, after the offending transactions have been examined with a view to simplification. Response time predictions are also less reliable than utilization predictions, and the average figure may have little relevance to an individual component of the workload. Response times are therefore not commonly a prime consideration during sizing.

4.5   Manual sizing

Using the sample workload characterized in Sec. 4.2.3 we are now in a position to demonstrate how sizing can be done manually. We will assume that allowances for growth and peak volumes have been made, so that the utilization guideline figures can be used directly to size the machine without further safety margins.

4.5.1   *CPU sizing*

We require $10\,000 \times 1.0 = 10\,000$ B10 CPU equivalent seconds per hour. Since there are only 3600 real elapsed seconds in an hour we cannot achieve our objective on a model B10. We need a CPU that is faster by at least a factor of $10\,000/3600 = 2.8$ approximately. On top of this we cannot allow the high-priority interactive work to use anywhere near 100 per cent of the CPU; this would cause lengthy queuing delays as well as leaving no capacity for concurrent lower-priority batch work.

We have proposed that 70 per cent is a reasonable peak utilization for high-priority work. The factor therefore becomes 2.8/0.7 = 4.0. From Fig. 2.1 in Sec. 2.1 we see that a Model 200/2031 or a Model 300/2040 would fit the bill. If we were not too confident about the accuracy of the input data and wished to leave some margin for error, we could select a Model 200/2032 or a Model 300/2041 at 5.8 × the internal performance of a B10. The estimated peak CPU utilization for the interactive workload would then be 0.7 × 4/5.8 = 0.48.

Finally we would recognize that a Model 200/2032 is currently top of the range in the 9402 packaging type. If growth beyond the capability of the 2032 CPU is likely within a year or two, we would probably choose the Model 300. The 2040 CPU is bottom of the easily expandable 9406 range and has the same internal performance as the Model 200/2031.

4.5.2   Disk sizing

The workload will generate 360 000 disk I/O requests per hour (or 100 I/Os per second). We noted earlier that the service time for one I/O using 9336 drives is about 20 ms. This means that one 9336 actuator can perform 1/0.02 = 50 I/Os per second working flat out, so our workload seems to be equivalent to 2 × 9336 access arms.

As with the CPU, queuing delays are again a consideration which prevents us from using 100 per cent of the throughput capacity. We have established that a sensible design threshold is for 9336 disk actuators to reach no more than 50 per cent busy. The net effect is that one 9336 actuator can handle 0.50 × 50 = 25 I/Os per second, and we need a minimum of four actuators for our workload.

These can be supplied by two 9336 devices (either Model 010 or model 020) with appropriate additional features. The disk storage capacity that accompanies the actuators ranges from 1.88G to 3.42G depending on the precise models and features selected. If the amount of online data requires more space than 3.42G we will have to provide additional access arms beyond the minimum of four required for performance reasons alone.

This discussion has ignored the existence of an *internal* disk provided as part of the base system unit of the 2040. This is protected by a battery power unit and is designed primarily to enhance recoverability following a power failure. However, it also adds to the data storage and throughput capacity of the system.

Similar arithmetic using the service time data in Table 2.2 can derive a suitable disk configuration based on other DASD. For example, if we choose a 9337 Model 215 subsystem, the device is roughly twice as fast as the 9336 and two actuators therefore give equivalent performance. However, the accompanying storage capacity is only 1.08G and our online storage needs may force us to add further DASD. Additional internal disks are a practical alternative.

4.5.3   Main storage sizing

The throughput is $10\,000/3600 = 2.8$ transactions per second. On average, each of the hundred users are generating $10\,000/100 = 100$ transactions per hour, or one transaction every 36 seconds. In reality, it is much more likely that only 50 users will be active, working at twice this rate, but the argument is not affected. How many users are likely to want their job to be *active*, i.e. occupying main storage concurrently?

To estimate this we need the average response time components due to CPU and disk activity. This tells us how long the average transaction needs to occupy memory:

- From Fig. 2.1 we see that a 300/2040 has 4.0 times the internal performance of a B10. The CPU service time required on the 2040 is $1.0/4.0 = 0.25$ second. The queuing multiplier is $1/(1 - 0.7) = 3.3$ giving a CPU response time of 0.83 second.
- The disk time required is $36 \times 0.019 = 0.68$ second. The queuing multiplier of $1/(1 - 0.50)$ leads to a disk response time component of 1.36 second.
- The total time spent in memory by an average transaction is therefore approximately 2.2 seconds.

Bearing in mind our previous result that 2.8 transactions per second are being processed, during the active life of one average transaction it is reasonable to expect that, on average, 2.8×2.2 ($= 6.2$) transactions will start and the same number of different transactions will end. If we could schedule all new transactions to start immediately after old transactions finished we could ideally manage with just 6.2 (say, 7) concurrent transactions.

Looking at the worst case, all the new transactions might start in a bunch just before a bunch of transactions end. Memory would then be demanded for double the number of concurrent transactions. This is an application of the well-known 'Murphy's Law' (if anything can go wrong, it will).

Note that the argument starts from average reponse time and throughput figures. The real workload will be far from homogeneous and transaction start and end times will be random. We should therefore take the conservative side of the previous discussion and assume that Murphy's Law applies:

Activity level estimate $= 2 \times 2.8 \times 2.2 = 12.3$ at peak periods

A more rigorous statistical analysis of this problem confirms that the above calculation does provide a reasonable estimate. Because the average working set size is 1 MB the starting point for sizing a pool for our workload is therefore 12.3 MB. This is a multi-server situation, so we can allow the utilization to get quite high, but a threshold of 80 per cent is advisable. The required pool size is then $12.3/0.8 = 15.4$ MB. Rounding up to 16 MB this allows for a maximum of 16 concurrently active transactions.

The system also requires memory for the machine pool, spool writer pool, *BASE pool and any concurrent batch streams. Making typical allowances for these items as recommended in Chapter 9, we arrive at a minimum total requirement of 24 MB. The base memory size on the 300/2040 is 8 MB and the increments are also 8 MB. We therefore select a 24 MB model 300/2040 for the sample workload.

4.6   Measured workloads

We have shown that it is not too difficult to size an AS/400 correctly providing we have the relevant workload parameters to hand. The question of how we come by them cannot be put off any longer.

To a prospective purchaser the most convincing approach might be a 'test drive', i.e. a series of benchmarks in which the proposed workload is generated and the performance of real hardware alternatives is demonstrated and measured. Unfortunately the difficulty and cost of setting up reproducible interactive benchmarks even for one workload situation rules this out for all practical purposes.

The best we can normally hope to do is to use the AS/400 performance measurement tools to measure the workload or various subsets of the workload once, running on a well-tuned and fully loaded AS/400 system. Experience shows that such measurements are good enough to accurately size machines for combinations and multiples of the measured workloads.

The process has already been illustrated by manual calculation but would generally be carried out using a tool such as BEST/1(*), as described in Chapter 6. This tool not only facilitates the process but allows the effects of a range of workload, configuration and system changes to be explored without further measurement.

Since the method extrapolates from actual performance and workload data it can only be applied where the application software is available in its final form and running in a live or realistic environment. *This should be the case with packages purchased from software suppliers.* A workload and performance profile suitable for input to BEST/1 should be available for all major modules and functions from the software vendor. Sizing for any combination of functions and for any specific mix of throughput figures will then be precise and trouble-free.

Similar considerations apply if you are planning to install a system at a remote site to run central site applications locally. Precise sizing can be achieved based on performance tool profiles from the central machine adjusted via BEST/1 for different overall volume and mix of workload components.

4.7   Predefined workloads

Predefined workloads are standard workloads which are built into the BEST/1 capacity planner. Where measured workloads are not available, the predefined ones can be used to represent proposed real workloads. The nature of the built-in workloads must be understood and carefully matched to the proposed workloads if the resulting sizing estimates are to be of any value at all.

Some of the predefined workloads exist as applications and have been used to perform extensive benchmarks in IBM performance-evaluation centres. The results of some of these measurements are presented in Chapter 5 together with a description of the test environment. The main purpose of the benchmarks is to compare the performance of different systems, but they also allow system developers to validate or calibrate the BEST/1 model.

The following sections describe the predefined workloads to assist the process of matching with proposed new workloads.

4.7.1   RAMP-C

This is a group of interactive commercial application functions written in Cobol. There are four transaction types defined covering a range of complexities. They are described in Table 4.2.

Of course, real commercial applications contain a very wide range of transaction types, some of which may be comparable to the RAMP-C classes in terms of

Table 4.2.   Logical characteristics of RAMP-C transaction types

Transaction type	Class 1	Class 2	Class 3	Class 4
Transaction name	Inquiry	Simple update	Multiple-entry update	Complex processing
Description	Single record lookup by key	Entering order consisting of one-line item	Entering order consisting of six-line items	Updating ten records in a file
Number of DB Files accessed	2	3	3	5
Logical DB I/Os				
Indexed reads	1	3	11	25
Sequential reads	0	2	5	5
Indexed updates	0	1	6	10
Sequential adds (log file)	1	1	1	1
Total logical DB I/Os	2	7	23	41
Size of files (except log file)	30 000 records	30 000 records	30 000 records	30 000 records
Workstation I/O				
Fields				
Input	1	5	0	0
Input/output	0	5	30	54
Output	23	18	8	8
Constant	36	36	12	12
Characters				
Input	8	40	0	0
Input/output	0	40	230	414
Output	120	80	21	21
Constant	425	439	154	154
Subprogram calls	0	0	0.2[a]	0.2[a]
COBOL program statements compiled/executed	403 99	462 131	560 345	652 625

[a]One in five executions of this transaction result in a single subprogram call.

Table 4.3. Standard RAMP-C transaction mix used for benchmarks

Transaction type	Percentage of terminals running each transaction type	Key/think time (seconds)	Percentage of total transactions
Class 1	20	7.5	35
Class 2	20	10.0	25
Class 3	40	18.2	30
Class 4	20	26.0	10

complexity. In our experience real workloads often contain a significant proportion of transactions which are more complex than class 4, and in some cases the average transaction may even exceed class 4 in complexity.

Nevertheless, a mix of the RAMP-C classes has been used as a standard for extensive benchmarking activity. The results documented in Chapter 5 are extremely valuable as a means of comparing the capabilities of different machines, but in most cases the absolute throughput figures attained in the benchmarks are not representative of results with typical real workloads.

The same warning applies equally to use of the default RAMP-C predefined workload when sizing with BEST/1. The mix is shown in Table 4.3 and in general it will be much simpler than the workload we wish to support. Providing we are aware of this and do not assume that standard RAMP-C is likely to be representative of our workload there is no problem. We simply adjust the mix of classes to suit our predictions or use some other workload for sizing.

Don't overlook the fact that transaction throughput and complexity is insufficient to define a workload. The number of terminal users generating that throughput is another important factor. A particular throughput could be achieved by a number of users working relatively slowly, or by a smaller number of users working faster. The latter workload would place a smaller resource demand on the system because of the smaller number of concurrent jobs which has to be managed. It would be expressed as a smaller physical disk I/O and CPU demand by the average transaction.

4.7.2 SPOOL workload group

Two types of spool application are defined within BEST/1 and can be specified when sizing with this tool:

- *AFP(*NO)*. This workload is representative of the majority of printing done on AS/400 systems. It is straightforward printing of normal text without data conversion or other complex facilities.
- *AFP(*YES)*. This workload represents high-speed and complex printing. It involves data conversion and support for high-speed printers, leading to a

higher than normal demand for performance resources. This sort of printing may result from use of the Advanced Function Printing support to create images, overlays and graphics.

4.7.3   BATCH workload group

Five different predefined batch workloads are defined within BEST/1 and can be selected to represent batch activities on your system where no relevant measured data is available.

1. *Commercial orders.* This is intended to simulate typical commercial end-of-day or end-of-month jobs which retrieve, update, print and copy data from multiple files with a relatively small amount of processing of the data. Three consecutive steps are performed which simulate order validation, order processing and file copy functions. Eighteen physical files are used and each file has ten logical files involving nine indexes built over it.
2. *Development.* This simulates the sort of batch processing which accompanies application development activities. It includes a compilation of a large RPG program, compilations of a small RPG program, and library save activities using data compression. The workload is fairly CPU intensive during the compilations but has more synchronous I/O activity during the saves.
3. *Complex query.* This is a CPU-intensive query running over a 100 000 record database file. It produces a report based on 30 per cent of the records and a subset of fields. It sequences the report on a derived field and uses summary functions on three of the fields.
4. *Summary query.* This medium-complexity query also tends to be CPU intensive and runs against a 144 000-record database file. It selects six out of the 49 fields in every record and produces a report using summary functions on all selected fields.
5. *Sort query.* This query sequences a 50 000 record database file on two fields for which no access path exists and produces a report based on all the records in the file.

Table 4.4 summarizes the approximate characteristics of the above five workloads when run as dedicated batch jobs. The range of I/O rates quoted arises because faster processors are able to make I/O requests at a higher rate.

Table 4.4.   Predefined batch workload characteristics

Batch application	Logical I/Os per second	Synchronous I/Os per second	Asynchronous I/Os per second
Commercial Orders	70–200	7–20	20–60
Development	2–25	3–35	1–10
Complex query	0.1–1.0	2–15	3–30
Summary query	0.2–2.0	1–12	1–15
Sort query	0.2–2.0	2–15	3–20

4.7.4   Office workload group

These workloads are all based on the IBM Systems Application Architecture(*) OfficeVision(*) licensed program and are only relevant if you use this product. Five different workload types are provided, designed to be representative of the main categories of user (e.g. secretary, professional, manager or word processing specialist).

Each type of user has its own characteristic default mix of the basic office functions. The basic functions include items such as update calendar, create small document, revise large document and work with mail. Each function corresponds to a fixed number of computer transactions.

Each type of user also has three built-in modes of activity (steady, interrupted or casual) which allocate default key/think times to the transactions. The BEST/1 user can, of course, override the default key/think times as well as the default function mixes to define a workload which simulates any desired pattern of office activity.

4.7.5   SQL RTW workload group

The RTW (Relational Transaction Workload) is the final predefined workload built into BEST/1. It simulates the functions of an inventory tracking and stock control application, and is written in COBOL/400(*) with database I/O functions performed by static SQL/400(*) statements.

Use of SQL rather than high-level language record I/O statements is growing in line with the growth of client/server environments. SQL is also appropriate where portability is a prime concern and applications need to run without change on the IBM SAA platforms (Mainframe, AS/400 and PS/2(*)).

4.7.6   Additional predefined workloads

IBM have announced for availability with Version 3 Release 1 of the performance tools a range of 22 new predefined workloads drawn from measurements on installed customer machines in a variety of industry groups. The groups include Finance, Manufacturing, Insurance and Education. Two predefined client/server workloads are also promised.

An additional batch workload, exemplifying a background server job, was provided with Version 2 Release 3. At the time of going to press we have had no opportunity to assess these workloads, but they could provide a very useful set of model input options, and an improved chance of realistically matching requirements.

4.8   *User-defined workloads*

If measured workload data are not available (e.g. software development is not completed) and some components of your anticipated workload cannot be matched by predefined workloads, BEST/1 allows direct input of user-defined workload data. You would need to provide all the information normally obtained by measurement including:

1. *Transaction data.* CPU time, synchronous and asynchronous database reads and writes, synchronous and asynchronous non-database reads and writes, and permanent writes are required. Permanent writes are physical output operations of permanent data, as opposed to transient data which is stored only during the execution of a job. To correctly model the effect of the checksum recovery facility which does not protect against loss of temporary data the classification of writes into permanent and temporary is necessary.
2. *Throughput data.* Key/think time, transactions per function, and functions per hour per user must be specified.

The degree of confidence which can be placed on completely artificial workload data being representative of your future workload is very small, even if your specifications are based on experience and understanding. As the outcome of any sizing exercise is determined by the input, and there is no magic way by which a model such as BEST/1 can come up with the 'right' answer if it is asked the wrong question, this facility should be used with extreme caution and as a last resort.

If user-defined workloads are used at all they should preferably form a small part of the overall workload. A user-defined workload is probably best entered by making changes to an existing measured or predefined workload, rather than by inventing the whole set of data from scratch. Care needs to be taken that the various parts of the data are mutually consistent if the model results are to be reliable.

If sizing must be done to budget for hardware costs using user-defined or predefined workloads only, the confidence level in the predictions must be rated very low or, at best, low. The sizing exercise should be repeated as application development proceeds, and more realistic measured data becomes available, to progressively increase the confidence level.

4.9   Estimation of batch run times

The BEST/1 model is designed primarily to predict interactive performance and offers no explicit batch run-time prediction facility. However, batch throughput is modelled as part of the overall workload and it is not difficult to use the output to get the answers we want about the effect of configuration changes on batch run times.

We showed in Sec. 1.3 how simple it is to calculate the effect of CPU and disk changes on batch run times in a dedicated environment. In fact it is quicker to do this manually than to use the modelling tool. In either case we must have measured performance data as a starting point.

If our input data comes from a mixed workload where the batch job of interest was running concurrently with other jobs the manual approach is still possible but becomes more complicated:

1. First, queuing for CPU and disk has to be considered, and because some of the workload is probably higher priority than batch we would need to use more elaborate variations of the queuing multiplier formulae than we have yet come across.
2. Identification of synchronous I/Os is more difficult. Although the performance tool reports list 'synchronous I/Os' by job, the figures do not include I/Os which were requested in parallel (i.e. asynchronously) but did not complete prior to the data being needed.
3. Exceptional waits due to contention for application objects may also occur.

We can work our way around problem 1 with additional arithmetic, or, by the deservedly popular least-effort principle, use BEST/1 for the job. The queuing multiplier (QM) for CPU response or run time is given by the following formula, where $U1$ is the utilization due to higher priority work, $U2$ is the utilization due to all jobs at the priority of the job we are considering, N is the number of such jobs, and P is the number of processors.

$$QM = 1 / (1 - (U1 + (U2 \times (N - 1)/N))^P)$$

Problem 2 can be sorted by querying the QAPMJOBS file, used for data collection by the performance tools. The file has records for each job, containing a counter field with the missing information.

JBWIO is the number of asynchronous I/Os that were waited on.

The recommended procedure is to add this value to the reported synchronous disk I/Os for the job.

Problem 3 is application dependent and difficult to predict. In general we can say that increasing the number of concurrent jobs (both batch and interactive), which we will presumably choose to do on a more powerful system, will tend to increase lock contention. On the other hand, if the number of jobs sharing a particular item does not increase, then the enhanced performance of the lock holders and lock seekers will tend to cancel out as the hardware is upgraded. Changes to all performance resources, not just the CPU, are likely to affect the issue.

Given a particular situation, with knowledge of the way contention objects are used by the applications, and of planned configuration and operational changes, it should be possible to make commonsense estimates of the effects on exceptional wait times.

4.10   Disk space sizing

Finally, with the more difficult part of the sizing job done, we must ensure that
sufficient disk space is provided for all online items. We sized the disks in terms of
the number and speed of actuators needed to handle the workload. Without
changing these specifications significantly, we have the freedom to choose a
variety of disk subsystems which have varying amounts of associated storage
capacity.

If the maximum storage-per-actuator model fails to satisfy our storage needs,
then we will increase the number of DASD as necessary. Space will be required not
only for application data and software but also for a variety of user-related
permanent and temporary objects, system software and data, work space, room for
growth, and storage for redundant information when high-availability disk
protection techniques are used.

4.10.1   System requirements

Every system will have some of the items listed in Table 4.5 stored on disk. The
'Min' column is the approximate size of a single item, compressed where possible.
The 'Max' column is the approximate decompressed size of the item or items listed.
In the case of compilers, all possible variations are included such as S/36(*) and
S/38(*) compatible, previous release and ILE versions. You will need to estimate
the storage needed for your particular environment and selection of products. For
information about individual product sizes refer to the current *New Products
Planning Information* manual (see Bibliography).

4.10.2   Application requirements

Application requirements will make up the bulk of the storage demand, and only a
few general remarks can usefully be made here. The space for programs, display
files and some other application objects will be known precisely. The larger storage
requirements for database files and access paths will depend not only on the
application design but also very much on the details of your particular business
and how you run it.

Such obvious variables as number of customers, number of suppliers, number of
products, and period of historic data to be maintained online are just a few factors
which can multiply file sizes and help to determine the storage requirement. If
journalling is used, the rate at which database changes occur, and housekeeping
options chosen for journal receiver management, control the extra space needed.
Quite accurate estimates can normally be made by the application provider
(whether within your own organization or not) from relevant input provided by
you.

Table 4.5. Disk space for system, operating system and related software

Material stored on disk	Possible disk space usage (M) min/max
Licensed internal code (9402/9404 or 9406)	76/94
Operating system licensed programs	
OS/400 base support	135/190
OS/400 normal options	71/115
OS/400 other options	20/25
PC Support/400	13/54
Online manuals	180/300
Main storage dump space (MB × 1 048 576 bytes)	4/1611
Internal objects:	
IOP and DASD LIC space (1.05M × number of actuators)	1/267
History and error logs	
Temporary storage for active jobs (PAGs etc)	
General utilities licensed programs	
Performance tools	12/23
Advanced function printing and fonts	49/140
Cross-application licensed programs	
Query, BGU, PBX support, Cryptographic support	1/13
Telex, fax and image support	
Communications utilities licensed programs	
Comms, TCP/IP, OSI, point of sale	2/52
CICS/400	30/76
Network management utilities licensed programs	
Application development licensed programs	
ADT, SEU, ADM	10/22
Application dictionary services	10/18
Application program driver	12/17
Compilers (RPG, Cobol, SQL, C, Pascal, PL/I . . .)	1/50
CODE	14/15

Note: The sizes given in the above table are derived from figures given in the Version 2 Release 3 (V2R3) *New Products Planning Information* manual. See the Bibliography for the V3R1 manual form number which may apply to subsequent software release levels.

In case you are faced with doing some of this work yourself, notes on deriving database and spool file sizes are provided below Table 4.6. Spool files are, of course, stored on disk prior to printing, and may be saved on disk after printing. Business requirements and system housekeeping policies will control the space to be reserved.

4.10.3 Allowance for work space and growth

When the machine is fully loaded and running live it is probably wise to avoid exceeding 90 per cent disk space utilization. This is partly a margin to avoid the risk of filling up the disks completely (which stops the machine) but also to avoid possible less dramatic performance impact. Particularly on a small disk configuration, 10 per cent free space is not a lot, and it may be highly fragmented. When it comes to allocating space for large objects the overheads of finding and using multiple extents can be significant.

Table 4.6. Disk space for application software and data

Material stored on disk	Possible disk space usage (M) min/max
Spool files[a]	
SAA OfficeVision/400	
Licensed program materials	6.0/33
Language dictionaries/400	24
Documents and search database[b]	
PC files, mail, calendars and directories[b]	
Other application 1	
Application code	
Application data[c]	
Repeat the above three lines for each application	
Job accounting and security journals (if used)[d]	

[a]Multiply the expected maximum number of spool files by the average number of print lines per file and then by 100 for a guide. Allow for end-of-month or other periodic peaks.

[b]An average calendar for one user requires 190 K plus 1.5 K times the number of calendar entries. Assuming, say, 50 entries per month, the space for 6 months of calendar entries for one user is:

$$190 \text{ K} + 300 \times 1.5 \text{ K} = 45 \text{ MB}$$

Multiply this by the number of users, including rooms, equipment, etc. to estimate the space. Fifty users would require $50 \times 0.64 = 32$ MB. A document requires roughly 14 K for the first page and 8 K for subsequent pages. Assuming 50 users owning about 30 documents each, of around 3 pages average size:

$$\text{Space required} = 50 \times 30 \,(14 + 2 \times 8) \text{ K} = 640 \text{ KB}$$

A folder for up to 18 documents occupies 8 K. An extension to 24 K allows for up to 82 documents, which may be a typical average size. Fifty users with two folders each require about

$$100 \times 24 \text{ K} = 2.4 \text{ MB}.$$

Disk space for office mail can be estimated from the following formula:

$$\text{Space} = N \times (((I + P)/58) \times 18 \text{ K} + R \times 40 \text{ K} + R \times (S + 1) \times 0.5 \text{ K})$$

where N = number of mail users
           I = average incoming mail items
           P = average outgoing mail items with confirmation of delivery
           R = average outgoing mail items
           S = average number of recipients per distribution.

Fifty mail users with 100 incoming items and 75 outgoing items (of which 25 request COD) with two recipients per distribution amounts to 154 MB. Relatively small amounts of space will be occupied by system directory entries, user enrollments, distribution lists and personal directories, plus temporary storage for work areas while users are active. Allow around 10 MB per 50 users. Note that journalling is used when documents are created, deleted and changed. The journal receiver will grow steadily until it is detached, saved and deleted.

[c]*Physical file data space*
The space in bytes required to store data records in a physical file is the sum of:

$$1024 + 5120 \times \text{(number of members)} + \text{(number of records} + 1) \times \text{(record length} + 1)$$

Note that the number of records includes deleted records, which remain in the file until re-used, or dropped by file reorganization.

Keyed sequence access path
The space in bytes required for a physical or logical file keyed access path is approximately:

$$4096 + \text{(number of keys)} \times \text{(key length} + 8) \times 1.48$$

Note that the factor of 1.48 is the product of an estimated 0.8 for key compression arising from partial key value redundancy, and 1.85 for index insertion space.

Logical file space
Excluding access path space the size of a logical file is:

$$1024 + 2560 \times \text{(number of members)}$$

Database record formats
Every physical or logical file record which does not share an existing format requires:

$$512 \text{ bytes} + 96 \times \text{(number of fields)}$$

Database sharing directories
There are three relevant system directories, each of which requires in bytes:

$$272 + 16 \times \text{(number of entries)}$$

If a record uses an existing format, an entry is created. A physical file member generates an entry for each logical file member using the data. An access path generates an entry for each logical file member sharing the access path.

[d]Space requirements are extremely variable, depending on options selected, activity on system and housekeeping policy. It is best to introduce these facilities after a 'running-in' period and budget for additional space if the pilot suggests it is necessary.

Naturally, an allowance for growth must be made on top of the immediate system and application requirements. This will be based on your business plans over the period to be supported by the current hardware. In addition, do not overlook the need for such things as temporary file copies, test files, and online save files. Data compression is an option when saving to a save file, but it is best to assume that the size is equal to that of the objects being saved.

Another large amount of space may be needed for access path journalling, and this is not easy to estimate. Space is also taken up by device configuration, user and security objects. There is bound to be uncertainty in estimating all this, so we suggest you work on 67 per cent occupancy. That means whatever your sums amount to, multiply by 1.5 to get the disk space requirement.

Round this up to a whole number of 1.97G DASD and compare this with the access arm requirement. If the number of DASD is greater than or equal to the number of access arms required you have the starting point for your disk configuration. If not, switch to 970 M or 542 M disks to increase the number of actuators. If necessary accept excess storage space in order to get sufficient actuators.

4.10.4 Allowance for high-availability options

User auxiliary storage pools (ASPs) are frequently reserved for journal receivers and save files, and sometimes for subsetting the application libraries. By fragmenting auxiliary storage you multiply the number of separate areas where space and actuator activity need to be considered. Low space utilization and/or activity in one ASP implies extra space and/or actuators in other ASPs to cope with the skewed demand. This may well result in additional DASD requirements beyond that calculated for a single ASP.

If you plan to use disk mirroring to allow continuous availability through disk unit failures, each mirrored ASP (usually all ASPs) will require double the calculated number of DASD and appropriate IOPs (see Sec. 5.5.1 for DASD mirroring). For IOP-level protection further DASD IOPs may also be necessary. Spare disk units are sometimes kept ready to replace failed units, thereby minimizing the time spent running without mirrored protection following a failure.

Device parity protection as implemented with the 9337 requires the equivalent of one redundant disk per unit. If you have eight disks per unit, effectively seven are used for data storage, so you need to multiply your estimate by about 1.15. With only four disks per unit the multiplier is 1.34. This is less costly than mirroring (multiplier 2.0) for disk unit level availability, but does not deliver normal performance following a disk failure.

Checksum protection provides device-parity protection somewhat analogous to the 9337 HA models, for disks that do not have this capability built in. Continuous availability is not provided, but following replacement of a disk the contents are rebuilt and restoration of the database is avoided. The space overheads are more

Table 4.7. Approximate size limits in current OS/400 implementation

Description	Maximum value
Size of a file member	266.757G
Size of an access path	4.294G
Number of records in a file member	2147 million
Size of record (bytes)	32 766
Size of key in physical or logical file (characters)	2000
Size of key for SQL 'ORDER BY' or OPNQRYF 'KEYFLD' (bytes)	10 000
Number of key fields in a file	120
Number of fields in a record	8000
Character or DBCS field size (bytes)	32 766
Zoned decimal or packed decimal field size (digits)	31
Number of keyed logical files over one physical file	3686
Number of physical file members in one logical file member	32
Number of members participating in join function	32

difficult to calculate (see the Advanced Backup and Recovery Guide) but, roughly, disks are divided into sets of up to eight similar devices, and one of each set is effectively redundant. Additional CPU, main storage and disk actuator resource will also be needed to implement this function.

4.10.5 Maximum object sizes

Maximum object sizes are a detail of the implementation which may change from release to release of the system software, or even by means of a mid-release PTF (program temporary fix). Probably database files are the largest and most variable size objects on the system, so the current limits for database related items should be borne in mind (Table 4.7).

5
AS/400 performance examples

The purpose of this chapter is to give some idea of the performance of the current range of AS/400s. These are the F02 to F97 and the Advanced Series. The information shown here is based on benchmarks performed by IBM on sample systems. The hardware configurations shown will be superseded by new ones in the future. However, IBM have traditionally supplied performance comparison information for new models as they appear, so that it should be possible for the reader to make use of this chapter in conjunction with any new information publicly available from IBM and its business partners.

5.1   AS/400—a system for business

The division of IBM responsible for manufacturing and marketing the AS/400 is based in Rochester, Minnesota, in the USA. This division was previously responsible for the smaller System/360s(*), System/3(*), System/32(*), and System/34(*), all regarded in their time as small business computers and aimed squarely at the commercial marketplace.

These machines influenced the development of the System/36(*) and System/38(*). The System/38 was a machine whose architecture was conceived in the massive IBM 'Future Systems' project in the 1970s, to design the 'next generation' of computer systems to replace the System/370(*) mainframes. AS/400 is a natural successor to the System/38 and to the System/36 although its architecture is firmly rooted in that of the System/38.

This background characterizes the AS/400 as a general-purpose, mid-range computer catering for a wide range of business applications. There are a huge number of commercial application packages available which position the system in marketplaces such as:

● Banking
● Insurance
● Manufacturing

- Distribution
- Retail
  and many more

Where the AS/400 is used in organizations which are not so commercially oriented (e.g. local government, hospitals, religious organizations) it has traditionally been used to support the commercial side of the operation such as:

- Financial ledgers
- Inventory
- Invoicing
- Work scheduling
- Personnel
- Membership recordkeeping
- Payroll

In summary, the AS/400 and its predecessors have been used mainly for business applications and its internals have been optimized to perform well in this arena. That is one reason why the benchmarks shown here employ multi-user business applications, and why the results are expressed in terms relevant to business needs such as transactions per hour and average interactive response time. While measures commonly used to represent raw computing power such as Mhz or MIPs may be appropriate for evaluating computers needed for weather forecasting or advanced graphics, they are almost meaningless to a business needing a system that will allow it to process 5000 customer orders per day.

AS/400 has a unique architecture with its high-level machine interface, single-level storage and object management. Although it has been criticized as proprietary in the past by some, it has the major advantage that new technology may be implemented much more quickly and easily than with some systems that are claimed to be 'open' rather than proprietary, where the intricacies of each flavour of UNIX(*) must be considered carefully by developers. Hence, it is reasonable to assume that the AS/400 may well branch out into different areas as time goes by. For example the recent announcement of the AS/400 Server models point to its future use as a high-powered, high-function database server—an area where it has not previously had significant impact.

5.2   AS/400—a mid-range system?

Traditionally, the AS/400 has been seen as a mid-range computer positioned between small multi-user systems and the mighty mainframes. Today the smallest AS/400s in the range are typically used by organizations to support three or even fewer online users. The larger systems can connect up to 4800 local workstations plus˙ 96 multi-point lines and eight LANs. The practical supportable limit obviously depends on the activity of the attached terminals.

Larger, multiprocessor systems up to top mainframe level are being planned for the mid-1990s. Indeed IBM have publicly stated that the top AS/400 will soon house the fastest processor of any IBM machine. In addition, with OptiConnect/ 400(*) now available on AS/400 systems, it is possible to effect 'horizontal' growth by enabling up to seven AS/400s to have transparent, fast database access between systems using optical bus technology. Bearing in mind also that a portable version has been announced, it may be true to describe it as a full-range computer, with a single operating system supporting the entire range.

5.3   Benchmarks in general

5.3.1   The benchmarks in this chapter

The benchmark results in this chapter give an idea of the relative power and capabilities of the models in the AS/400 range. They are not intended to allow you to size an AS/400. The systems used in each case were large configurations for each model. The main commercial benchmark used is IBM RAMP-C. This is an interactive workload which allows commercial performance comparisons between different models of the AS/400 and with systems having different architectures (see Sec. 4.7.1).

Remember that RAMP-C is a particular interactive workload which is not representative of any specific customer environment. Results in other environments may vary significantly. You cannot assume either that it corresponds to any 'typical' commercial workload. A benchmark result may show that an AS/400 Model X could support 300 busy workstations performing the RAMP-C workload. However, your business may well require a larger configuration to support 300 busy workstations using your applications. In the banking environment, for instance, because of the nature of the work to be done, a typical application is likely to be very much more complex than RAMP-C. In order to estimate the configuration you might require, use BEST/1 as discussed in Chapter 6.

Remember also that an average response time shown in the benchmark results is exactly what its name suggests. The average is made up of individual response times, many of which will be longer than the average and many of which will be shorter.

In summary, view these benchmark results with caution. They reflect results from situations that cannot be compared with your own, and do not address all the factors that may concern you.

5.3.2   Other benchmarks

There are other benchmarks used in the industry for comparing commercial systems. The Transaction Processing Performance Council (TPC)* is an independent organization devoted to the specification and standardization of publicly available measures of computer performance. In July 1992, the TPC approved the definition of a benchmark known as TPC-C(*). This is a public benchmark that is designed to evaluate a computer system and associated software in the commercial environment taking ownership costs into account.

When using a benchmark to compare the performance of systems, you must assess its applicability to your situation. As with RAMP-C, do not assume that any benchmark is representative of your own workload. Ensure that comparison between systems is done on a like-for-like basis. For instance, comparing a client/server configuration against a non-client/server configuration may not be valid. This is because, in the client/server configuration, some of the workload will be handled by the client.

5.4   The RAMP-C benchmarks

When examining the RAMP-C throughput versus average response time line graphs note the following:

- Average response time is given in seconds.
- Throughput is given in transactions per hour.
- The throughput and average response time performance varies between systems.
- The square symbol on the line graphs marking 70 per cent system capacity refers to the number of interactive transactions which can be executed by a system at an acceptable and consistent response time. The symbol shows at what throughput the CPU utilization hits 70 per cent, or the DASD utilization 40 per cent, or the response time starts to become intolerable, whichever comes first.

5.4.1   AS/400 native performance

Figures 5.1 and 5.2 show results for various AS/400 systems executing the RAMP-C commercial benchmark in the native environment. Native means that the applications used were written for the AS/400 and not, for example, migrated applications run in the System/36 Environment(*).

Notice the similarities between the throughput of certain models such as the F06 and F10, the F25 and F35 and the Advanced Series models 200 with feature code 2031 and 300 with feature code 2040. Decisions about which system to select will often depend on the ability to upgrade within the same range.

Figure 5.3 is in the form of a capacity bar chart. It depicts:

- The interactive commercial throughput of systems at 70 per cent capacity (as previously described in Sec. 5.4)
- The relative interactive performance between various systems executing RAMP-C.

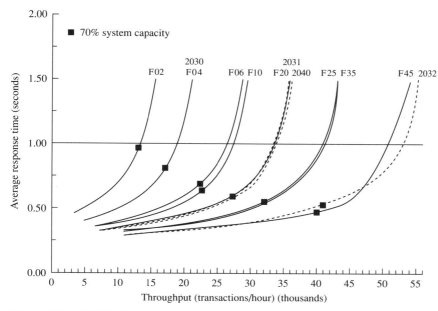

Figure 5.1. AS/400 V3ROM5 native RAMP-C performance: (lower end of range). Data shown here is based on the IBM RAMP-C interactive commercial benchmark, which is not representative of a specific customer requirement. Results in other environments may vary significantly.

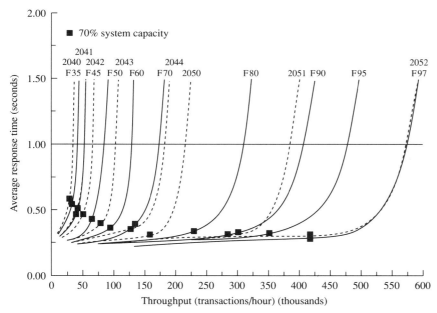

Figure 5.2. AS/400 V3ROM5 native RAMP-C performance: (higher end of range). Data shown here is based on the IBM RAMP-C interactive commercial benchmark, which is not representative of a specific customer requirement. Results in other environments may vary significantly.

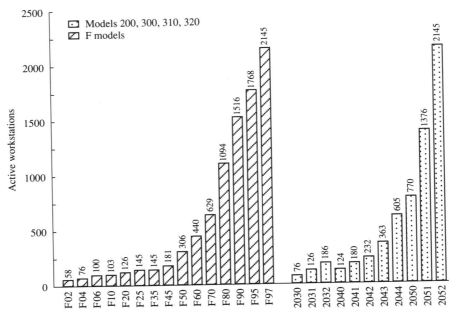

Figure 5.3. AS/400 V3ROM5 native RAMP-C performance: (large configurations at 70 per cent system capacity). Data shown here is based on the IBM RAMP-C interactive commercial benchmark, which is not representative of a specific customer requirement. Results in other environments may vary significantly.

5.4.2 AS/400 System/36 Environment performance

The System/36 (S/36) Environment is a special environment on the AS/400 allowing a user to run migrated S/36 applications in much the same way as on the S/36. In most cases, the S/36 user only has to use the AS/400 System/36 Migration Aid(*) (5727-MG1) to migrate S/36 applications. The migrated application may then be executed on an AS/400 in the S/36 Environment (Fig. 5.4).

This section compares the performance of the S/36 family with the performance of AS/400. These comparisons are made with the RAMP-C benchmark running on the AS/400 in the S/36 Environment. To facilitate valid comparisons, source code for programs and files used by the RAMP-C benchmark on the S/36 is migrated to the AS/400 using the above-mentioned migration aid. The migrated source code is then used to re-create programs and files on the AS/400 for execution in the S/36 Environment.

The S/36 Environment RAMP-C and AS/400 native environment RAMP-C 70 per cent system capacity numbers published in this document and elsewhere have led many people to draw the conclusion that the S/36 Environment has a 30–50 per cent performance degradation compared to the native environment. This conclusion is incorrect and is typically based on misinterpretation of data.

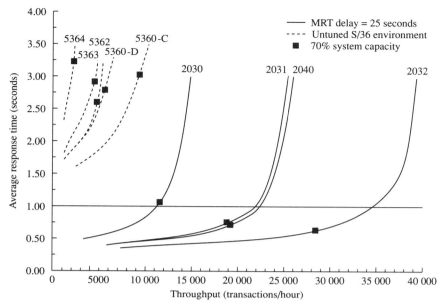

Figure 5.4.   AS/400 V3R0M5 S/36 Environment RAMP-C performance. Data shown here is based on the IBM RAMP-C interactive commercial benchmark, which is not representative of a specific customer requirement. Results in other environments may vary significantly.

The native RAMP-C application has been migrated from the S/38 to the AS/400 native environment whereas the S/36 Environment RAMP-C application was migrated from the S/36 to the AS/400 S/36 Environment. These are two distinctly different implementations which both satisfy RAMP-C design requirements.

In summary, it is the difference in the RAMP-C applications which causes the difference in performance between AS/400 native RAMP-C results and AS/400 System/36 Environment RAMP-C results, not any overhead caused by the System/36 Environment. Therefore, applications with similar characteristics and design to RAMP-C when migrated to the AS/400 can be expected to perform less efficiently than native applications. In fact, it is possible to 'tweak' many S/36 applications in order to make them perform almost equivalently to a native application performing similar functions. This can often be done with little effort.

5.5   Performance with recovery options

There are many facilities on the AS/400 that enhance recoverability. Naturally, some of these have performance implications. This section discusses the impact of some of the more common recovery options on performance.

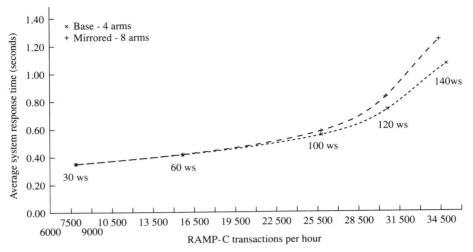

Figure 5.5.   Effect of mirroring on RAMP-C performance.

5.5.1   *DASD mirroring*

The option to mirror the disk storage on the AS/400 is available to any user with the appropriate amount and type of disk units and the required level of OS/400. What happens in a mirrored environment is that all mirrored data is duplicated—it is stored in two places on separate disk units. On the failure of a mirrored DASD unit, the AS/400 continues to operate by using the data on the partner unit. Obviously, storing the data twice requires twice the amount of DASD storage. A unit must also be mirrored by another unit of the same type and capacity.

The effect of DASD mirroring on run-time performance on a system which is not overloaded is generally small, since the CPU and main storage requirements of the mirroring function are low. Figure 5.5 shows a comparison between an AS/400 using DASD mirroring and one which is not using mirroring. When looking at the graph, note:

- Measurements made on Version 2 hardware using V2R1 software
- 9406 D model systems have two internal 2800-001 disk devices (four arms)
- Average response time is in seconds
- Throughput is in RAMP-C transactions per hour
- One of the curves has mirrored protection active

In some cases, mirroring can actually improve performance. Improvements of 0–5 per cent are reasonable expectations. This is particularly true where there is a high proportion of read activity—data can be read from the actuator with the shortest request queue. However, be aware that mirroring can have an adverse effect on performance where there is a large amount of write activity, since the number of disk writes required is doubled. This is particularly true where disk arms are busy. A degradation of 3–5 per cent is a reasonable expectation.

During synchronization of data after a failed unit has been repaired or replaced, you can expect some performance degradation. You may want to consider when to perform the synchronization in order to minimize the effect on your end users. You can also choose to synchronize only one mirrored pair at a time which carries less overhead than synchronizing all mirrored pairs at the same time. Even though some degradation in system performance can be expected at this stage, the system will be up and running.

5.5.2 RAID-5

The High Availability (HA) models of the 9337 Disk Array Subsystem and the disk controllers which support RAID-5 contain an implementation of the RAID-5 technique. RAID stands for 'redundant array of independent disks' and RAID-5 is a way of using redundancy to provide availability protection. This involves reserving a portion of the disk storage for parity information such that a lost unit can be dynamically reconstructed using the information from the other units. On a 9337 configured with four arms 25 per cent of the storage is required for parity information. The same area is sufficient to hold the parity information for a further four arms. Thus on a 9337 Model 2XX configured with eight arms, only 12.5 per cent of the storage is required for parity information.

Figure 5.6 compares 9337-225 HA with 9337-120, 9336 'standard' and 9336 mirrored. Each curve is marked with the DASD type (e.g. 9337-120) and quantity of arms (e.g. four) and possibly the quantity (e.g. two) of 9337s. The mirrored configurations contain double the DASD configuration specified at the top of the

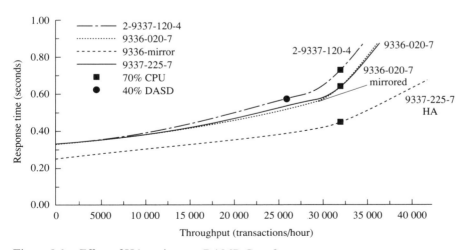

Figure 5.6. Effect of HA options on RAMP-C performance.

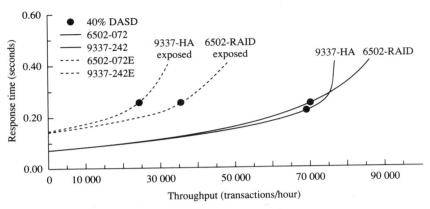

Figure 5.7.   Effect of DASD failure on RAMP-C performance.

figure. The term 'standard' refers to a DASD configuration that does not use the HA models of 9337 or mirroring.

RAID-5 places zero overhead on AS/400 CPU and memory. In addition, when a write is requested to a 9337-2XX, 9337-4XX, 6502 or 6522, the unit writes the data to the write cache and to the non-volatile cache backup, and the application is allowed to continue. The unit will then manage the write cache and write the data, compute the parity information stripe and write it. Through a combination of the write cache and non-volatile memory, the unit ensures the integrity of the data even if a failure should occur. Thus with 9337-2XX, 9337-4XX, 6502 and 6522 there is virtually no additional disk service time incurred in providing RAID-5 protection.

RAID-5 performance overhead increases when a DASD fails. To read from a failed DASD, RAID-5 must read *all* remaining arms in the set. (For 9337 configurations, this means anywhere from three to seven total reads, where one was sufficient previously.) With a write to a failed DASD, all DASD in the set must be read and then one write will be done to the parity information. Figure 5.7 compares the impact of one failed DASD on two configurations. The graph lines marked 'exposed' indicate where one DASD has failed.

5.5.3   Journalling and commitment control

The primary purpose of journal management is to provide a method to recover database files. Additional uses related to performance include the use of journalling to decrease the time required to back up database files, and the use of access path journalling for a potentially large reduction in the length of abnormal IPLs. Commitment control is an extension to the journal function that allows users to ensure that all changes related to a transaction are either completed or automatically backed out. This section focuses on the performance impacts of physical file journalling and commitment control.

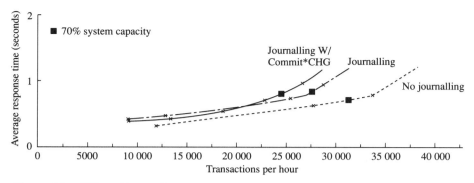

Figure 5.8. Effect of journalling on RTW performance.

The use of journalling adds application overheads in terms of both CPU and disk I/Os as file changes are entered into the journal. The use of commitment control adds two more journal entries, one at the beginning of the committed transaction and one at the end, resulting in additional CPU and I/O overhead. Record-level locks are also held longer with the use of commitment control. Figure 5.8 illustrates the effect of journalling and commitment control.

The Relational Transaction Workload (RTW) is used to provide an indication of the performance impact of adding physical file journalling and commitment control to an application in Version 1 Release 3. The performance data from three environments is provided: RTW without journalling, RTW with journalling, and RTW with commitment control with *CHG specified. Other environments may see more or less performance impact than RTW, depending primarily on the number of writes made to the database.

Figure 5.8 is composed of a combination of measured and modelled data. The AS/400 system consisted of a Model B50 with 48Mb of main storage. There were eight 9335 actuators in the System ASP and two actuators on the user ASP containing the journal receiver. PURGE (*NO) was specified.

5.6   Performance in a communications environment

There are two aspects to performance in a communications environment:

● The performance of the communications job
● The effect of the communications job on the general performance of the system.

There are many different forms of communications job ranging between:

● Display stations pass through from one AS/400 to another—the user appears to be connected to the target system for interactive work, and

- Volume batch data transfer using something like the Remote Job Entry function.

These are very different types of work. The performance of the first will be characterized by the response time to the end user. The performance of the second will be characterized by the time to send/receive the data. Critical factors in the performance of communications jobs are the speed of the line, how busy that line is and also, in some cases, the settings of various parameters which control how the communications is done—such parameters as Systems Network Architecture(*) (SNA) pacing counts, block sizes and many more.

To achieve acceptable performance on a communications job it is important to ensure that the line speed is adequate, that the utilization of the line is kept to an acceptable level, that all relevant parameters are set to the optimum for the type of job and the link involved, and that the AS/400s and any other systems involved have sufficient capacity to support the job.

The AS/400 provides a wide variety of options for communication with remote terminals and with remote systems. All forms of communications on the AS/400 involve system overhead but, for all practical purposes, the impact of communications activity on the general performance of a system is mainly dependent on the type of work being done. For instance, an interactive user passing through from another AS/400 performing normal end-user work on the target system will have a similar impact on general performance to any other user on that system. However, a batch transfer of a large amount of data running at high priority will have a similar impact on general performance to a long query run at high priority.

Since there are hundreds of different scenarios, involving many different forms of communications, it would not be particularly helpful to provide benchmark results to reflect the effect of communications on the AS/400 workload.

5.7   Save/restore performance

Once you have decided on the save/restore strategy appropriate to your organization, you must then ensure that your save/restore device and your AS/400 capacity will allow you to achieve the saves you require in the time you have available on the system. The figures in this section give some idea of the save/restore speeds that you can expect on various systems and tape devices.

5.7.1   Save/restore workloads

The following workloads were designed to help evaluate save/restore performance. Familiarization with the make-up of the workloads will help with an understanding of the differences in the save/restore rates presented below.

- The User Environment workload consists of four libraries containing 640 objects with a total size of 250 MB. The majority of the total size is represented by 240 1 MB files. The four libraries were saved using a single SAVLIB command and restored using four consecutive RSTLIB commands. This combination of data, being heavily weighted toward large database files, is meant to represent a typical daily save of an average customer.

- The Source File workload is a file of 2 MB with 200 source members (a member is equivalent to an object), saved using the SAVOBJ command and restored using the RSTOBJ command. This workload represents the worst-case performance scenario because of its large number of very small objects.
- The 200 MB Large File workload is a single file of 200 MB saved using the SAVOBJ command and restored using the RSTOBJ command.

5.7.2 Save/restore rates

The save/restore rates specified in Figs 5.9–5.12 were obtained from a restricted state measurement. A restricted state measurement is performed when all subsystems are ended using the ENDSBS *ALL command. All restore measurements were conducted such that each workload was new to the system. This represents the worst-case performance scenario for restore.

The rates in Figs 5.9–5.12 include the processing time required to start and complete the operation. The leftmost rates do not include the time required for rewind or for operator handling. This rate represents two drives with overlapped rewind being used during the operation. The two drive rates are followed by an estimate of the achievable rates if only one tape drive is used. The one tape rates include time required for rewind and operator handling. The estimated rates assume the following:

- Rewind time is the average tape drive rewind time. Retension time for the $\frac{1}{4}$ inch tape drives is added to the rewind time when calculating single tape rates. The tape cartridge is automatically retensioned when inserted into the tape drive. The rewind time, retension time, and operator handling time are all components of the total time required to switch cartridges when multiple tape cartridges of data are processed.
- For $\frac{1}{2}$-inch reel media a 2400-foot tape is assumed.
- Operator handling time is an estimate of the necessary time to load and unload a tape, and respond to the console prompt. In these estimates operator time for reel tape devices is 90 seconds, and for 36-track devices, like the 3490E, the rewind time is 1 second.
- The compression ratio (using HDC) for User Environment was 2.4:1, for a 200 MB large file it was 2.0:1 and for a Source File it was 2.0:1.
- All reels and cartridges are assumed to be filled to capacity.
- For the 3490E devices an uncompressed cartridge with a capacity of 800 MB was used.

F35	80M								
4 × 2800 8 × 9337									
Tape Drive			User Environment		Source File		Large File (200 MB)		
Unit	Density	IPS	2 Tape	1 Tape	2 Tape	1 Tape	2 Tape	1 Tape
SAVF SDC			726		254		721	
SAVF			1409		340		1732	
7208-02 HDC	43200	0.43	1200	1190	58	58	1251	1240
7208-12 HDC	86400	0.44	2375	2335	97	97	2465	2422
9348 HDC	6250	125	3364	2202	245	236	3820	2392
3490E HDC	*FMT3490E	79	3677	3621	263	263	4560	4458
6368	*QIC1000	80	1952	1812	204	202	1825	1702

IPS = Inches per Second   HDC = Hardware Data Compression
SDC = Software Data Compression

Figure 5.9.   F35 save rates (megabytes/hour)

- All configurations use one DASD IOP for each four 9336 disk units or four 9335 B01 units.
- Device types 3480, 3490 and 3490E are the $\frac{1}{2}$-inch tape units. The cartridges on this unit hold 800 MB of unformatted data. All these devices support IDRC, while only the 3490E Model E does not support HDC. The default for the

F80	768M								
4 × 2800 42 × 9337									
Tape Drive			User Environment		Source File		Large File (200 MB)		
Unit	Density	IPS	2 Tape	1 Tape	2 Tape	1 Tape	2 Tape	1 Tape
SAVF SDC			2403		350		2717	
SAVF			2990		446		3687	
7208-02 HDC	43200	0.43	1254	1243	60	60	1267	1256
7208-12 HDC	86400	0.44	2555	2509	108	108	2979	2916
9348 HDC	6250	125	3391	2300	284	272	3936	1713
3490E HDC	*FMT3490E	79	7041	6839	334	333	10307	9799
6368	*QIC1000	80	2014	1865	217	215	1768	1652

IPS = Inches per Second   HDC = Hardware Data Compression
SDC = Software Data Compression

Figure 5.10.   F80 save rates (megabytes/hour).

| F35 | 80M | | | | | | | | |
| 4 × 2800 8 × 9336 | | | | | | | | | |

Tape Drive			User Environment		Source File		Large File (200 MB)	
Unit	Density	IPS	2 Tape	1 Tape	2 Tape	1 Tape	2 Tape	1 Tape
SAVF SDC			862		174		1026	
SAVF			1774		186		3434	
7208-02 HDC	43200	0.43	1188	1178	112	112	1443	1428
7208-12 HDC	86400	0.44	1672	1652	143	143	3160	3090
9348 HDC	6250	125	1856	1439	174	169	3406	2223
3490E HDC	*FMT3490E	79	2053	2035	166	166	5104	4976
6368	*QIC1000	80	1436	1359	163	162	1826	1703

IPS = Inches per Second   HDC = Hardware Data Compression
SDC = Software Data Compression

Figure 5.11.   F35 restore rates (megabytes/hour).

3480/3490/3490E series is to use IDRC. This is not the best-performing scenario. The best performance will be gained from using just HDC. (In the case of the 3490E Model E, the IDRC hardware is as fast as the HDC hardware.)

| F80 | 768M | | | | | | | | |
| 4 × 2800 42 × 9337 | | | | | | | | | |

Tape Drive			User Environment		Source File		Large File (200 MB)	
Unit	Density	IPS	2 Tape	1 Tape	2 Tape	1 Tape	2 Tape	1 Tape
SAVF SDC			1521		247		1947	
SAVF			2444		249		3456	
7208-02 HDC	43200	0.43	1286	1274	141	141	1506	1490
7208-12 HDC	86400	0.44	1157	1147	174	174	2193	2159
9348 HDC	6250	125	2141	1604	238	229	3456	1662
3490E HDC	*FMT3490E	79	3538	3456	222	222	9960	9484
6368	*QIC1000	80	1618	1520	229	227	1853	1726

IPS = Inches per Second   HDC = Hardware Data Compression
SDC = Software Data Compression

Figure 5.12.   F80 restore rates (megabytes/hour).

- The device type SAVF refers to the online save file. The save file for these tests was created in the system ASP. The use of a user ASP with two or more DASD actuators can show slightly better throughput than a save file in the system ASP due to separation of I/O between the data being saved and the data being written.

The density columns of the figures are units of bytes per inch, with a few exceptions. The 8mm tape cartridge device (7208) has units of bits per inch. The save and restore rates in Figs 5.9–5.12 are expressed in terms of megabytes per hour.

The figures in this section show no save or restore rates for the 3490E Model EXX attached via a 6501 IOP. Performance of 3490E EXX models with IDRC is significantly better than the 3490E CXX models using IDRC. The percentage improvement will vary with the type of data being saved and other factors.

5.8   AS/400 in a client/server environment

5.8.1   AS/400 Server Series

Until recently all AS/400 models have been optimized for a commercial workload on a multi-user system where, in the main, the required data access, processing and terminal handling is managed by the AS/400 itself. The computer industry recognized some time ago the very strong trend towards client/server computing. This means that some proportion of the processing, terminal handling and possibly data access is handled by the machine on the user's desktop.

Where this becomes the environment for most users, a system optimized in a different way from the traditional AS/400 can be expected to give better performance. The AS/400 Server Series are specifically optimized to give better performance for client/server applications, enabling the AS/400 to compete as a server with PC and UNIX-based servers.

The AS/400 Server Series 9402 Model 20S or Model 100 configuration is intended primarily for a distributed client/server environment supporting up to 15 typical users and a limited need for vertical growth. This model is designed for a small workgroup who have need to share information stored in relational databases and access the information through *ad hoc* query tools.

The 9406 Model 30S-2411 or Model 135 Server Series configurations are intended primarily for a larger distributed client/server environment supporting up to 30 typical users with a wide range of shared data and applications needs as well as being a platform for client/server application development. These configurations are the most appropriate for larger workgroups and development teams with a broad range of sharable resources to access in a common workgroup.

The 9406 Model 30S-2412 or Model 140 Server Series configurations are intended for large standalone environments and larger development environments supporting up to 75 typical users.

Table 5.1. Server Series performance data

	Model 20S Model 100	Model 30S-2411 Model 135	Model 30S-2412 Model 140
Interactive	F02	F10	F20
Client/server	F45	F50	F70
Approx. number of clients	10–30	20–60	50–140

Client/server applications make extensive use of communications and database functions, which require long and complex code paths. While the operating system for the Server Series models is the same as for the rest of the AS/400 product family, the AS/400 Server Series models have improved hardware performance in key areas. They also implement a workload-balancing algorithm that gives highest priority to non-interactive jobs. This is directly opposite to the prioritization techniques used for traditional interactive applications, where display response time is given higher priority.

As a result, the AS/400 Server Series models display a two-part performance curve (interactive and client/server) that reflects the optimization toward non-interactive workloads. Table 5.1 indicates the relative throughput capability of the AS/400 Server Series models compared to other AS/400 models for the same types of workloads.

The number of clients supported on a given Server Series model is a function of the actual workload. Two workloads were used as examples in setting the range of clients listed in Table 5.1. These workload were variations of an **IBM** internal client/server benchmark used to evaluate the performance of the AS/400 Server models.

- *Dynamic SQL.* This workload represents the lower range of clients listed in Table 5.1. The application exists primarily on the clients, but sends several database requests to the AS/400 using dynamic SQL via PC Support.
- *Stored OS/400 program.* This workload represents the upper range of clients that can be supported. The client application accesses the AS/400 via PC Support Remote SQL to invoke an RPG program with static SQL procedures.

These two benchmarks indicate the wide variation in number of users that the AS/400 Server models may support.

The Model 30S-2412 and Model 140 are two-way processors. Thus single-job streams (e.g. single interactive terminal or single batch job) which can run only on one processor at a time will run at the speed of one of the processors (Table 5.2).

Table 5.2. Speed and capacity of Server Models 30S-2412 and 140

	Single job (speed)	Multiple jobs (throughput or capacity)
Interactive	F04	F20
Client/server	F60	F70

5.8.2   FSIOP and LAN Server/400

The client/server applications discussed in Sec. 5.8.1 refer to situations where the database accessed consists of native AS/400 database files. Another type of server environment is where PC-type files are stored on the AS/400 DASD. This function has hitherto been provided by shared folders under PC Support/400. The best performance for this type of file serving is provided by the File Server I/O Processor(*) (FSIOP) and LAN Server/400(*).

The FSIOP contains a 486 66 MHz processor and a highly optimized Operating System/2(*) (OS/2) LAN Server using High Performance File System(*) (HPFS) to connect PCs on a LAN to the AS/400. This software is call LAN Server/400. The FSIOP can be configured with 16 MB, 32 MB, 48 MB or 64 MB of memory. Portions of the memory are used to cache the data being requested by the attached PCs: the more memory, the larger the cache.

The AS/400 main processor and bus are involved in file serving requests only when the data needs to be read from or stored to the AS/400 DASD. In this environment the FSIOP delivers performance approximately equivalent to a similarly configured OS/2 LAN 486 66 MHz PC-based file server. The FSIOP can be used on the D, E and F models, Server models and the Advanced Series models. It can provide an improvement in response time of up to eight times compared to using Version 2.3 shared folders.

The FSIOP can also be used as a normal token ring or Ethernet adapter, for instance to connect a PC to the AS/400 using Client Access/400(*) to access shared folders, workstation function and AS/400 database.

5.9   The real world

It is all very well to look at the results of benchmarks carried out in a sterile laboratory environment but what happens in the real world? In an attempt to make this chapter come alive we visited a number of organizations using AS/400 to support their businesses. In the following sections we present brief profiles of what they do on their systems and the performance that they see. All the machines were well tuned and were not overloaded.

5.9.1   User 1

Business: User 1 is in the manufacturing industry sector.
Configuration: E45 with 80 MB main storage and 6 × 9335 disks.
Users: 115 interactive users with somewhat less than half the transaction throughput coming from users located at remote sites. During a typical peak period about 45 users will be actively using the system.

Applications: Manufacturing and accounting using well-known packages with home-grown modifications, *ad hoc* queries, development work and operations activities.

Workload: 5400 tr/h with average characteristics:

> 0.35 second CPU time
>
> 22 synchronous disk I/Os
>
> 0.2 second exceptional wait time

Multiple batch streams.

Performance:

1.5 seconds average response time

58 per cent high-priority CPU utilization

85 per cent total CPU utilization

12 per cent average actuator utilization

24 page faults per second total.

5.9.2   User 2

Business: User 2 is in the finance industry sector.

Configuration: F80 with 384 MB main storage and 40 × 9337 disks.

Users: 300 interactive users of which most are programmable terminal users attached through a token ring LAN. During a peak period about a hundred users will be actively using the system.

Applications: Commercial loans and general ledger deal input, SWIFT message processing, money market deals, futures, complex enquiries, front and back office functions.

Workload: 31 000 tr/h with average characteristics:

> 0.13 second CPU time
>
> 12 synchronous disk I/Os
>
> 0.25 second exceptional wait time

Multiple batch streams.

Performance:

0.8 second average response time

67 per cent high-priority CPU utilization

80 per cent total CPU utilization

13 per cent average actuator utilization

58 page faults per second total.

5.9.3   User 3

User 3 is an organization which runs a number of large exhibition centres and provides associated services such as equipment and furniture hire and maintenance. There are a number of separate companies included in the organization and different applications are required for these. They run five AS/400s, two Risc System/6000s(*) (RS/6000) and 220 PCs of which 40 are directly attached to AS/400s and 80 are attached to the AS/400s via the local area network. The local AS/400s and RS/6000s are all connected via a token ring, and a remote AS/400 and a remote workstation controller are attached on 64 000 BPS permanent connections. The number of AS/400s is partly a matter of history because of company acquisition.

Users use Display Station Pass-through to attach to the machine they require on the network and all AS/400s have access to a common name and address database on one system via DDM. The numbers of users specified in the table below are attached users, but some will be passed through to another system at any point.

AS/400 configurations

	System 1	System 2	System 3	System 4	System 5
Model	B45	B45	F35	B35	E10
Memory	40 MB	40 MB	48 MB	40 MB	
Disks	3.2 GB	2.8 GB	4.7 GB	2.4 GB	
No. of users	80	35	60	16	5

Core interactive applications on the four larger AS/400s

- Payroll
- Personnel
- Box Office
- Multiple Accounting Ledgers
- Purchase Orders
- Planned maintenance of hall equipment
- Multiple Order Entry Systems
        Stand orders
        Catering
        Electrical and Stand Fitting
        Furniture Hire and Stock Control
        Telephone Line Hire
- Hall managers' database
- Sales and Marketing
- Space Allocation
- Contracting
- Invoicing
- AS/400 OfficeVision for electronic mail
- Text Processing

The E10 supports five application developers using a CASE development tool.

The IT department have two staff with the skill to monitor and tune performance. They are by no means full time on this but spend a total of 2 or 3 days per month, on average. In the main, performance is good. Occasional slowdowns are attributed to particularly heavy processing requirements in some packages used.

Here we have an example of an AS/400 network supporting an extremely mixed set of applications for multiple companies. The use of DDM to access a common name and address database avoids data duplication and the associated currency problems. The main accounting system is very high function and hence complex.

Performance data for system 2:

Workload: 1869 tr/h with average characteristics:

> 0.43 second CPU time
>
> 14 synchronous disk I/Os

Multiple batch streams.

Performance:

0.8 second average response time

16 per cent high-priority CPU utilization

26 per cent total CPU utilization

5 per cent average actuator utilization

6 page faults per second total.

6
Use of BEST/1 for sizing

To help to understand the process of sizing, we gave an example in Chapter 4 of how to approach it with just a pencil, paper and calculator. In practice, there are many reasons why this method is inadequate.

1. First, we considered only the primary performance resources. There are a number of other configuration items which could possibly limit throughput and should be included in the exercise, for example:
   - Disk I/O processors
   - Disk controllers
   - Local workstation I/O processors
   - Communications I/O processors
   - Communication lines
   - Remote workstation controllers.
2. We did not consider the effect that memory availability has on the apparent complexity of transactions. The number of I/Os and the working set size were treated as independent and constant attributes of a transaction. In fact the number of disk I/Os required to complete a given function will normally decrease down to a fixed minimum value, as more memory is made available to store objects referred to. Conversely, as memory is removed, the number of I/Os increases without limit.

   If memory is unconstrained referenced items will only be brought from disk once, however many times they are used. With limited memory, items will be overwritten according to the LRU algorithm as new material is brought from disk. Subsequent references will cause repeat fetching of the same pages, i.e. more I/Os for the same function. Within limits, the measured complexity of a transaction therefore depends inversely on the size of the pool in which it will run.

   The working set size of a transaction can be defined as the minimum amount of memory in which it will run, such that additions cause no significant improvements in response time.

3. Some simplifying assumptions were made to reduce the amount of arithmetic. For example, no allowance was made for the effect of concurrent higher-priority work on the behaviour of an interactive workload, and there was no provision for different components of the workload to run in different pools at different priorities.

4. Perhaps the main limitation is that sizing will often be a repetitive procedure, trying out the effect of various workload and system facility assumptions on the configuration, and hence the cost of the hardware. The tedious repetitive computation and presentation of results makes this process a classic candidate for automation.

BEST/1 is the capacity planning component of the Performance Tools/400 licensed program (5738-PT1). With this tool we can evaluate all sorts of 'what if' ideas with speed, accuracy and convenience. Alternative workload projections, use of mirroring or checksum data protection, and trade-offs between memory and disk can all be investigated and documented in the course of a terminal session.

6.1   Overview of the tools

BEST/1 is developed in alliance with BGS Systems Inc., who have produced similar products for other platforms. It does *not* form part of the Performance Tools Subset/400 licensed program (5798-RYP) which is therefore inadequate for our purposes. With V3R1 software the performance tools are packaged slightly differently. The 'Agent' version includes the BEST/1 capability of creating models as well as the functions of the previous subset. It does not allow model analysis. The 'Manager' version is the complete package, required for sizing and capacity planning.

Compared to MDLSYS, which was the capacity planning component in earlier versions of the performance tools, BEST/1 has significant enhancements which include the following major items:

- Models interactive workload generated by PWS (programmable workstations) as well as 'dumb terminals' (also called dependent workstations or DWS).
- Models interactive workload due to DSPT (display station pass-through) source and target, and DDM (distributed data management) activities.
- Better modelling of batch workloads including PC Support/400 file transfer, server jobs fed by data queues, OS/400 and LIC tasks as well as traditional batch jobs.
- Handles explicit CPU priority specification including multiple interactive priorities.
- Handles explicit main storage pool and activity level specification, which allows jobs of a single class (interactive say) to be split between multiple pools,

and jobs of different classes to share a pool. See the exercise later in this chapter, and the one in Chapter 13, for some guidance on the modelling of memory changes in the current (V2R3) version of the product.

- Handles multiple ASP's (auxiliary storage pools) including modelling the effects of checksum and mirroring by ASP.
- Access is allowed to the CPU and disk hardware performance parameters. The file can be edited to permit modelling of newly announced hardware without having to wait for a new version of the capacity planner.

6.1.1   BEST/1 concepts

The following notes define the terms used in modelling with BEST/1 and Fig. 6.1 shows the relationship between the corresponding concepts.

- *Model.*   A complete representation of the hardware, workload and performance information necessary for input to BEST/1.
- *Configuration.*   The hardware resources employed, e.g. CPU, DASD, memory and communications facilities.
- *Workload.*   A set of interactive and non-interactive transactions associated with a set of jobs, including throughput and performance resource consumption figures. It can be measured, predefined or user-defined. A number of workloads can be combined with a configuration to create a model.

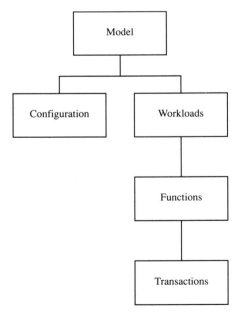

Figure 6.1.   BEST/1 terminology.

- *Function.* A 'business transaction' consisting of a set of computer trans- actions associated with a user. A function can contain a mixture of interactive and non-interactive transactions. A set of functions with corresponding throughput figures constitutes a workload.
- *Transaction.* A definition of an interactive transaction was given in Chapter 1 and the term has been used freely since. A non-interactive transaction is a novel idea and is defined arbitrarily in BEST/1 by the user. For example, you can specify a certain number of logical I/Os or a certain number of print lines as one transaction.

  This allows BEST/1 to express the throughput of the non-interactive job in transactions per hour. The default is 100 logical I/Os per transaction, but given a knowledge of the processing cycle it may well be more meaningful to override with a number of logical I/Os that correspond to some external milestone, such as one order, or one page of printout. A set of characterized transactions with throughput and performance resource demands, when associated with a user, becomes a function.

Configurations, workloads and models are stored in separate files by BEST/1, as are other items used in the sizing process such as hardware characteristics, analysis guidelines, results, graph formats and job-classification criteria. This means that multiple versions of all these things can be saved separately, edited and combined as required for a particular sizing or capacity-planning exercise.

6.1.2 The menu structure

There is a great deal of function and flexibility built into BEST/1 and a newcomer to the tool will find it easy to get lost when trying to familiarize with the facilities. That is why we will adopt an authoritarian style when it comes to explaining the tool, and give directions on how to perform a particular function, rather than attempting to deal with all the options at once.

As an additional navigation aid we provide two figures. Figure 6.2 is an overview of how to reach the main functions of BEST/1 from the initial menu (invoked by the command STRBEST). Figure 6.3 is simply a continuation of the previous figure starting from the 'Work with BEST/1 Model' screen in the third level of the hierarchy. For clarity, many minor functions and links have been excluded.

In each box after the first the top line contains the option number(s) and/or function key(s) which route to this box from the previous level. The abbreviation 'NTR' is used to indicate use of the ENTER key. The rest of the text describes the corresponding functions. Where necessary, the normal AS/400 command language abbreviations have been employed. We hope that other words which have been shortened remain decipherable.

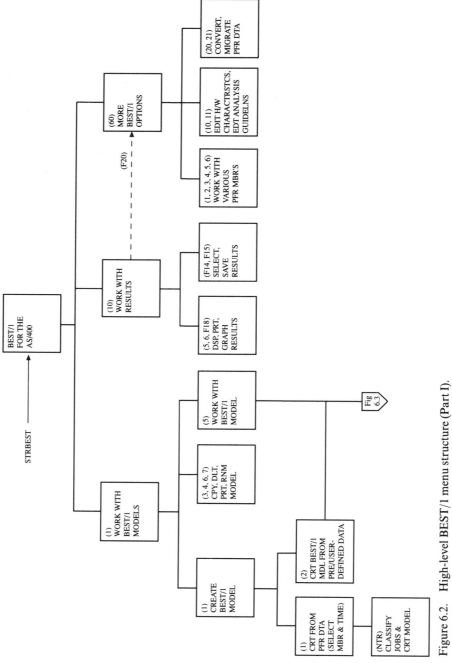

Figure 6.2. High-level BEST/1 menu structure (Part I).

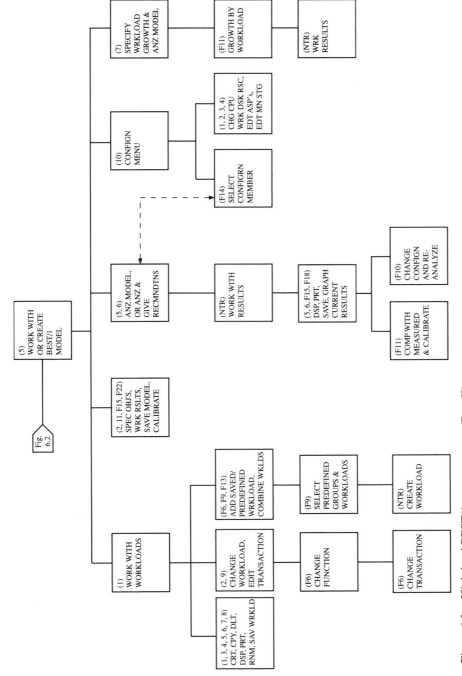

Figure 6.3.   High-level BEST/1 menu structure (Part II).

6.2   Obtaining the input

It is important to take into account all sources of work when building a model workload. A common mistake is to cater for the core application activities, but to overlook or fail to allow sufficiently for items such as *ad hoc* queries, and operator and technical support activities.

For each distinct interactive workload component you need to estimate the number of active users (often 35–45 per cent of the signed-on users) and the throughput in transactions per hour (often derivable from business transactions per hour). These figures should include any allowance you wish to make for uncertainty, and for growth potential. Finally you need a profile (preferably measured) of the character of each component.

6.2.1   Measured data

To provide a reliable basis for sizing, the input data must be representative of the workloads which will run on the proposed machine. In the case of measured data (which ideally would constitute the bulk of the input) this does *not* mean that the configuration, throughput and number of users have to match or approximate to the proposed machine environment. All that is necessary is that the complexity of the workload should match. The model handles the effect of the other variables.

Careful consideration of the quality of the input data is still essential. To ensure that it is suitable for the purpose, the following criteria should be observed:

1. The workload measured should contain a typical mix of interactive and batch functions, matching the activities which you expect to run on your machine during a peak period. A single measurement containing all the proposed activities in the correct mix is not necessary. Component functions can be measured independently and combined by the model in whatever proportions are representative of the expected workload. Other irrelevant applications may be running on the machine at the same time, but will not form part of the measured input.

   Strictly speaking, it is only the demand for performance resources of the average measured transaction which must match the proposed workload. The actual activities performed by the measured workload are irrelevant and could belong to a totally different application, providing they produce the same average performance demand.

   In a sizing situation we will always prefer to measure the proposed workload components rather than some notionally equivalent workload, because we cannot be sure of the equivalence until we know the performance characteristics of both. Only when the proposed workload is inaccessible for some reason (e.g. not yet finished development), might we decide to make do with measurements of a workload which we believe to be similar.

2. The measured system must be properly set up, e.g. have sensible priority, time slice, memory and activity level allocations, and appropriate system values. This topic is covered in Chapter 9.
3. The operating environment should also be normal, e.g. without excessive error recovery, and no high-priority batch work or concurrent save/restore activity unless these are an essential feature of the proposed workload. Above all, the machine must not be heavily overloaded.
4. The measured machine should be working hard, somewhere near its through-put limits. Total interactive and higher priority CPU utilization should be in the range 50–75 per cent. This does not imply that the measured workload must be responsible for all the utilization; it could be only a small component.
5. The data collection period should be in the range 20 minutes to 1 hour, and during this time the workload should be stable in character and volume.

It is clear from the above that neither a random spot check nor an all-day average measurement are likely to meet the need. Measurements must be planned and the results must be carefully examined before they are accepted as input for sizing. The procedure is similar to that required for capacity planning and is described in Chapter 12.

This is true whether you are producing the data yourself or accepting it from an application provider. You need to be confident about the provenance of any sizing data, and fully aware of any simplifying assumptions, or divergence from the five criteria. Measurements that do not conform to the criteria are effectively useless. Any attempt to short-circuit the approach described here by using experience-based 'rule-of-thumb' methods should be viewed with suspicion, and probably rejected.

It is not necessary to be so fussy if you are prepared to 'suck it and see', and budget for immediate upgrades should the initial machine prove to be inadequate. Similarly, you may be prepared to build in a large allowance (100 per cent or more perhaps) to compensate for lack of confidence in the sizing. This chapter is directed mainly at those who do not fit either of these descriptions.

6.2.2   Predefined data

There is no way you can size for a workload if nothing is known about its character. You must at least assume something, and be prepared to revise the estimates as better information arrives. Perhaps the best way to handle this situation is to assume that the undefined application is similar (in complexity) to one for which you already have measurements (e.g. a component of the existing workload).

If there are no measurements available of an equivalent workload, we will have to rely on knowledge (or assumptions) about the logical character of the proposed workload. From a detailed knowledge of the mix of transactions, and the number of logical I/Os in each, we may be able to equate the proposed workload to some mix of RAMP-C transaction classes or some other predefined workload, as described in Chapter 4.

Quite apart from any uncertainty in estimating the logical character of the workload, we have already explained the large inherent uncertainties in translating this into real physical resource demands. The use of predefined interactive workloads for sizing should therefore be minimized, and should be done conserva٤ ˥ly (i.e. guess high on complexity and volume). Do not place any more confidence in the modelling results than you do in the input.

6.3   Sizing example

As an introduction to BEST/1 we will take you on a guided tour of some of the necessary facilities illustrated by sample screen panels. There are two limitations that restrict what we can do at this point to simulate a realistic sizing exercise. First, we can't provide you with sample measured workloads, that we have said should be the major components of the input. Therefore we cannot navigate with you through a realistic process showing the same screens that you will see.

Second, although sizing comes logically before capacity planning (after all, you need to get a machine before you can tune it and plan for growth) the use of BEST/1 is most naturally developed through capacity planning; a kind of simplified sizing process. Therefore we will first look at sizing with predefined data only, as an introduction to the tool. At the end of Chapter 13 there is another exercise which involves the saving of workloads and configurations from measured data. This output can be used as a basis for further exploration of BEST/1 sizing facilities.

6.3.1   Input to sizing example

We need to estimate the machine configuration required to support the following peak workload:

• A hundred active terminal users performing the interactive work represented by the following mix of RAMP-C predefined transaction classes:
  Class 1: 20 per cent/Class 2: 0 per cent/Class 3: 40 per cent/Class 4: 40 per cent
• Twenty active terminal users performing OfficeVision tasks on an 'interrupted' basis
• Five concurrent batch streams; one CPU intensive, one for application development work, and the rest for mixed commercial jobs
• Seven active print writers; one serving a 1400 lpm line printer and five serving workstation printers

```
                        BEST/1** for the AS/400

Disclaimer:

The performance estimates presented are approximations which are
believed to be sound.  The degree of success which you may achieve in
the use of IBM equipment and programs is dependent upon a number of
factors, many of which are not under IBM's and BGS Systems' control.
Thus IBM and BGS Systems neither warrant nor guarantee that you can or
will achieve similar results.  It is your responsibility to validate the
estimates furnished and to determine their relevance to your operation.

Any configuration recommended by the capacity planner should be verified
since the capacity planner does not consider all attachable devices.

BEST/1 is a registered trademark of BGS Systems, Inc., Waltham, MA, USA.

(c) Copyright 1975-1993, as an unpublished work.  All rights reserved.
Contains confidential information and trade secrets proprietary to BGS
                                                              More...

Press Enter to continue.

F12=Cancel
```

Figure 6.4. The disclaimer screen.

6.3.2 Building a model

1. Assuming the model data and results are to be kept in a library called MODELS, enter the following commands:
   CHGCURLIB   MODELS
   STRBEST

```
                        BEST/1 for the AS/400

Select one of the following:

     1. Work with BEST/1 models

    10. Work with results

    50. About BEST/1
    51. Moving from MDLSYS to BEST/1

    60. More BEST/1 options




Selection or command
===> 1

F3=Exit    F4=Prompt    F9=Retrieve    F12=Cancel
```

Figure 6.5. The initial BEST/1 menu.

```
                        Work with BEST/1 Models

  Library . . . . .    MODELS         Name

  Type options, press Enter.
    1=Create   3=Copy   4=Delete   5=Work with   6=Print   7=Rename

  Opt  Model       Text                                    Date      Time
   1   MDL1

    (No mo⌐⌐ls in library)




                                                                    Bottom
  Command
  ===>
  F3=Exit    F4=Prompt    F5=Refresh       F9=Retrieve   F12=Cancel
  F15=Sort by model       F16=Sort by text  F19=Sort by date and time
```

Figure 6.6.   Work with BEST/1 models: create MDL1.

2. The disclaimer screen appears, after an extended response time.
3. If you are unfamiliar with the content, read the disclaimer (Fig. 6.4). It is intended to protect the suppliers against unduly high user expectations.
4. Press *Enter*.
5. The initial BEST/1 menu appears (Fig. 6.5). Key selection '*1*' and press *Enter*.
6. The 'Work with BEST/1 Models' screen appears (Fig. 6.6). There will be a list of any models previously created on the system in the MODELS library, with associated text, date and timestamp, plus option fields to the left. Alterna-

```
                        Create BEST/1 Model

  Select one of the following:

       1. Create from performance data
       2. Create from predefined and user-defined workloads










  Selection
     2

  F3=Exit    F12=Cancel
```

Figure 6.7.   Selection '2' from create BEST/1 model screen.

```
                        Create BEST/1 Model

Model/Text:    MDL1

Select one of the following:

      1. Work with workloads
      2. Specify objectives and active jobs

      5. Analyze current model
      6. Analyze current model and give recommendations
      7. Specify workload growth and analyze model

     10. Configuration menu
     11. Work with results

     50. About BEST/1

                                                         Bottom
Selection or command
===> 1
F3=Exit    F4=Prompt    F9=Retrieve    F12=Cancel    F15=Save current model
F20=More BEST/1 options
```

Figure 6.8.   Selection '1' from main create BEST/1 model screen.

tively, the message shown in Fig. 6.6 is displayed. Preceding this list or message is an input field. Key the model name '*MDL1*' into the input field and option '*1*' against it to indicate that you wish to create a new model. Press *Enter*.

7. The 'Create BEST/1 Model' screen appears (Fig. 6.7). Key selection '*2*' and press *Enter*.

8. The main 'Create BEST/1 Model' screen appears (Fig. 6.8). Key selection '*1*' and press *Enter*.

```
                      Work with Workloads

Model/Text:    MDL1

Type options, press Enter.
   1=Create   2=Change   3=Copy   4=Delete   5=Display   6=Print   7=Rename
   8=Save workload to workload member        9=Edit transactions

Opt    Workload       Text


   (No workloads defined)




                                                         Bottom
F3=Exit    F6=Add saved workload    F9=Add predefined workload    F12=Cancel
F13=Combine workloads
```

Figure 6.9.   Work with workloads: press F9.

```
                    Select Predefined Workload Group

   Library . . . . .   QPFR           Name

   Type option, press Enter.
     1=Select

             Workload
   Opt       Group        Text
     1       BATCH        IBM Supplied (BATCH)
     1       COMMERCIAL   IBM Supplied (Includes RAMP-C)
     1       OFFICE       IBM Supplied (OfficeVision/400)
     1       SPOOL        IBM Supplied (SPOOL)




                                                                    Bottom
   F3=Exit    F12=Cancel
```

Figure 6.10.   Select predefined workload group screen.

9. The 'Work with Workloads' screen appears (Fig. 6.9). Currently our model has no workloads specified. Press *F9*.

10. The 'Select Predefined Workload Group' screen appears (Fig. 6.10). Key option '*1*' against *BATCH*, *COMMERCIAL*, *OFFICE* and *SPOOL* and press *Enter* to select these workload groups.

11. The 'Select Predefined Workload' screen appears for the BATCH group (Fig. 6.11). These workloads were described briefly in Sec. 4.7.3. The complex query meets the CPU-intensive requirement. We will ignore the other batch streams

```
                    Select Predefined Workload

   Group . . . . . . . . . :   BATCH

   Type option, press Enter.
     1=Select

   Opt       Predefined Workloads
             Commercial orders
             Development orders
     1       Complex query
             Summary query
             Sort query
             Background batch server




                                                                    Bottom
   F3=Exit    F12=Cancel
```

Figure 6.11.   Select predefined workload (batch group).

```
                              Create Workload

Type changes, press Enter.
     Workload  . . . . . . . .    BATXXX        Name
     Workload text . . . . . .    Complex query
     Workload type . . . . . .    *NORMAL       *NORMAL, *BATCHJOB
     Usage mode  . . . . . . .    4             1=Casual, 2=Interrupted, 3=Steady,
                                                4=N/A

                              Functions  Avg K/T  ------Tns per Function------
     Function Text            per User   (secs)      Inter         Non-inter
     Complex query               1.00      .0         .00             61.00








                                                                      Bottom
     F3=Exit   F6=Work with functions   F9=Specify chars to comm line resources
     F10=Specify I/Os to ASPs   F11=Show functions with volume   F12=Cancel
```

Figure 6.12.   Create workload (CPU intensive batch).

in the sizing example input for two reasons. First, the complex query will be enough to use up most of the excess CPU cycles on its own, so the other jobs are redundant because they should be relatively inactive. The workload we are sizing for is the interactive workload, and batch is just running when it can in the background. Second, if they *are* added the model apears to make them more active than would be expected in a real environment. The I/O rate then becomes very high and an unduly large CPU is suggested (at V2R3). Key option '*1*' against '*Complex query*' and press *Enter*.

12. The 'Create Workload' screen appears for the Complex query workload (Fig. 6.12). Key the name '*BATXXX*' for the new workload and press *Enter*.

13. The 'Select Predefined Workload' screen appears for the COMMERCIAL group (Fig. 6.13). Key option '*1*' against '*RAMP-C*' and press *Enter*.

14. The 'Create Workload' screen appears for the RAMP-C workload (Fig. 6.14), with 'Functions per User' for each transaction type corresponding to the standard transaction percentages used in the benchmark measurements (see Chapter 4).

   Suppose we try to change these numbers to represent the more complex mix for our workload. Key '*ITV*' as the workload name, enter the 'Functions per User' figures shown in Fig. 6.14 and press *Enter*. The error message shown on the bottom line is displayed.

15. The reason for this is the relationship between throughput and key/think (k/t) time, discussed in Chapter 1. The RAMP-C throughput per user is 225 tr/h. The average k/t plus response time (= cycle time) is then 3600/225 = 16 seconds. To keep the input self-consistent, as the throughput of a transaction type goes up, the k/t time must go down—and vice versa. In fact the model

```
                      Select Predefined Workload

   Group . . . . . . . . . :     COMMERCIAL

   Type option, press Enter.
     1=Select

   Opt     Predefined Workloads
    1      RAMP-C
           SQL RTW




                                                              Bottom
    F3=Exit    F12=Cancel
```

Figure 6.13.   Select RAMP-C commercial interactive workload.

allows us to change the k/t times, and will then respond by making the appropriate inverse change to the functions per user figures. Experiment with
changes to the k/t fields as shown in Fig. 6.15, and finally adjust the functions
per user to match our requirements. Press *Enter*.

16. The 'Select Predefined Workload' screen appears for the OFFICE group (Fig.
    6.16). Five different mixes of the basic office functions are provided, corre-
    sponding to four common types of end user, plus the standard IBM Office

```
                          Create Workload

   Type changes, press Enter.
     Workload  . . . . . . . .    ITV          Name
     Workload text . . . . . .    RAMP-C
     Workload type . . . . . .    *NORMAL      *NORMAL, *BATCHJOB
     Usage mode  . . . . . . .    2            1=Casual, 2=Interrupted, 3=Steady,
                                               4=N/A

                              Functions  Avg K/T  ------Tns per Function------
   Function Text               per User   (secs)      Inter        Non-inter
   Inquiry                       20.00      8.0        2.21            .02
   Simple updates                  .00     10.3        2.36            .03
   Multiple entry updates        40.00     18.5        2.20            .03
   Complex processing            40.00     26.3        2.29            .08




                                                              Bottom
    F3=Exit    F6=Work with functions    F9=Specify chars to comm line resources
    F10=Specify I/Os to ASPs   F11=Show functions with volume    F12=Cancel
    Average key/think time of 19.6 exceeds cycle time of 16.08
```

Figure 6.14.   Create RAMP-C workload: incorrect input.

```
                        Create Workload

Type changes, press Enter.
   Workload  . . . . . . . .    ITV          Name
   Workload text . . . . . .    RAMP-C
   Workload type . . . . . .    *NORMAL      *NORMAL, *BATCHJOB
   Usage mode  . . . . . . .    2            1=Casual, 2=Interrupted, 3=Steady,
                                               4=N/A


                            Functions  Avg K/T  ------Tns per Function------
   Function Text            per User   (secs)      Inter         Non-inter
   Inquiry                    20.00     14.5        2.21              .02
   Simple updates              .00      10.3        2.36              .03
   Multiple entry updates    40.00      17.0        2.20              .03
   Complex processing        40.00       7.0        2.29              .08




                                                               Bottom
   F3=Exit    F6=Work with functions   F9=Specify chars to comm line resources
   F10=Specify I/Os to ASPs   F11=Show functions with volume   F12=Cancel
   Functions per user is changed because key/think time changed
```

Figure 6.15.   Create RAMP-C workload: acceptable input.

Benchmark. Assume that our users are best described as professional. Key option '*1*' against '*Professional*' and press *Enter*.

17. The 'Create Workload' screen appears (Fig. 6.17). We have the opportunity of changing the proportions of different functions and the key/think times to tailor this workload further, but we will assume it already reflects our estimates. Key the name '*OFC*' for this workload and press *Enter*.

```
                   Select Predefined Workload

   Group . . . . . . . . . :    OFFICE

   Type option, press Enter.
     1=Select

   Opt     Predefined Workloads
           IBM Office Benchmark V2
           Secretarial
           Managerial
     1     Professional
           Correspondence center







                                                               Bottom
   F3=Exit    F12=Cancel
```

Figure 6.16.   Select professional office predefined workload.

```
                          Create Workload

Type changes, press Enter.
   Workload  . . . . . . . .   OFC          Name
   Workload text . . . . . .   Professional
   Workload type . . . . . .   *NORMAL      *NORMAL, *BATCHJOB
   Usage mode  . . . . . . .   2            1=Casual, 2=Interrupted, 3=Steady,
                                               4=N/A

                            Functions  Avg K/T  ------Tns per Function------
Function Text                per User   (secs)     Inter         Non-inter
Update one calendar            1.00      83.0       7.00             2.65
View one calendar              1.00     207.9       3.00             2.54
Process heavy mail             1.00      17.8      32.00             5.49
Create small document         1.00      34.6      11.00             2.79
Revise small document          1.00      39.3      15.00             2.75
View directory entry           1.00      99.2       7.00             2.58

                                                                   Bottom
F3=Exit    F6=Work with functions    F9=Specify chars to comm line resources
F10=Specify I/Os to ASPs    F11=Show functions with volume    F12=Cancel
```

Figure 6.17.   Create professional office workload: press Enter.

18. The 'Select Predefined Workload' screen appears for the SPOOL group (Fig.
    6.18). We need to model only one sort of spool activity in this example. Key
    option '1' against 'Simple print AFP(*NO)' and press Enter.
19. The 'Create Workload' screen appears for the simple print workload (Fig.
    6.19). Key the name 'PRTS' and press Enter.


```
                      Select Predefined Workload

   Group . . . . . . . . . :    SPOOL

   Type option, press Enter.
     1=Select

   Opt     Predefined Workloads
    1      Simple print AFP(*NO)
           Simple print AFP(*YES)
           Complex print AFP(*YES)




                                                                   Bottom
   F3=Exit    F12=Cancel
```

Figure 6.18.   Select SPOOL predefined workload.

```
                          Create Workload
Type changes, press Enter.
     Workload  . . . . . . . .    PRTS          Name
     Workload text . . . . . .    Simple print AFP(*NO)
     Workload type . . . . . .    *NORMAL       *NORMAL, *BATCHJOB
     Usage mode  . . . . . . .    4             1=Casual, 2=Interrupted, 3=Steady,
                                                   4=N/A

                             Functions   Avg K/T  ------Tns per Function------
     Function Text           per User    (secs)      Inter        Non-inter
     Simple print AFP(*NO)       1.00       .0         .00           881.00




                                                               Bottom
     F3=Exit   F6=Work with functions   F9=Specify chars to comm line resources
     F10=Specify I/Os to ASPs   F11=Show functions with volume   F12=Cancel
```

Figure 6.19.   Create non-AFP spool workload.

6.3.3   *Modelling the proposed volumes*

20. The 'Work with Workloads' screen reappears with all the component work-
    loads required for our sizing exercise. Press *Enter* or *F12* or *F3* to return to the
    'Work with BEST/1 Model' screen (Fig. 6.20). Then key selection '*2*' and
    press *Enter* to specify the number of users required for each workload.

```
                         Create BEST/1 Model
     Model/Text:    MDL1

     Select one of the following:

          1. Work with workloads
          2. Specify objectives and active jobs

          5. Analyze current model
          6. Analyze current model and give recommendations
          7. Specify workload growth and analyze model

          10. Configuration menu
          11. Work with results

          50. About BEST/1

                                                              Bottom
     Selection or command
     ===> 2
     F3=Exit    F4=Prompt   F9=Retrieve   F12=Cancel   F15=Save current model
     F20=More BEST/1 options
```

Figure 6.20.   Return to create BEST/1 model screen and select objectives.

```
                        Specify Objectives and Active Jobs

     Model/Text:    MDL1

     Type changes, press Enter.

                           Workload    Active   ----Interactive-----   Non-inter
     Workload   Connect   Type        Jobs    Rsp Time    Thruput    Thruput
     BATXXX     *LOCAL    *NORMAL      1.0      .0            0           0
     BATXXX     *LAN      *NORMAL       .0      .0            0           0
     BATXXX     *WAN      *NORMAL       .0      .0            0           0
     ITV        *LOCAL    *NORMAL    100.0      .0            0           0
     ITV        *LAN      *NORMAL       .0      .0            0           0
     ITV        *WAN      *NORMAL       .0      .0            0           0
     OFC        *LOCAL    *NORMAL     20.0      .0            0           0
     OFC        *LAN      *NORMAL       .0      .0            0           0
     OFC        *WAN      *NORMAL       .0      .0            0           0
     PRTS       *LOCAL    *NORMAL      7.0      .0            0           0
     PRTS       *LAN      *NORMAL       .0      .0            0           0
     PRTS       *WAN      *NORMAL       .0      .0            0           0
                                                                    More...

     F3=Exit    F11=Show positive quantities    F12=Cancel
     F15=Sort by connect type    F19=Work with workloads
```

Figure 6.21.   Specifying number of active jobs.

21. The 'Specify Objectives and Active Jobs' screen appears (Fig. 6.21). Each workload appears three times because of the three possible attachment types. We will assume that all jobs are local. We simply need to specify the number of jobs required for each defined workload. Remember batch will be represented by only one job. Key the 'Active Jobs' figures shown in Fig. 6.21 and then press *Enter*.

Note that we could also specify response time and/or throughput objectives for the interactive users. It is not recommended at this stage. Satisfying the additional constraints could require a more powerful machine than would otherwise be the case. The result would be a lightly loaded large machine, possibly very much too large (and expensive) if the specified response time was unrealistic.

22. The 'Create BEST/1 Model' screen reappears (Fig. 6.22). We are now almost ready to let the model size a machine for the proposed workloads. Before it will do this we have to suggest an initial configuration, and let it criticize our choice. Key selection '6' (Analyze current model and give recommendations) and press *Enter*.

23. The 'Select Configuration Member' screen appears, with a message telling us that the model, as yet, lacks a configuration (Fig. 6.23). A list of sample configurations is shown. Note that these are supplied in library QPFR. If we have previously saved configurations from measured data or elsewhere (see Chapter 13) we could use them at this point. Alternatively, we could build a configuration from scratch after selecting '10' from the previous menu.

We will take the easy route, and also show naive optimism by selecting the

```
                        Create BEST/1 Model

Model/Text:    MDL1

Select one of the following:

      1. Work with workloads
      2. Specify objectives and active jobs

      5. Analyze current model
      6. Analyze current model and give recommendations
      7. Specify workload growth and analyze model

     10. Configuration menu
     11. Work with results

     50. About BEST/1

                                                          Bottom
Selection or command
===> 6
F3=Exit    F4=Prompt    F9=Retrieve    F12=Cancel    F15=Save current model
F20=More BEST/1 options
```

Figure 6.22.   Key selection '6' into create BEST/1 model screen.

Model 300/2040 configuration. Key '*1*' against the 2040 member and press *Enter*.

24. The message 'Analyzing model. Please wait' appears; then after a while we get the 'Work with Results' screen (Fig. 6.24). You can browse through all the output if you wish, to see where utilization guidelines have been exceeded. However, for a summary of these exceptions and a list of recommendations to fix them, all we need is to look at the recommendations report. Key option '*5*' against 'Recommendations' and press *Enter*.

```
                      Select Configuration Member

Library . . . . .    QPFR            Name

Type option, press Enter.
   1=Select

Opt   Member      Text                                 Date       Time
      A20S_2010   Sample 9402 configuration            07/09/94   18:01:20
      A200_2030   Sample 9402 configuration            07/09/94   18:01:20
      A30S_2412   Sample 9404 configuration            07/09/94   18:01:20
      A30S_2411   Sample 9404 configuration            07/09/94   18:01:20
      A200_2032   Sample 9402 configuration            07/09/94   18:01:19
      A200_2031   Sample 9402 configuration            07/09/94   18:01:19
   1  A300_2040   Sample 9406 configuration            07/09/94   18:01:19
      A300_2041   Sample 9406 configuration            07/09/94   18:01:19
      A300_2042   Sample 9406 configuration            07/09/94   18:01:19
      A310_2043   Sample 9406 configuration            07/09/94   18:01:19
      A310_2044   Sample 9406 configuration            07/09/94   18:01:19
      A320_2050   Sample 9406 configuration            07/09/94   18:01:19
                                                                   More...
F3=Exit    F5=Refresh    F12=Cancel    F15=Sort by member    F16=Sort by text
F19=Sort by date and time
Model has no configuration
```

Figure 6.23.   Select model 300/2040 configuration.

```
                         Work with Results

     Printed report text . . . . . .



     Type options, press Enter.
       5=Display    6=Print

     Opt     Report Name
             Analysis Summary
      5      Recommendations
             Workload Report
             ASP and Disk Arm Report
             Disk IOP and Disk Arm Report
             Main Storage Pool Report
             Communications Resources Report
             All of the above


                                                             Bottom
     F3=Exit    F12=Cancel    F14=Select saved results    F15=Save current results
     F18=Graph current results    F19=Append saved results    F24=More keys
     CPU cannot handle specified load                                      +
```

Figure 6.24. Work with results screen: display recommendations.

25. We have clearly been over-optimistic (Fig. 6.25). The number of actuators is totally inadequate (though the model does not tell us yet what to do about this), the CPU is not up to the job, and a huge memory upgrade appears to be necessary. Before taking all this at face value, note the messages:

'Sync reads per second exceeded ...' and
'Unable to find configuration ...'.


```
                      Display Recommendations

     *****  Analysis Exceptions  *****
     Sync reads per second exceeded for pools other than pool 1 (*MACH)
     Disk utilization of 122.82 for ASP 1 exceeds objective of 40.00
     Disk IOP utilization of 73.88 for IOP MFIOP exceeds objective of 70.00
     CPU is saturated
     CPU cannot handle specified load
     Disks on ASP 1 cannot handle specified load
     Unable to find configuration that met all specified objectives

     *****  Analysis Recommendations  *****
     Change Pool 1 size to 34816 KB
     Change Pool 2 size to 17921 KB
     Change Pool 3 size to 96006 KB
     Change Pool 4 size to 15097 KB
     Change storage size to 160 MB
     Change CPU model to 2042

                                                             Bottom
     Performance estimates -- Press help to see disclaimer.
     F3=Exit    F10=Change to recommended configuration and re-analyze    F12=Cancel
     F15=Configuration menu    F17=Analyze multiple points    F24=More keys
```

Figure 6.25. Evaluator recommendations.

```
                          More BEST/1 Options

Select one of the following:

     10. Hardware characteristics menu
     11. Analysis parameters menu














Selection or command
===> 11


F3=Exit    F4=Prompt    F9=Retrieve    F12=Cancel
```

Figure 6.26.   More BEST/1 options: select analysis parameters menu.

These suggest that a threshold related to the page fault rate has been exceeded, and second, that the largest available AS/400 is too small! This is a case where the default analysis guidelines (as provided at V2R3) need adjustment. Press *F12* to return to the results screen.

26. If you have not already done so, look at the other reports, including the 'Main Storage Pool Report' and note the synchronous read rates. These are what caused the 'Unable to find configuration ...' message. Other resources are grossly overloaded, but can be upgraded without difficulty. Now press *F20* to get to the 'More BEST/1 Options' menu (Fig. 6.26). Selection '10' would let us modify hardware performance data, e.g. to support a newly announced CPU. Our immediate needs are different. Key '*11*' and press *Enter*.

27. The 'Analysis Parameters' screen appears (Fig. 6.27). You can look at the utilization guidelines if you like, to compare with those in Table 4.1. They should normally be left as delivered: the resulting CPU, disk, IOP and line upgrade recommendations are realistic and reliable. In our experience (with V2R3) the synchronous read guidelines are not in the same category, and frequently need to be adjusted. Key '*2*' and press *Enter*.

28. The 'Edit Sync Reads Guidelines' screen appears (Fig. 6.28). Take time to have a good look at it. Note that the highest threshold value is 100, which was exceeded by the model's predicted rate: hence the problem. The guideline value for our selected CPU is 30, and that for the biggest currently available machine is 60. These seem to be too low when compared with actual measurements on installed machines, and with model predictions. A rather drastic circumvention of this difficulty would be to disable the synchronous read rate

```
                        Analysis Parameters

Select one of the following:

      1. Edit utilization guidelines
      2. Edit sync reads guidelines
      3. Edit paging behavior values












Selection or command
===> 2

F3=Exit   F4=Prompt   F9=Retrieve   F12=Cancel
F14=Replace with saved analysis parameters   F24=More keys
```

Figure 6.27.   Select edit synchronous reads guidelines.

criteria, by keying '*NONE ' where the specified value is '*GUIDE'. We suggest a slightly less permissive approach.

29. First, the default figures shown are the V2R3 page fault rate guidelines, not the V3R1 figures discussed in Chapter 9, and fully documented in the Work Management Manual. Due to AS/400 developments, the figures are under review and likely to be substantially revised upwards for the more powerful machines. Figure 6.29 shows the likely V3R1 recommendations. Second, synchronous read rates are often 1.5–2.0 × the fault rates. This can be repre-

```
                     Edit Sync Reads Guidelines

Type changes, press Enter.  Values are used for Analysis recommendations.

   Max sync reads . . . . . . . . . .    *GUIDE     *GUIDE, *THRESH, *NONE

                                         ------Pool 1 (*MACH)------
   CPU relative performance              Guideline       Threshold
   2.0 or less . . . . . . . . . . . .   2               5
   Greater than 2.0 . . . . . . . . .    1               3

                                         -----All Other Pools------
   CPU relative performance              Guideline       Threshold
   2.0 or less  . . . . . . . . . . .    20              25
   3.0 or less  . . . . . . . . . . .    25              35
   10.0 or less . . . . . . . . . . .    30              45
   30.0 or less . . . . . . . . . . .    40              50
   50.0 or less . . . . . . . . . . .    50              65
   100.0 or less  . . . . . . . . . .    60              80
   Greater than 100.0 . . . . . . . .    70              100

                                                                  Bottom
F3=Exit   F12=Cancel
Relative performance of current CPU (2040) is 4.00
```

Figure 6.28.   Default synchronous reads guidelines.

```
                    Edit Sync Reads Guidelines

Type changes, press Enter.  Values are used for Analysis recommendations.

    Max sync reads . . . . . . . . . .   *THRESH   *GUIDE, *THRESH, *NONE

                                        ------Pool 1 (*MACH)------
    CPU relative performance             Guideline      Threshold
    2.0 or less . . . . . . . . . . . .  2              5
    Greater than 2.0 . . . . . . . . . . 1              3

                                        -----All Other Pools------
    CPU relative performance             Guideline      Threshold
    2.0 or less . . . . . . . . . . . .  15             25
    3.0 or less . . . . . . . . . . . .  25             40
    10.0 or less . . . . . . . . . . . . 35             60
    30.0 or less . . . . . . . . . . . . 80             130
    50.0 or less . . . . . . . . . . . . 180            300
    100.0 or less . . . . . . . . . . .  250            440
    Greater than 100.0 . . . . . . . . . 300            500

                                                              Bottom
F3=Exit    F12=Cancel
Relative performance of current CPU (2040) is 4.00
```

Figure 6.29.   Modified guidelines.

sented quite well by using '*THRESH' in combination with the revised figures. Make the changes shown and press *Enter*.

30. Returning to the 'Analysis Parameters' screen you can then use F15 to save the modified guidelines for future use. The default set are in QPFR library, and others can be invoked via *F14*. Using Enter repeatedly gets you back to the 'Create BEST/1 Model' screen and this time selection '6' causes the analysis and recommendation function to take place. After a time the 'Work with

```
                       Display Recommendations

***** Analysis Exceptions *****
Sync reads per second exceeded for pools other than pool 1 (*MACH)
Disk utilization of 122.82 for ASP 1 exceeds objective of 40.00
Disk IOP utilization of 73.88 for IOP MFIOP exceeds objective of 70.00
CPU is saturated
CPU cannot handle specified load
Disks on ASP 1 cannot handle specified load

***** Analysis Recommendations *****
Change Pool 1 size to 27727 KB
Change Pool 2 size to 10612 KB
Change Pool 3 size to 56633 KB
Change Pool 4 size to 3332 KB
Change storage size to 96 MB
Change CPU model to 2043
Create 1 6602-050 disk ctl(s)
Create 2 6602-050 arm(s)
                                                              More...
Performance estimates -- Press help to see disclaimer.
F3=Exit    F10=Change to recommended configuration and re-analyze    F12=Cancel
F15=Configuration menu    F17=Analyze multiple points    F24=More keys
```

Figure 6.30.   Recommendations after re-analysis.

```
                         Work with Results

Printed report text . . . . . .



Type options, press Enter.
  5=Display    6=Print

Opt      Report Name
  5      Analysis Summary
  5      Recommendations
  5      Workload Report
  5      ASP and Disk Arm Report
  5      Disk IOP and Disk Arm Report
  5      Main Storage Pool Report
         Communications Resources Report
         All of the above


                                                         Bottom
 F3=Exit   F12=Cancel   F14=Select saved results   F15=Save current results
 F18=Graph current results   F19=Append saved results   F24=More keys
 Configuration has been changed                                    +
```

Figure 6.31.   View results after re-analysis.

Results' screen appears. Key option '*5*' against '*Recommendations*' and press
Enter. This time the model can and does find a configuration to match the
workload (Fig. 6.30). Press *F10* after viewing the second screen, to accept the
recommendations and re-analyse.

31. The 'Work with Results' screen reappears (Fig. 6.31). Key option '*5*' to
    display results and check them for reasonableness. Press *Enter*.
32. The 'Analysis Summary' shows that the CPU, disk arms and IOPs are all com-
    fortably below guideline utilizations, and the average response time is sub-

```
                     Display Analysis Summary

CPU Model . . . . . . . . :   2043
Main Storage  . . . . . . :   96     MB
               •
                                Quantity    Predicted Util
CPU . . . . . . . . . . . . . . . . :   1          64.0
Disk IOPs . . . . . . . . . . . . . :   2          14.3
Disk ctls . . . . . . . . . . . . . :   5           .9
Disk arms . . . . . . . . . . . . . :   6          28.7
Local WS ctls . . . . . . . . . . . :   5          21.7

                                                          More...
                                Interactive   Non-interactive
CPU utilization % . . . . . . . . . . . . . :   36.4          27.6
Transactions per Hour . . . . . . . . . . . :   23880         7084
Local response time (seconds) . . . . . . . :    .4            .9
LAN response time (seconds) . . . . . . . . :    .0            .0
WAN response time (seconds) . . . . . . . . :    .0            .0

Performance estimates -- Press help to see disclaimer.
F3=Exit    F10=Re-analyze      F12=Cancel   F15=Configuration menu
F17=Analyze multiple points   F18=Specify objectives   F24=More keys
```

Figure 6.32.   Analysis summary after automatic upgrade.

```
                        Display Recommendations

*****  Analysis Exceptions  *****
All the specified objectives have been met









                                                          Bottom
Performance estimates -- Press help to see disclaimer.
F3=Exit    F12=Cancel       F15=Configuration menu   F17=Analyze multiple points
F18=Specify objectives   F19=Work with workloads
```

Figure 6.33. Recommendations after upgrade: machine is adequate for workload.

second (Fig. 6.32). If the CPU looks a bit too comfortable, remember that some of the non-interactive utilization is high-priority system work. Also, the next smaller CPU is significantly less powerful. Press *Enter*.

33. The 'Recommendations' are exactly what we wanted to see (Fig. 6.33). Press *Enter*.

34. The 'Workload Report' shows predicted CPU utilization, throughput and response time by workload component (Fig. 6.34). The non-interactive utilization due to ITV and OFC only adds 6.4 per cent to the 36.4 per cent interactive

```
                        Display Workload Report

Period:    Analysis
                     CPU      Thruput   -------Response Times (Secs)-------
Workload    Type    Util     per Hour  Internal   Local     LAN       WAN
ITV          1      33.7       22380      .3        .4       .0        .0
OFC          1       2.7        1500      .3        .5       .0        .0
BATXXX       2      20.8          60     68.7      68.7      .0        .0
ITV          2       4.6           0      .4        .4       .0        .0
OFC          2       1.8          73     1.1       1.1       .0        .0
PRTS         2       .4         6167      .0        .2       .0        .0




                                                          Bottom
Type: 1=Interactive, 2=Non-interactive, 3=*BATCHJOB
Performance estimates -- Press help to see disclaimer.
F3=Exit    F10=Re-analyze   F11=Response time detail      F12=Cancel
F15=Configuration menu     F17=Analyze multiple points    F24=More keys
```

Figure 6.34. Workload report following upgrade.

```
                    Display Disk IOP and Arm Report

Period:    Analysis
                                   ---------Disk Arm Averages---------
                 I/Os       IOP     Pct     I/Os    Msecs    Queue
IOP      Arms   per Sec    Util    Busy   per Sec  per I/O  Length
IOP0      2      50.2       8.5    19.3    25.1     10.7      .3
MFIOP     4     100.3      20.1    33.4    25.1     21.4      .5




                                                            Bottom
Performance estimates -- Press help to see disclaimer.
F3=Exit   F10=Re-analyze    F11=Display ASP and Disk Arm report   F12=Cancel
F15=Configuration menu     F17=Analyze multiple points   F24=More keys
```

Figure 6.35.   Disk activity.

utilization. Perhaps a 2042 CPU (RIP = 7.2) would be OK from this point of view. Figure 2.2 shows that a 2043 RIP = 10.9, so the utilization due to high-priority work on the smaller CPU would be about $42.8 \times 10.9/7.2 = 64.8$ per cent which is below the 70 per cent guideline. Press *Enter*.

35. The 'Disk IOP and Arm Report' shows that predicted access arm and disk IOP utilizations are within guidelines (Fig. 6.35). Note that the I/O activity is spread evenly over the six actuators. The actuators on IOP0 have a much faster service time than those on the MFIOP: therefore the 'Pct Busy' figure is

```
                    Display Main Storage Pool Report

Period:    Analysis
Pool     Act    Size    Ineligible    -----Avg Number-----    Sync Reads
 ID      Lvl    (KB)    Wait (sec)    Active    Ineligible     per Sec
  1       0    27727       .0          .1          .0            .0
  2       0    10612       .0         1.3          .0           9.0
  3       0    56633       .0         1.8          .0          55.2
  4       0     3332       .0          .0          .0           2.0




                                                            Bottom
Performance estimates -- Press help to see disclaimer.
F3=Exit   F10=Re-analyze       F12=Cancel    F15=Configuration menu
F17=Analyze multiple points   F18=Specify objectives    F24=More keys
```

Figure 6.36.   Main storage activity.

correspondingly lower. We could edit the configuration and move arms to the faster IOP, but will not choose to do so in this exercise. Press *Enter*.

36. The 'Main Storage Pool Report' includes 'Sync Reads per Sec' (Fig. 6.36). These total 66.2, which exceeds the threshold of 60 for a CPU of RIP = 10 or less (Fig. 6.29). This is presumably why the model recommended a 2043 rather than a 2042. We don't have to slavishly follow model recommendations. We might opt for a 2042 with some more memory (say, 128 MB) to reduce page fault rates. In real life more memory reduces fault rates (and sync reads) in a way that the model currently does not seem to reflect. In this exercise we are not working from measured data; and therefore need a moderate margin for error. We'll stick with the 2043 and explore how large a margin this gives us. Press *Enter*.

6.3.4   *Modelling growth and saving the results*

37. The 'Work with Results' screen reappears. Press *F12* to return to the 'Create BEST/1 Model' screen (Fig. 6.37). Select '7' and press *Enter* to explore the growth capacity.

38. The 'Specify Growth of Workload Activity' screen appears (Fig. 6.38). The default growth per period is 20 per cent compound. We can specify whatever growth we like, vary it by period and rename the periods. In this exercise we'll take the defaults for these values. Key '*Y*' and '*5*' as shown to examine five periods and recommend upgrades as necessary. Press *Enter*.

39. Messages appear at the bottom of the screen charting progress, and finally the 'Work with Results' screen reappears. Option '*5*' against 'Analysis Summary'

```
                          Create BEST/1 Model

    Model/Text:    MDL1

    Select one of the following:

         1. Work with workloads
         2. Specify objectives and active jobs

         5. Analyze current model
         6. Analyze current model and give recommendations
         7. Specify workload growth and analyze model

        10. Configuration menu
        11. Work with results

        50. About BEST/1

                                                            Bottom
    Selection or command
    ===> 7
    F3=Exit    F4=Prompt    F9=Retrieve    F12=Cancel    F15=Save current model
    F20=More BEST/1 options
```

Figure 6.37.   Selection of workload growth analysis.

```
                     Specify Growth of Workload Activity

 Type information, press Enter to analyze model.
   Determine new configuration . . . . . . . . . .  Y    Y=Yes, N=No
   Periods to analyze . . . . . . . . . . . . . .   5    1 - 10

   Period 1 . . . . . . . . . . . . .   Period 1      Name
   Period 2 . . . . . . . . . . . . .   Period 2      Name
   Period 3 . . . . . . . . . . . . .   Period 3      Name
   Period 4 . . . . . . . . . . . . .   Period 4      Name
   Period 5 . . . . . . . . . . . . .   Period 5      Name

              ------Percent Change in Workload Activity------
 Workload     Period 1  Period 2  Period 3  Period 4  Period 5
 *ALL             .0      20.0      20.0      20.0      20.0

                                                              Bottom
 F3=Exit   F11=Specify growth by workload   F12=Cancel
 F13=Display periods 6 to 10   F17=Analyze using ANZBESTMDL
```

Figure 6.38.   Specify workload growth.

presents a new version of this display with the predicted effects of growth over
the five periods (Fig. 6.39). We see that 20 per cent growth (period 2) requires
no further hardware, 44 per cent growth (period 3) requires two extra disk
arms, 69 per cent growth requires a CPU and memory upgrade.

40. The more extreme predictions are less reliable, but we can see that the 2043
    has a good margin for growth or input error, and is the best choice for the
    sizing exercise. We can document the results by returning to the previous

```
                        Display Analysis Summary

            CPU    Stor     CPU   -Disk IOPs--   -Disk Ctls--   -Disk Arms--
 Period     Model  (MB)     Util  Nbr   Util     Nbr    Util    Nbr    Util
 Period 1   2043    96      64.0   2    14.3      5      .9      6      28.7
 Period 2   2043    96      77.1   2    17.6      5     1.1      6      35.3
 Period 3   2043    96      93.1   2    21.9      7     1.1      8      34.7
 Period 4   2044   128      63.6   2    24.3      7     1.2      8      38.6
 Period 5   2051   192      35.0   2    28.2      9     1.2     10      37.0

                                                                      Bottom
            ----Inter Rsp Time----   -------Inter--------  -----Non-Inter------
 Period     Local    LAN      WAN    CPU Util   Trans/Hr   CPU Util   Trans/Hr
 Period 1    .4      .0       .0      36.4       23880       27.6       7084
 Period 2    .5      .0       .0      43.7       28656       33.4       8501
 Period 3    .5      .0       .0      52.7       34387       40.5      10201
 Period 4    .4      .0       .0      36.2       41265       27.4      12241
 Period 5    .4      .0       .0      19.9       49518       15.1      14689

                                                                      Bottom
 F3=Exit     F10=Re-analyze    F11=Alternative view       F12=Cancel
 F15=Configuration menu        F17=Analyze multiple points  F24=More keys
```

Figure 6.39.   Analysis summary showing growth.

```
                        Work with Results

Printed report text . . . . . .    Sizing Exercise Output



Type options, press Enter.
  5=Display    6=Print

Opt      Report Name
         Analysis Summary
         Recommendations
         Workload Report
         ASP and Disk Arm Report
         Disk IOP and Disk Arm Report
         Main Storage Pool Report
         Communications Resources Report
  6      All of the above


                                                          Bottom
F3=Exit    F12=Cancel    F14=Select saved results    F15=Save current results
F18=Graph current results    F19=Append saved results    F24=More keys
```

Figure 6.40.   Printing the results.

screen (*F12*) and printing all the reports (Fig. 6.40). They could also be saved via *F15*. Key option '*6*' against "*All of the above*' and press *Enter*.
41. Use *F3* to return until you reach the 'Exit BEST/1 Model' screen (Fig. 6.41). Key option '*1*' and press *Enter*.
42. The 'Save Current Model' screen appears (Fig. 6.42). This will save the model complete with its workloads and configuration. Results are not saved unless

```
                        Exit BEST/1 Model

Type choice, press Enter.

   Option . . . . . . . . . .    1       1=Save and exit
                                         2=Exit without saving
                                         3=Resume









F12=Cancel
```

Figure 6.41.   Save and exit BEST/1 model.

```
                         Save Current Model

Change values if desired, press Enter.

Save to Model member:
  Member . . . . . . . . . . .    MDL1            Name
    Library . . . . . . . . .      MODELS         Name
  Text . . . . . . . . . . .     Sizing Exercise
  Replace . . . . . . . . .      N               Y=Yes, N=No

Externally described member information:
  Save . . . . . . . . . . . .    N               Y=Yes, N=No
  Member . . . . . . . . . . .    *MEMBER         Name, *MEMBER
    Library . . . . . . . . .      *LIB           Name, *LIB
  Text . . . . . . . . . . .     Sizing Exercise Output
  Replace . . . . . . . . .      *REP            Y=Yes, N=No, *REP




F12=Cancel
```

Figure 6.42.   Save model details.

you did it previously with F15 from the results screen. Key the descriptive text
and press *Enter*.
43. The 'Work with BEST/1 Models' screen reappears with our model listed, and
    a message confirming the save (Fig. 6.43). Use *F3* to return to the main menu
    and then *F3* again to exit BEST/1. Congratulations on completing the
    exercise.


```
                      Work with BEST/1 Models

Library . . . . .    MODELS        Name

Type options, press Enter.
  1=Create   3=Copy   4=Delete   5=Work with   6=Print   7=Rename

Opt   Model      Text                               Date      Time

      MDL1       Sizing Exercise                    10/08/94  12:15:14




                                                                    Bottom
Command
===>
F3=Exit    F4=Prompt    F5=Refresh       F9=Retrieve   F12=Cancel
F15=Sort by model      F16=Sort by text  F19=Sort by date and time
Member MDL1 has been saved
```

Figure 6.43.   Confirmation of save.

6.3.5 Other relevant functions

For reasons partially discussed at the start of Sec. 6.3, this exercise has introduced some of the main functions of BEST/1 modelling, but has not included all the activities which will be required in a real sizing job. Some of these will be covered in the course of the exercise in Chapter 13. Other functions which are often required, and which you may wish to explore at a future time, include the following items.

1. *Changing workload attributes.*   Measured workloads include pool numbers from the measured machine, which may well not match those in your selected configuration, or those from other measured workloads. From the 'Work with Workloads' screen you can use option '9' to edit the transactions in any workload. This includes changes to the pool assignments. It is a good idea to edit all workloads that you intend to use for sizing so that they conform to a standard pool layout, for example:

   System non-interactive   pools 1 and 2
   Spool   pool 3
   Interactive   pool 4
   Batch   pool 5.

   You should then save these workloads and delete the original versions.

2. *Editing the hardware configuration.*   Rather than allowing the model to do the upgrade, you may prefer to exercise more control by trying out the effect of various configuration alternatives. From the main 'Create BEST/1 Model' screen select '10', and then from the 'Edit Hardware Configuration' screen you can change all sorts of hardware options including CPU, memory, IOPs, disks, lines and LANs. The F4 prompt facility means that you don't have to know details such as feature numbers, so it is quite easy to do.

   One pitfall deserves a mention. If you select '5' (Work with communications resources) to add a LAN or WAN IOP, this is not recognized as part of the configuration until you edit the CPU (selection '1') to explicitly specify the IOP. If any of your measured workloads contain jobs that were connected via a LAN or WAN, you will have to add appropriate hardware to your configuration, or set the number of such jobs to zero on the 'Specify Objectives and Active Jobs' screen.

   If you change the memory size, you will be forced to edit the pool allocations (option '4' from the 'Configuration menu'). The easiest approach is to press F17, which rescales the pools based on the current sizes. You can, of course, move memory about manually, but you have to ensure that the pool sizes add up to the correct total.

3. *Specifying distribution of characters across alternative workstation connections.*   If your configuration contains multiple connection types, you will be prompted to specify for each workload, what proportion of the workstation

I/O is to go via each connection type. Simply take option '2' on the 'Work with Workloads' screen and then press F9. If the required information is not known, you can press F17 to make the distribution in proportion to the hardware attachment speeds.

7
Service-level agreements

7.1 The need for service level agreements

Service management is the collective term for procedures laid down and followed in order for the IT department to ensure that the computer users receive a consistent effective service through all the planned and unplanned changes a business experiences over a period of time, e.g.:

- Increased business volumes
- New applications
- Hardware problems
- Software bugs
- Unexpected disaster.

Organizations that run their main business applications on an AS/400 tend to have a variety of data processing histories:

- Manual system prior to AS/400
- Migrated/converted from S/36, S/38 or other mid-range business computer system
- Converted from a mainframe-type system.

The service management procedures in place vary considerably from advanced procedures of the type you would find in a mainframe environment to very little service management at all.

Obviously, you should select the type of service management procedures appropriate to your type of installation based on such considerations as:

1. How critical are the applications to your business?
2. How long can you afford to have the computer down?
3. How complex is the computing environment?
   - Use of telecommunications, LANs
   - Use of PCs

4. How many users rely on the system to perform their daily work?
5. How much change is going on?

This chapter will be of little use to you if you have a background of advanced service management with problem and change management procedures and service level agreements (SLAs) in place. However, there may be others in IT management who would like to improve their effectiveness in this area. They may feel a heavy burden of responsibility to their users for the computer service, and the factors which can affect that service are not always fully under their control. This is a very difficult position to maintain, as those of us who have experienced it know only too well.

There are many aspects to service management other than the management of performance—ability to recover from system failure or a disaster of some type, ensuring the security of the system against unauthorized access, management of your service through problems and changes. This book deals specifically with performance management but you may find that agreeing service levels with your users will highlight requirements for more stringent procedures in the other areas.

Performance as viewed by the IT manager tends to consist mainly of:

- Interactive response time
- Batch throughput.

A user might add:

- Service availability (time of day and days of the week)
- Availability of critical reports on business deadlines.

Users tend to have their own opinions about what they regard as acceptable performance in both interactive and batch. The IT department may have different opinions. Unless these differing opinions are discussed and a common view agreed, problems and misunderstandings will almost always occur. Consider the following situation.

A group of users has been using an order entry application for some months. It is fairly simple and gives a consistent response time of under 2 seconds. An enhancement is to be implemented to allow the users to find available parts using a variety of search arguments keyed at run time. The function is implemented via an online SQL data extraction. Let us say that with the current hardware configuration and the application as written, the response to that search will never be under 5 seconds. When the enhancement goes live users may see this 5-second response as a degradation in their service. The result is potential dissatisfaction among these users.

How might conflict have been avoided? If the users had been told during development of the enhancement that they should expect a response time of 5 seconds to this transaction, they might have:

- Upon consideration, accepted the situation and agreed to live with it
- Presented a genuine case that this would be unacceptable for business purposes, for instance if the transaction were to be used while the user is on the phone to a client.

In the latter case a plan could have been made to:

- Change the application so as to satisfy the requirement in a different way if possible
- Put a business case to higher management for additional hardware to provide a shorter response to the transaction as written.

If an SLA had been in place where response times were stipulated and proper performance testing of the application had been carried out, the IT department would have known that this new transaction would be outside the terms of the agreement and should have alerted the users as a matter of course and performed a capacity plan to recommend an upgrade which would bring the new transaction within the response time stipulated.

Thus one basic purpose of an SLA is to provide a focus for discussion between the users and the IT department in order to avoid user dissatisfaction. Notice that success in this area depends upon performing all aspects of performance management—sizing, capacity planning, performance testing of applications and on communicating with the users.

The resulting discussion between users and the IT department should give the users an understanding of the costs associated with performance. They will realize that the organization must pay for any improvements in service which they require.

7.2   How to establish an SLA

7.2.1   Forum for agreement

The key to good relations with the users is a regular, healthy dialogue between all user departments and the IT department. One way of achieving this is to have representatives of each user department in a user group or committee which meets regularly with the appropriate IT personnel. However, if this means that you will have a large number of users at one meeting battling for attention, you might choose to split this down so that the IT department meets with representatives of the various user departments separately.

The selection of the right user representatives is important. They must carry sufficient weight and also be close enough to the coal face to properly represent all the users in their department.

It is likely that the users will look to the IT department for a lead in setting service levels. Matters will be dealt with more quickly if IT present the users with a draft agreement for discussion. Ability to meet specified service levels may then be tested prior to the negotiations.

The keys to the success of putting service levels in place is:

* To ensure that the service levels are achievable and are met initially
* To ensure that the service levels continue to be met as things change
* To ensure that service levels are modified with the changes in the business and applications as time goes by
* Understanding and communicating the cost of service to the users.

In other words, the dialogue must go on. If service levels are set correctly and kept current, the time spent in maintaining the dialogue with the users and drawing up documentation will be far outweighed by the time that would otherwise have been spent dealing with dissatisfaction and sudden crises.

7.2.2   Items to consider for inclusion in your SLA on system performance

One important point about the SLA is that it should be as brief and comprehensible as possible. If you create one which covers reams of paper it will be difficult to understand and to maintain.

Workload

You have a specific hardware resource available to you. The performance which that hardware resource can supply for a particular set of applications is dependent upon the workload. Thus an SLA must document the anticipated workload on the various applications. It is vital this be reviewed regularly with the user departments and kept current.

Interactive response time

In an ideal world it would be possible to guarantee all your users sub-second response times for all their transactions forever. However, this is not an ideal world. The first task therefore is to group your users into similar sets, i.e. users of the same set of applications, local and remote users, and then to estimate what average response time is achievable for each group. The AS/400 performance tools can assist with this, either by measuring the existing workload and response times or by modelling planned workload and predicting average response times.

Remember to allow for some growth in volumes. Do not commit to a response time measured on a heavily loaded machine such that a small increase in throughput could prevent objectives being met. Use the tools to model an increase in workload to arrive at a reasonable average response time target. If variability of response times is an issue, the target can be expressed in terms such as '90 per cent of response times should be less than $x.y$ seconds'. This threshold value will, of course, be greater than the average. Compliance with this sort of objective can be monitored using the performance tools for local screens, and for remote screens attached to control units with the necessary data collection function (e.g. 5494).

Whatever turns out to be your measured or predicted average response time for any one group, you need to add various provisos for unusual situations. For instance, if your system is planned to allow for a particular peak load, there may be times when the actual workload is higher than this for a short period. You can cater for this by stipulating that the target will only be met in a percentage of cases. In addition, the users need to understand what average response time means, i.e. that some of their responses will be well within the target and some will be outside the target. They must also understand that some of their transactions, because they are more complex, will always have longer response times than more simple ones. If there is likely to be a significantly differing average response time between applications for the same user group, it may be advisable to specify different target response times for the two applications.

Users should be made aware that situations can occur which will degrade their service. Examples of this are:

- Peak workload exceeded
- Hardware malfunction, e.g. re-synchronization of mirrored data after a disk failure
- High error rate on a remote communications line.

If user departments are made aware of such problems when they arise, they are more likely to be understanding and work around the degraded service.

Batch job turnaround

The IT department cannot be expected to know the inner workings of each user department. In order, therefore, to provide the optimum service for batch jobs, the users should specify which batch jobs are time-critical and also the business deadlines to which they work. With this information, the IT department can tune the system to:

- Allocate resource such that time-critical batch jobs do not wait upon long-running non-critical ones
- Reallocate resource as appropriate for specific business deadlines, e.g. set up a separate batch queue for monthly sales figures at the end of the month
- Allocate resource such that each department has access to a 'fast' batch queue for short jobs.

System availability

In these days of flexible working hours and remote home working, users need to know when they can have access to the system. Discussions with user departments will tell you when the users wish this access. This will allow you to plan any necessary downtime, e.g. for backup, and to set procedures in place to ready the required subsystems automatically after downtime.

Once more, the users need to be aware that out-of-line situations may occasionally affect the system availability. Again, the key to managing this is communication with the users.

7.3   Maintaining the service day-to-day

7.3.1   *Communication with the users*

Once agreements are in place with the users, the job of the IT department is to keep its side of the bargain. In order to do this in the short term, there must be an ever-open channel of communication with the users. Most organizations find this best achieved by a help desk. It is a focus for all user problems. The implementation of an effective help desk means that users can always get a prompt answer to their problems and also keeps the IT department fully in touch with what is going on out there.

The main keys to running an effective help desk are:

- The desk must be manned at all times when the computer service is available.
- The front-line call taker(s) must have access to the appropriate specialist for any type of user problem. Application specialists may well be members of user departments.
- Problems must be recorded and tracked through to satisfactory resolution.
- Users must be kept informed of the progress towards resolution.
- Out-of-line situations must be reported up the line in the IT department.

There are many help desk applications available to assist with recording, tracking and escalation.

7.3.2   *Performance monitoring*

You should appoint someone in the IT department to be responsible for monitoring the service and producing short regular reports describing the service provided to the users. This can be done with the aid of the AS/400 Performance Tools which should be run at least weekly at a time when the system is at its busiest. Reports and graphs can be produced giving the key performance indicators so that performance can be measured against targets. Downtime for any service and any user complaints related to performance should be logged and reported. You can then use these reports to review the service with the user groups to check that their perception of performance is the same as yours. There are also various tools available which give very graphic representations of performance information. These include Performance Investigator/400.

The production of such reports will also enable you to spot trends in workload, and in fact form part of the input to the capacity planning process as described in Chapter 12. If the reports show that service levels are not always being met, you can investigate the cause and take action to rectify before the degradation can become a user issue.

7.4   Maintaining the service into the future

One advantage of having an SLA in place is that the IT department have documentation of the users' expectations. When planning for implementation of additional work or new applications, you know what the requirements of the existing users and applications are. Thus, you will be able to use the modelling tools discussed in this book to add workload and check whether or not the system can cope with the additional work and still satisfy the users' expectations. If not, you have full supporting documentation to use in a business case for a hardware upgrade, and you will have the users behind you.

In addition, the existence of service targets will assist you in specifying performance targets for new applications. This can help you to ensure that designers take performance fully into account when planning new applications, and carry out performance testing as a natural process in the development cycle.

7.5   Sample SLA on system performance

Purpose of this document.   To define the system performance which users can expect from the AS/400 and the applications which it provides.

Date of this document.   1 September 1994.

Workload.   The normal peak workload is shown in Table 7.1.

Average interactive response time during normal operations.   This is defined as the average time from the user pressing the Enter key or a function key to the computer responding with the next screen format.

Table 7.1

Department	No. of workstations	Peak computer trans/h
Accounts	15	1200
Order Processing	24	2000
Telesales	15	1200
Management Enquiries	9	400

Table 7.2

Department	Average response time (s)
Accounts local workstations	1.5
Accounts remote workstations	3.5
Order Processing local workstations	2.0
Order Processing remote workstations	4.0
Telesales	1.0
Management local workstations	2.0
Management remote workstations	4.0

The average response times shown in Table 7.2 represent the average response time currently experienced during the normal peak workload on the last Monday of the month between 10 am and 12 noon. Should activity exceed this peak by more than 10 per cent, average response times will degrade.

The figures shown are averages of all response times experienced over the working period. Some actual response times experienced will be faster than average and some slower.

There are some particular transactions which require the system to perform more work than any other transactions and responses to these are always likely to be longer than the average. These include:

- Context search on customer name
- *Ad hoc* queries using the XYZ query front end or Query/400.

Such transactions will also adversely affect other users of the system and, hence, they are designed to be used only on a casual basis. Over-use of these functions can cause general performance degradation. The frequency of their use is checked regularly. The batch option should be taken for all file queries except where used in direct response to a customer phone query.

Critical batch job turnaround. The batch jobs shown in Table 7.3 have been registered as time-critical and have the following target turnaround times during normal operations. The definition of turnaround time is the time from job submission to completion of job, including printing if applicable. This assumes that they are submitted for processing by the deadline shown.

System availability during normal operations. The system and all applications will normally be available from 6 am to 10 pm each day including most weekends. The exception to this is the first weekend in every month which is reserved for planned maintenance.

Table 7.3

Batch job	Deadline	Target turnaround time
Daily Invoices	6 pm	by 9 am next day
Cheques	2 pm	4 pm

Performance outside normal operations. Some abnormal situations will cause the system performance to degrade or even cause the system to be unavailable. These include hardware malfunction, network malfunction, software malfunction. Where such situations occur, user department representatives will be informed within 15 minutes of the IT Department detecting the problem. Within 1 hour of this, user department representatives will be given an initial estimate of time to correct the problem. Progress bulletins will thereafter be provided to user departments every 3 hours during the business day.

Monthly performance reports. These will be circulated to user department representatives. They will include:

- Average response time and transactions per hour recorded for each set of users during the regular monthly peak period
- Average response time and transactions per hour recorded for each set of users during any periods of activity higher than the regular monthly peak period
- Record of critical batch job turnaround during the period
- Report of all abnormal situations causing performance degradation or non-availability
- Report of any periods of non-availability of any part of the service

Part III
AS/400 system tuning

8
Preparations for system tuning

8.1   Introduction to system tuning

The primary aim of system tuning is to set up the machine to make optimum use of the performance resources. This does not necessarily imply that we will meet users' performance expectations or needs, or even our own objectives. We simply make the best of what we have. If the initial sizing was realistic, sensible service levels were agreed and capacity planning is going on, we can then, of course, also be confident of satisfying our users.

The process we will carry out will identify and implement beneficial system tuning changes and, once the initial status has been established, should take less than a day to complete. It can be done by following the checklist of activities outlined in Sec. 8.2 and detailed in Chapter 9.

Before getting on with that there are some preliminaries to deal with. For example, what is the best way to measure the effects of changes, so that we will know when we have succeeded? Most of this chapter is concerned with answering this question. Performance evaluation is the first step in system tuning because we have to document the 'before' situation prior to making changes.

8.1.1   System tuning expectations

We should not expect to make a dramatic impact on performance by system tuning measures unless the initial set-up is wildly eccentric. Anything near to the default arrangements will give reasonable performance, after initial tailoring at the machine installation stage. However, system tuning is relatively quick and so should always be done. Heroic performance improvements are much more likely to come from considering the specific needs of individual applications, and catering for these preferentially (Chapter 10).

As you might suspect there is no single right way to tune an AS/400. The optimum way of allocating the various system resources will depend on the workload the system is required to handle, for example:

- Number of interactive users
- Mix and characteristics of the workload components
- Number of batch job streams

and on any requirements to favour particular workload items.

There is a limited amount of initial tuning which should be done when an AS/400 is first installed, before the characteristics of the workload are fully known. This is dealt with in Sec. 9.18. Our main interest, however, is the potentially far more rewarding task of improving the performance of a system which has been running for a time. Normally one is asked to do this because there is a perceived problem. Remember that a performance problem could be caused by:

- Work overload—the system is just not big enough to handle the workload
- Inefficient application design or coding.

If either of these is the case, system tuning may be able to improve the situation marginally, but will not fix the problem. You should set the expectation of your management at the outset that system tuning is not a panacea. The recommendation at the end of the exercise may be to conduct a review of a certain application, or to evaluate the effect of adding hardware.

8.1.2   *Documenting the process*

In order to get the most out of the time and effort you will put into the exercise, we recommend that you fully document the findings and actions. System tuning is not usually a job which needs to be done once only. The workload on the system will grow and change and your tuning requirements may change too. Documentation will record the situation before and after the tuning exercise, and will prove invaluable the next time you or your successor come to examine system tuning.

To assist you in this we have provided forms for recording the information. These are shown at the appropriate point in the text, and are also available in a larger size in Appendix 1. You can photocopy the larger ones as required.

8.2   **Action list**

This section gives a skeleton system tuning action list. Each individual item is expanded in a later section of the chapter, or in Chapter 9.

1. Record the current workload, performance, system values and storage pool status as follows:
   - (a) Measure the workload and performance (Sec. 8.4.2) and screen the data for suitability (Sec. 8.4.3).
   - (b) Record relevant system value settings (Sec. 8.4.4).

(c) Gather information from users about perceived performance problems and document your understanding (Secs 8.4.5 and 8.4.6). Get agreement that you have stated the problems accurately.

(d) Document the physical locations of the workstations and the method of connection to the AS/400 (Sec. 8.4.7).

(e) Record the division of main memory into system pools and their use by subsystems (Sec. 9.1).

2. Observe the effect of automatic performance adjustment support (Sec. 9.2).
3. Note the recommendations of the performance advisor in Performance Tools/400 (Sec. 9.3).
4. Examine the settings of system values affecting performance and record recommendations for changes (Sec. 9.4).
5. Estimate desirable main storage pool allocations (Sec. 9.5).
6. Make initial tuning changes (Sec. 9.6).
7. Record and assess storage pool activity and modify pool sizes and/or activity levels (Sec. 9.7). This action should be repeated after any changes which might affect storage pool activity.
8. Review CPU and disk utilization (Sec. 9.8). This action should be repeated after any changes which might affect CPU and/or disk utilization.
9. Review time-slice values (Sec. 9.9).
10. Review purge values (Sec. 9.10).
11. Consider use of separate pool(s) for batch work (Sec. 9.11).
12. Consider use of multiple pools for interactive work (Sec. 9.12).
13. Consider use of Expert Cache (Sec. 9.13).
14. Consider System/36 Environment tuning (Sec. 9.14).
15. Review operational procedures and practice with respect to performance (Sec. 9.15).
16. Review performance of communications (Sec. 9.16).
17. Review performance of attached personal computers (Sec. 9.17).

8.3 Performance evaluation and monitoring

Performance evaluation is what we do to assess the effects of tuning. Performance monitoring is a regular activity that is part of the capacity planning process we describe in Chapters 12 and 13. Both involve the same sort of measurements, but each is performed in a different way and used for a different purpose.

Performance evaluation is done on an irregular, as required basis. Performance monitoring is a routine installation management responsibility that involves the collection of performance and workload data during peak periods of activity. One of the prerequisites for using this data in capacity planning is that it must be gathered from a system tuned for optimum performance. Hence performance evaluation and system tuning must precede the establishment of capacity-planning disciplines.

Optimum tuning means that the system should be set up to execute the given workload with the best possible performance outcome. Primarily we measure this in terms of low average interactive response time and high batch throughput. Low response times usually result from reducing page fault rates, other disk I/O rates and CPU utilization caused by interactive jobs. The increased share of system resources thereby left for batch in a normally tuned system automatically improves batch throughput.

The data that we need for performance evaluation appears on performance tools' reports, which can be generated at any time and which are regularly produced by the performance-monitoring process. They are also available in large part from normal interactive commands, which you may prefer to use in a more impromptu way to view the results of changes. In practice the performance tools' reports are more convenient and comprehensive, and will be the preferred source.

8.4   External performance

We use a number of parameters to indicate the effects of tuning, but the real measure of any success we have is improved performance. We may seek this in one or more of the following areas, and will be prepared to distribute system resources accordingly:

- Reduced interactive response times
- Increased interactive throughput
- Increased batch throughput.

The second objective in the list implies that we are already running the machine at its limit and wish to increase the throughput capacity without adding hardware. To measure the effect of tuning changes we would need to run 'saturation' tests where the interactive workload is pushed to its peak attainable value. This is not necessarily convenient or even perhaps possible in a live environment.

Response times, on the other hand, can be measured during normal operations. A reduction in response time normally indicates reduced consumption of system resources and therefore potential for increased throughput. Increasing throughput naturally increases response times, but if we find a way to reduce response time for a given throughput, then there is scope to increase throughput without exceeding the original response time.

From this viewpoint we can consider the first two objectives as equivalent. The third objective, in contrast, potentially conflicts. It is easy to increase batch throughput at the expense of interactive performance by redistributing system resources, e.g. reversing the relative priorities of batch and interactive or moving memory from interactive to batch pools. Generally this is not what we want to do.

A more likely requirement is to improve the efficiency of the batch work so that it can use virtually all of the CPU time remaining after interactive work has taken what it needs. In Chapter 10 we will see how to achieve this for individual batch jobs by minimizing synchronous I/Os. System tuning may achieve a similar effect by running multiple concurrent batch jobs such that the CPU is never left idle. In this way we aim to improve batch throughput with zero or minimal impact on interactive performance.

8.4.1   Use of WRKACTJOB for performance assessment

The command WRKACTJOB displays a list of all the jobs currently running on the system together with status information. Pressing F11 (Display elapsed data) gives some relevant performance data, which will be useful if we press F5 (Refresh) after an elapsed period of about 5 minutes. Figure 8.1 gives an idea of what you might see.

Under the heading 'Elapsed' we see the number of interactions (transactions), the total internal response time, the number of auxiliary disk I/Os and the average CPU utilization during the elapsed period. We can get the active jobs to the head of the list by moving the cursor to the 'Int' or 'CPU' column and pressing F16 to sort the displayed lines accordingly.

Some arithmetic is needed to get interactive throughput or response time figures for a group of users. The throughput will be the sum of the 'Int' values scaled up to one hour from the measured time. Average response time over the period is the sum of the 'Rsp' values divided by the sum of the 'Int' values. For batch and spool jobs we can get a measure of throughput from the 'CPU' and 'Auxio' columns.

For the performance data to have any meaning they must be viewed in the context of the total workload as well as the system set up. To reduce the labour of documenting and examining all this performance data we clearly need a more convenient tool than the WRKACTJOB display.

```
                        Work with Active Jobs                    NBS400B
                                                   13/07/94  10:18:19
  CPU %:    40.5      Elapsed time:   00:06:29    Active jobs:   74

  Type options, press Enter.
    2=Change   3=Hold   4=End    5=Work with   6=Release    7=Display message
    8=Work with spooled files    13=Disconnect ...
                                       --------Elapsed---------
  Opt  Subsystem/Job  Type  Pool  Pty      CPU   Int   Rsp  AuxIO  CPU %
       QCTL           SBS    2     0       2.3                 0     .0
        QSYSSCD       BCH    2    10        .8                 0     .0
       QINTER         SBS    2     0      12.4                21     .1
        PE303L01S1    INT    4    20       5.6    14    .4     2     .4
        PE303L02S1    INT    4    20       9.5   100    .1     0    1.2
        PE303L03S1    INT    4    20      19.6    49    .7   147    3.4
        PE303L04S1    INT    4    20       6.5    29    .0    21     .5
        PE303L05S1    INT    4    20      22.5    26   1.4   204    3.6
        PE303L06S1    INT    4    20      12.1    18   1.2   145    1.9
                                                                More...
  Parameters or command
  ===>
  F3=Exit       F5=Refresh         F10=Restart statistics   F11=Display status
  F12=Cancel    F23=More options   F24=More keys
```

Figure 8.1.   WRKACTJOB display: elapsed data.

8.4.2   Use of the performance tools' reports to measure performance

Comprehensive performance and workload measurement can be requested simply by using the STRPFRMON command to submit a high-priority batch data collection job. Assuming you have the performance tools installed, the PRTSYSRPT and other commands will then produce nicely formatted and summarized figures relating to the measured period.

Selected subsets of the workload and sample intervals can also be characterized, and detailed analysis of any part of the workload down to the level of transitions within an individual transaction can be carried out subsequently if necessary. Chapters 12 and 13 explain how this is done in the context of capacity planning. Here we need to review the same data from a slightly different perspective.

For clarity and simplicity, we will adopt an authoritarian or cookbook style during the rest of this subsection. The following recipe produces an extract of performance and workload data to characterize a single before or after measurement period. The explanatory notes are optional reading.

1. Sample and trace performance data.
    (a) Select a period of medium to high interactive activity when you believe that the workload will be stable for at-least half an hour, and will include significant business functions. If the workload is too variable or unpredictable, you may have to consider setting up a test script where standard functions are performed by a group of users according to a repeatable schedule.
    (b) Enter the following command when the period of stable activity is under way:

```
STRPFRMON   MBR(name)
                TEXT('description of measurement')
                INTERVAL(5)
                HOUR(0)
                MINUTE(30)
                TRACE(*ALL)
          /* Other parameters take default values *
```

Note 1. This command submits a high-priority batch job to the QCTL job queue. The job collects sample data at 5-minute intervals in a set of database files, and a continuous trace of other data in the system trace table. The job terminates after 30 minutes and dumps trace data from the system table to a database file.

Note 2. The same files are used each time the performance monitor runs but a new member is added for each set of data, with the name specified in the MBR parameter. The name should start with a letter and contain self-identifying information such as date and a sequence letter. If you omit the

MBR parameter a system generated name is used containing the date and time when data collection started.

Note 3. The descriptive text will be attached to each member associated with this performance data within the multiple files, and by default will be used as a title for some subsequent reports.

Note 4. See the CL Reference manual for how the ENDTYPE, DAY, HOUR and MINUTE parameters control the measurement period. A period of 20 minutes should be considered the absolute minimum for this type of work. Periods longer than 30 minutes are fine so long as the workload remains homogeneous and the throughput is level, but give no extra benefit.

Note 5. Beware that dumping 30 minutes or more of trace data from a busy system is a significant workload in itself. If production work is suffering poor performance, you can avoid making things worse by specifying DMPTRC(*NO) as a parameter of the command.

Trace data is then left in the table. The DMPTRC command can be used subsequently, when the machine is less loaded, to complete the function. If you defer dumping the data you must be careful not to overwrite it by making further measurements. In addition, more job names will be unresolvable.

2. Print the System Report and the Component Report from the sample data collected above.

(a) Sign on as a user with authority to the private performance tools commands (QPGMR, QSRV and QSECOFR are delivered with appropriate rights) and enter the following commands after the data collection job of step 1 has terminated:

```
PRTSYSRPT   MBR(member name)
            /* Other parameters take default values */
PRTCPTRPT   MBR(member name)
            /* Other parameters take default values */
```

Note 1. These commands submit normal-priority batch jobs to the QBATCH job queue. The jobs generate reports summarizing the workload and performance during a specified measurement period. The member name should correspond to that specified or generated for the data collection. If you don't know the member name do the following:

enter the command GO PERFORM
enter selection 3 (print performance report)
review the names, text and timestamps
enter option 1 against the selected member
press F6 (print entire report)
press enter

enter option 2 against the selected member

press F6 (print entire report)

press enter.

3. Print the Job Summary Report from the trace data dumped earlier.

   (a) Enter the following command after the data collection job of step 1 has terminated:

```
PRTTNSRPT   MBR(member name)
            OPTION(*SS *HV)
            /* Other parameters take default values */
```

   Note 1. This command submits a normal priority batch job to the QBATCH job queue. The job generates a workload and performance report with summary and detail data at the job and transaction level. The member name should correspond to that specified or generated for the data collection. If you don't know the member name do the following:

   enter the command GO PERFORM

   enter selection 3 (print performance report)

   review the names, text and timestamps

   enter option 3 against the selected member

   key the OPTION values into the command prompt

   press enter.

4. Record key attributes of the measured workload and performance on forms similar to Tables 8.1 and 8.2.

8.4.3   Criteria for accepting data

Whatever the method used to assess performance, if we wish to gauge the effect of system tuning changes measurements must be made before and after the changes, and we must be sure that in other respects the environment we measure is unchanged. This is easy to achieve when measuring the performance of a dedicated batch job but quite the reverse for mixed interactive workloads.

In a live interactive environment we have to make before and after measurements when we believe the workloads are not significantly different, and then analyse the performance data to discover if the results are directly comparable. If not, we repeat the after measurements until we get a set that can be used. The criteria to permit comparison of before and after measurements are:

1. To make the machine sensitive to system tuning changes measurements should be made during periods of medium to high activity. Such periods will be identified as part of the capacity-planning process. If this is not yet under way at your installation and you do not have a clear idea of how the workload varies,

Table 8.1. Workload and performance summary data

Date[a]					
Start time[b]					
Average response time[c]					
Total interactive throughput[d]					
NPT tr/h[e]					
PCS tr/h[f]					
Passthrough tr/h[g]					
DDM target tr/h[h]					
S/36 tr/h[i]					
MRT tr/h[j]					
Total active interactive jobs[k]					
Active workstations (%)[l]					
CPU utilization @ > = priority 20[m]					
Machine pool NDB faults/s[n]					
Total DB and NDB faults/s[o]					
Average actuator utilization[p]					
CPU seconds per transaction[q]					
Synchronous disk I/Os per transaction[r]					
Exceptional wait per transaction[s]					

Most of these data items are easily located in the few subdivisions of the System Report; the remainder (l and s) are in the System Summary Data section of the Job Summary Report.

[a]Right side of the heading of every page (Fig. 8.2)

[b]Right side of the heading of every page (Fig. 8.2)

[c]'Average Response' column of 'Workload' report (Fig. 8.2). Note: This does not include line time and no distinction need be made between local and remote workload components for our purposes. This is our prime measure of the efficacy of system tuning measures

[d]Total of 'Tns/Hour Rate' column of 'Resource Utilization' report (Fig. 8.3)

[e]'Tns/Hour Rate' figure identified as 'Interactive' job type in the 'Resource Utilization' report (Fig. 8.3). Note: NPT = non-programmable terminal

[f]'Tns/Hour Rate' figure identified as 'PC Support' in the 'Resource Utilization' report (Fig. 8.3). This is the workstation function part of the PC activity

[g]'Tns/Hour Rate' figure identified as 'Passthru' in the 'Resource Utilization' report (Fig. 8.3). This represents transactions executed on the measured machine by virtual devices, associated with workstations attached to another machine in the network

[h]'Tns/Hour Rate' figure identified as 'DDM Server' in the 'Resource Utilization' report (Fig. 8.3). This represents the Distributed Data Management requests satisfied by the measured machine for transactions running on other machines in the network

[i]'Tns/Hour Rate' figure identified as 'S/36' in the 'Resource Utilization' report (Fig. 8.3). All S/36 environment jobs that are not MRT jobs are counted

[j]'Tns/Hour Rate' figure identified as 'MRT' in the 'Resource Utilization' report (Fig. 8.3). These are a special type of S/36 environment transaction

[k]'Nbr Jobs' figure for interactive job type in 'System Summary Data' section of 'Job Summary' report (Fig. 8.4). Note that the total 'Active Jobs Per Interval' figure from the 'Resource Utilization' report is likely to be too large, due to the way PC Support jobs are counted

[l]'Est Of AWS' from right-hand side of 'System Summary Data' section of 'Job Summary' report (Fig. 8.4). Divide this by the total active jobs figure and note the percentage

[m]'Cum Util' figure against the lowest-priority 20 job type in the 'Resource Utilization Expansion' report (Fig. 8.5)

[n]Top figure in the 'Non-DB Fault' column of the 'Storage Pool Utilization' report (Fig. 8.6)

[o]Sum of the two totals under the 'Non-DB Fault' and 'DB Fault' columns of the above report (Fig. 8.6)

[p]Average figure under the 'Percent Util' column of the 'Disk Utilization' report (Fig. 8.7)

[q]Average figure under the 'CPU Seconds' column of the 'Resource Utilization' report (Fig. 8.3)

[r]Average figure under the 'Sync Disk I/O' column of the 'Resource Utilization' report (Fig. 8.3)

[s]'Excp Wait/Tns' figure from 'System Summary Data' section of the 'Job Summary' report (Fig. 8.4)

Note: The MSRPRF parameter of the PRTSYSRPT command defaults to a value of '*NONE'. If a profile name is specified, an extract of the data is stored under the specified name and an additional part of the System Report is printed, containing what appears to be much of the information we need in a compact list. Beware that this data ignores any PC Support and Pass through transactions.

Table 8.2.   Record of pool activity

System pool no.	Pool size (K)	Activity level	DB faults per second	NBD faults per second	AW trn/min	WI trn/min	AI trn/min
1	N/A						
2							
3							
..							
15							
Totals							

Note: These data items are easily located in the 'Storage Pool Utilization' section of the System Report (Fig. 8.6).

collect sample data and check for peaks over a period of at least a week, as described in Sec. 12.2.1.

2. The total interactive throughput should be the same (within 5 per cent).

   (a) Compare the logged values in row (d) of Table 8.1 against this criterion. If the response time (c) shows an improvement and the 'after' figure is more than 5 per cent out on the *high* side, your results still prove the change was beneficial but do not quantify the benefit well.

3. The number of active users should be the same (within 10 per cent).

   (a) Compare the logged values in row (l) against this criterion. Again, a divergence on the high side may not be sufficient to completely negate the effects of tuning changes, but it will obscure the measurement of performance improvement.

4. The mix of application functions should be similar and should represent normal production activities. This includes batch and spool as well as interactive work.

   (a) Review the jobs that were active by scanning the 'Job Summary' section of the job summary reports (Fig. 8.8) and confirm that there are no obvious discrepancies in the type of work going on.

   (b) Compare the 'Interactive Program Statistics' sections of the job summary reports (Fig. 8.9). These rank the interactive programs used in activity sequence and provide a good indication of the application functions used.

   (c) The average transaction characteristics logged in rows (q) and (r) of Table 8.1 should be comparable if the workloads were similar. System tuning improvements could reduce the 'after' values, particularly the synchronous disk I/Os per transaction.

5. No abnormal activities or conditions that might distort the performance of production work should be present. These include console activity, excessive sign-off/on activity, unusually complex interactive transactions (such as long-running queries, file copies, access path builds and compilations), abnormal lock conflicts and error-recovery situations due to such things as persistent line faults or application errors.

System Report
Workload
After System Tuning Changes

(a) (b)

Member . . . : THU290794   Model/Serial . . . : F80/44-D5817   Main storage . . : 384.0 M   Started . . . . : 29/07/94 09:31:51
Library . . . : RSFPFRLIB   System name . . . . : WIDGETS   Version/Release : 2/ 2.0   Stopped . . . . : 29/07/94 11:26:36

Interactive Workload

Job Type	Number Transactions	Average Response	Logical DB I/O Count	----- Printer ----- Lines	Pages	Communications I/O Count	MRT Max Time
Interactive	975	.86	23,323	0	0	0	
DDM Server	1	.00	0	0	0	8	
PC Support	14,529	.84	633,248	452	42	0	
Total/Average	15,505	.84	656,571	452	42	8	

(c)

Non-Interactive Workload

Job Type	Number Of Jobs	Logical DB I/O Count	----- Printer ----- Lines	Pages	Communications I/O Count	CPU Per Logical I/O	Logical I/O /Second
Batch	21	36,692	303	1,878	0	.0085	20.4
Spool	32	107	975	20	0	.5689	.0
AutoStart	3	0	0	0	0	.0000	.0
Total/ Average	56	36,799	1,278	1,898	0	.0102	20.5

Average CPU Utilization . . . . : 77.9
CPU 1 Utilization . . . . : 77.9
CPU 2 Utilization . . . . : 77.9

Figure 8.2. System Report: workload section.

Member . . . : FRI200794   Model/Serial . . . : F80/44-D5817   Main storage . . : 384.0 M   Started . . . . : 29/07/94 09:31:51
Library . . : RSFPFRLIB   System name . . . : WIDGETS   Version/Release : 2/ 2.0   Stopped . . . . : 29/07/94 11:26:36

------------- Average Per Transaction -------------

Job Type	Response Seconds	CPU Seconds	Sync Disk I/O	Async Disk I/O	DB I/O
Interactive	.8	.10	12.3	3.6	23.9
DDM Server	.0	.37	133.0	28.0	.0
PC Support	.8	.13	11.8	7.1	43.5
Total/Average	.8	.13 (q)	11.8 (r)	6.9	42.3

Job Type	CPU Util	Tns /Hour Rate	Active Jobs Per Interval	Total I/O	Synchronous DBR	DBW	NDBR	NDBW	Asynchronous DBR	DBW	NDBR	NDBW
Interactive	2.7	1,956 (h)	15	8.6	1.7	1.1	2.8	1.0	.8	.8	.0	.1
DDM Server	.0	2	0	.0	.0	.0	.0	.0	.0	.0	.0	.0
PC Support	56.1	29,155 (f)	317	153.9	60.6	6.6	23.6	4.8	41.6	14.3	.0	2.0
Total/Average	58.9	31,113 (d)	332	162.7	62.4	7.8	26.5	5.8	42.5	15.2	.0	2.2

(e)

Figure 8.3.   System Report: resource utilization section.

172

Job Summary Report
System Summary Data
After Tuning Changes

Member . . . : FRI290794   Model/Serial . . . : F80/44-D5817   Main storage . . : 384.0 M   Started 29 07 94 10:01:00
Library . . . : RSFPFRLIB   System name . . . : WIDGETS   Version/Release : 2/ 2.0   Stopped 29 07 94 10:31:00

CPU AND DISK I/O PER JOB TYPE FOR ALL JOBS FOR TOTAL TRACE PERIOD.

Job Type	Nbr Jobs	CPU Seconds	CPU Util	Disk I/O Requests Sync	Async	CPU Sec/ Sync DIO	Sync I/O /Elp Sec
INTERACTIVE	380	7193.5	52.8	646658	301259	.0111	95.0
BATCH A,B,C,D,X	268	2641.0	19.4	131950	107194	.0200	19.4
SPOOL WTR/RDR	34	155.8	1.1	36387	2601	.0043	5.3
SYSTEM JOBS	25	26.9	.2	12311	698	.0022	1.8
SYSTEM TASKS	410	890.1	6.5	182339	693	.0049	26.8
** TOTALS **	1117	10907.3	80.0	1009645	412445	.0108	148.3

Planning Parameters

Elapsed Seconds = 1800
Tns Selected = 15762
TCPU= .0000 TDIO= 0
SCPU= .0000 SDIO= 0
BCPU= .0000 BDIO= 0
XSUM= .0000 PDIO= 0
29.24 Percent Selected

TIME RANGE SELECTED BEG = 100100   END = 103100
DATA FOR SELECTED TIME INTERVAL (OR TOTAL TRACE PERIOD IF NO TIME SELECTION)
INTERACTIVE TRANSACTION AVERAGES BY JOB TYPE.

Ty p	Prg	Nbr Jobs	Nbr Tns	Pct Tns	Tns /Hour	Avg Rsp (Sec)	CPU/ Tns (Sec)	Sync Disk I/O Rqs/Tns DB Read	DB Write	NDB Read	NDB Write	Sum	Async DIO /Tns	W-I Wait /Tns	Excp Wait /Tns	Key/ Think /Tns	Active K/T /Tns	Est Of AWS
I	NO		1586	10.1	3171	.959	.127	3	3	5	2	13	5	.020	.302	23.011	18.053	17
I	YES		14176	89.9	28352	.864	.134	7	1	3	0	11	7	.027	.256	9.676	8.797	76
I	***	380 (k)	15762	100.0	31524	.874	.133	7	1	3	1	12	7	.026	.261 (s)	11.008	9.722	93 (l)

EXCEPTIONAL WAIT BREAKDOWN BY JOB TYPE.

Type	Purge	A-I Wait /Tns	Short Wait /Tns	Short WaitX /Tns	Seize Wait /Tns	Lock Wait /Tns	Event Wait /Tns	Excs ACTM /Tns	Excp Wait /Tns	EM3270 Wait /Tns	DDM Svr Wait /Tns	Other Wait /Tns
I	NO	.000	.168	.000	.015	.003	.000	.116	.302	.000	.000	.000
I	YES	.000	.132	.000	.043	.003	.000	.078	.256	.000	.000	.000
I	***	.000	.136	.000	.040	.003	.000	.082	.261	.000	.000	.000

Figure 8.4. Job Summary Report: system summary data section.

System Report
Resource Utilization Expansion
After System Tuning Changes

Member . . . : FRI290794   Model/Serial . . . : F80/44-D5817   Main storage . . : 384.0 M   Started . . . . : 29/07/94 09:31:51
Library . . : RSFPPRLIB   System name . . . : WIDGETS   Version/Release : 2/ 2.0   Stopped . . . . : 29/07/94 11:26:36

Average Per Transaction

Job Type	Physical Disk I/O Synchronous				Physical Disk I/O Asynchronous				Logical Data Base I/O			Communications I/O	
	DBR	DBW	NDBR	NDBW	DBR	DBW	NDBR	NDBW	Read	Write	Other	Get	Put
Interactive	3.1	2.1	5.1	1.8	1.6	1.6	.0	.3	23.2	.3	.3	.0	.0
DDM Server	1.0	.0	121.0	11.0	.0	4.0	.0	24.0	.0	.0	.0	4.0	4.0
PC Support	7.4	.8	2.9	.6	5.1	1.7	.0	.2	39.8	.5	3.2	.0	.0
Total/Average	7.2	.9	3.0	.6	4.9	1.7	.0	.2	38.7	.5	3.0	.0	.0

Priority	Job Type	CPU Util	Cum Util	Disk I/O Sync	Disk I/O Async	CPU Per I/O Sync	CPU Per I/O Async	DIO /Sec Sync	DIO /Sec Async
000	Batch	.4	.4	1,700	918	.0089	.0165	.9	.5
	System	7.8	8.2	56,695	245	.0049	.1442	31.6	.1
010	Interactive	.0	8.3	664	52	.0043	.0550	.3	.0
	Batch	.0	8.3	147	28	.0035	.0187	.0	.0
	AutoStart	.0	8.3	0	0	.0000	.0000	.0	.0
015	Spool	.2	8.6	2,832	466	.0037	.0229	1.5	.2
020	Interactive	2.7	11.3	11,420	3,460	.0084	.0280	6.3	1.9
	DDM Server	.0	11.3	133	28	.0028	.0133	.0	.0
	PC Support	55.9	67.2	170,217	104,049	.0117	.0192	94.8	57.9
	System	.0	67.2 (m)	221	0	.0015	.0000	.1	.0
025	PC Support	.1	67.4	1,480	129	.0040	.0466	.8	.0
030	PC Support	.0	67.4	268	41	.0040	.0266	.1	.0
	Spool	1.3	68.8	14,275	677	.0035	.0741	7.9	.3
040	Batch	.0	68.8	0	0	.0000	.0000	.0	.0
	System	.0	68.8	80	97	.0084	.0069	.0	.0
050	Batch	8.3	77.2	18,071	16,369	.0165	.0182	10.0	9.1
052	System	.0	77.2	0	0	.0000	.0000	.0	.0
060	System	.0	77.2	0	0	.0000	.0000	.0	.0
Total/Average				278,213	126,559			155.0	70.5

Figure 8.5. System Report: resource utilization expansion section.

System Report
Storage Pool Utilization
After System Tuning Changes

| Member . . . : FRI290794 | Model/Serial . . . : F80/44-D5817 | Main storage . . . : 384.0 M | Started . . . : 29/07/94 09:31:51 |
| Library . . . : RSFPFRLIB | System name . . . : WIDGETS | Version/Release : 2/ 2.0 | Stopped . . . : 29/07/94 11:26:36 |

| Pool ID | Size (K) | Act Lvl | CPU Util | Number Tns | Average Response | --------- Avg Per Second --------- | | | | ---- Avg Per Minute ---- | | |
						DB Fault	DB Pages	Non-DB Fault	Non-DB Pages	Act-Wait	Wait-Inel	Act-Inel
01	42,000	000	6.7	0	.0	.0	.0	.8	6.7	24	0	0
02	33,716	006	6.2	56	.3	.3	32.6	1.8	9.1	6	0	0
03	6,500	003	1.6	0	.0	.4	1.2	7.5	20.6	81	1	0
04	8,000	004	1.3	584	.5	.2	1.0	3.8	15.4	21	0	0
05	15,000	004	5.7	1,601	.9	1.0	15.9	3.9	11.9	54	0	0
06	18,000	003	3.7	0	.0	.3	5.3	2.3	16.6	1	0	0
08	270,000	016	51.7	13,263	.8	22.0	1042.9	14.3	72.7	451	2	0
Total/ Average	393,216		77.2	15,504	.8	24.3	1099.2	34.8	153.5	642	4	0

(n) (o)

Pool ID	--	Pool identifier
Size (K)	--	Size of the pool in kilobytes at the time of the first sample interval
Act Lvl	--	Activity level at the time of the first sample interval
CPU Util	--	Percentage of available CPU time used
Number Tns	--	Number of transactions processed by jobs in this pool
Average Response	--	Average transaction response time
DB Fault	--	Average number of data base faults per second
DB Pages	--	Average number of data base pages per second
Non-DB Fault	--	Average number of non-data base faults per second
Non-DB Pages	--	Average number of non-data base pages per second
Act-Wait	--	Average number of active to wait job state transitions per minute
Wait-Inel	--	Average number of wait to ineligible job state transitions per minute
Act-Inel	--	Average number of active to ineligible job state transitions per minute

Figure 8.6. System Report: storage pool utilization section.

System Report
Disk Utilization
After System Tuning Changes

| Member . . . : FRI290794 | Model/Serial . . . : F80/44-D5817 | Main storage . . : 384.0 M | Started . . . . : 29/07/94 09:31:51 |
| Library . . : RSFPFRLIB | System name . . . : WIDGETS | Version/Release : 2/ 2.0 | Stopped . . . . : 29/07/94 11:26:36 |

| | | Size | IOP | IOP | ASP | CSS | --Percent-- | | Op Per | K Per | ----- Average Time Per I/O ----- |
Unit	Type	(M)	Util	ID	ID	ID	Full	Util	Second	I/O	Service	Wait	Response
0001A	2800	320	1.0	0-01	01	00	99.9	.5	.29	1.2	.016	.000	.016
0001B	2800	320	1.0	0-01	01	00	99.9	.6	.31	1.3	.019	.000	.019
0002A	9337	970	12.0	2-01	01	00	74.1	8.3	4.08	2.1	.020	.005	.025
0002B	9337	970	14.0	3-03	01	00	74.1	11.6	5.63	2.3	.020	.005	.025
0003A	9337	970	15.0	2-02	01	00	75.4	11.0	4.87	2.0	.022	.005	.027
0003B	9337	970	13.0	3-02	01	00	75.4	13.3	6.53	2.0	.020	.004	.024
0004A	9337	970	14.0	2-03	01	00	78.5	9.1	4.24	2.7	.021	.004	.025
0004B	9337	970	15.0	3-01	01	00	78.5	11.5	5.80	2.7	.019	.005	.024
0034A	2800	320	1.0	0-01	01	00	99.8	5.2	3.05	.9	.017	.004	.021
0034B	2800	320	1.0	0-01	01	00	99.8	6.7	3.67	1.0	.018	.002	.020
0037A	9337	970	12.0	2-01	01	00	70.0	12.6	6.58	3.6	.019	.005	.024
0037B	9337	970	14.0	3-03	01	00	70.0	16.2	8.27	3.4	.019	.007	.026
0038A	9337	970	12.0	2-01	01	00	70.0	12.3	5.96	3.0	.020	.008	.028
0038B	9337	970	14.0	3-03	01	00	70.0	15.7	7.67	3.2	.020	.006	.026
0039A	9337	970	12.0	2-01	01	00	70.4	12.4	5.88	2.9	.021	.004	.025
0039B	9337	970	14.0	3-03	01	00	70.4	15.6	7.71	2.9	.020	.004	.024
0040A	9337	970	13.0	3-02	01	00	72.3	12.3	6.10	2.0	.020	.006	.026
0040B	9337	970	15.0	2-02	01	00	72.3	16.2	7.77	2.3	.020	.005	.025
Average							72.2	12.8 (p)	6.39	3.0	.020	.005	.025

Unit   -- Disk arm identifier
Type   -- Type of disk
Size (M)   -- Disk space capacity in millions of bytes
IOP Util   -- Percentage of utilization for each Input/Output Processor
IOP ID   -- Input/Output Processor identification number (Bus-IOP)
ASP ID   -- Auxiliary Storage Pool ID
CSS ID   -- Checksum Set ID
Percent Full   -- Percentage of disk space capacity in use
Percent Util   -- Average disk operation utilization (busy)
Op per Second   -- Average number of disk operations per second
K Per I/O   -- Average number of kilobytes (1024) transferred per disk operation
Average Service Time   -- Average disk service time per I/O operation
Average Wait Time   -- Average disk wait time per I/O operation
Average Response Time -- Average disk response time per I/O operation

Figure 8.7. System Report: disk utilization section.

176

(a) Check the previously referenced 'Job Summary' sections (Fig. 8.8) of the job summary reports for the absence of all the above conditions except long lock delays, which are not highlighted there. Console and similar activity shows up as a priority of 10 in the 'Pty' column and a significant number of transactions in the 'Tot Nbr Tns' column. Sign-on/off shows as an '*' to the left or right of the job number. The total number of each occurrence is logged in the 'Interactive Transactions by 5 Minute Intervals' section of the job summary report (Fig. 8.10).

Complex transactions are highlighted by large values in the 'CPU Sec/Max' and 'Average DIO/Transaction/Synchronous/Max' columns of the Job Summary report combined with type 'I' in the 'Typ' column. These show, for each job, the most complex transaction measured. 'Unusually complex' can only be defined in relation to previously filed reports of typical workloads.

(b) The 'top ten' transactions encountered during the measurement period will also be listed in the 'Individual Transaction Statistics' section of the job summary report. Among the many 'top ten' listings, find those for longest CPU service time and largest synchronous disk I/O (Fig. 8.11). The programs responsible for excessively complex transactions should be noted down together with the CPU and I/O figures. What constitutes 'excessive' depends on the CPU model in use and the nature of the normal workload.

As a broad indication, most people would agree that 5 seconds of CPU and/or 500 I/Os characterize a transaction that we would hope to see only rarely in our interactive workload. Responses to such observations may well involve application changes, which are not the subject of this book. A system tuning response might involve adjustments to time slice and isolation of 'heavy' transactions by time slice end pool transfer (Secs 9.4.2 and 9.9). Sometimes a minor application change will allow us to run the 'heavy' functions in batch at a lower priority and/or in a separate pool.

(c) Seize/lock conflicts are probably insignificant unless they contribute largely to the exceptional wait component of the average transaction response time. We logged the exceptional wait previously in Table 8.1 from the 'System Summary Data' shown in Fig. 8.4. The bottom line of this report shows all the possible contributions to the exceptional wait figure in the line above, including 'Seize Wait/Tns' and 'Lock Wait/Tns'. If either of these contributes more than 10 per cent to the average response time, corrective action may be appropriate. Turn to the 'Longest Seize/Lock Conflicts' section of the job summary report for a 'top thirty' listing of the longest lock conflicts that occurred (Fig. 8.12).

The report shows the delayed job, the object it waited for and the job holding the lock that caused the conflict. A value of 2 seconds or more for a seize ('S' in column headed 'S/L') or more than 5 seconds for a lock ('L') should be rare. A seize conflict is an unsatisfied request for a system

After Tuning Changes

```
Member . . . : FRI290794    Model/Serial          F80/44-D5817   Main storage . . :  384.0 M    Started . . . . 29 07 94 10:01:00
Library . . . : RSFPFRLIB   System name . . . :   WIDGETS        Version/Release  :  2/ 2.0     Stopped . . . . 29 07 94 10:31:00
```

Job Name	User Name	*On/Off* Job Number	Pl	Typ	Pty	Prg	Tot Nbr Tns	Resp Avg	Resp Max	CPU Util	CPU Avg	CPU Max	DBR	NDBR	Wrt	Sum	Max	Async Sum	Async Max	Number Cft Lck Sze	K/T /Tns Sec
VLIC Log	Task	VLTASK	01	L	00							1.11					799	5	476	93	
		MNTASK	01	L	00							.41									
		DBIO000	01	L	20																
SCPF		000000	02	X	40							5.07					604		574	1	
QDBSRV1	QSYS	939105	02	S	52																
QPFRADJ	QSYS	939109	02	S	00																
QSPLMAINT	QSYS	939110	02	S	20							1.08					1002		243	3	
QSYSARB	QSYS	939102-	02	S	00							2.62					724		243	9	
QLUS	QSYS	939103	02	S	00							4.39					1364		91	1	
QPFRCOL	QPGMR	939477	02	A	10																
QCMN	QSYS	939487	02	M	00							3.57					2000		41		
QSPL	QSYS	939490	02	M	00							.32					166		3	3	
QINTER	QSYS	939491	02	M	00							6.61					2750		243	1	1
QBATCH	QSYS	939503	02	M	00							.79					337				
PRT01	QSPLJOB	939511	03	WP	15																
PRT02	QSPLJOB	939516	03	WP	15							2.10					769		98	1	1
PCS414S1	ROUSEM	*942830	08	I	20	Y	434	.6	15.8	.3	.09	1.16	7	1		8	169	2	22	8 16	4
PCS067S1	SMITHJ	*942831	08	I	20	Y	136	1.1	16.9	.2	.19	1.15	15	2	2	19	512	4	42	28	11
PCS031S1	COXALM	*942833	08	I	20	Y	69	.7	7.0		.11	.56	3	3		6	61		7	1	22
STMTS	JONESP	942835	02	B	50		28	24.4	157.7	19.1		624.07					8487	1013	13950		
PCS363S1	MACHEC	*942869	08	I	20	Y	21	.8	4.3	.6	2.35	13.59	53	6	17	76	873	5	21	26	34
PCS087S1	WATKIP	*942882*	08	I	20	Y				1.9	.16	.92	5	2	2	9	113		21		3
PCS002	TOUSLEMO	942883	02	BE	20					5.4		.10					32		7		
PCS002S1	RSF	*942885	05	I	20	N	4	1.2	3.3		.44	1.40	3	3	3	9	13	21	66		20
STMTS	SEEGEP	942878	02	B	50					5.2		3.24		17		17	343		249		
PCS100S1	WASSEB	*942888	04	I	20	Y	240	.5	20.8	.2	.07	1.64		17		17	1219	3	30	3	4
PCS212S1	MERRIP	*942891*	08	I	20	Y	24	.8	5.1	.5	.14	.72	3	2	2	7	86	7	68	2	12
PRTSYS	QSPLJOB	942897	03	W	30					.2		16.69					2776		257	4	
NPT4EVER	AMOS	*942874	05	I	20	N	42	.8	5.1	.1	.19	1.38	6	4	1	11	107	3	78	3	14
PCS080S1	DILLAD	*942877	08	I	20	Y	56	.9	4.7		.12	.69	7	2	2	11	68	2	20	8	20
PCS088S1	SAMANIN	*942903*	08	I	20	Y	10	.7	3.3	1.4	.12	.30	2	2			10	5	15	3	3

Figure 8.8. Job Summary Report: job summary section.

Job Summary Report
Interactive Program Statistics
After Tuning Changes

| Member . . . : FRI290794 | Model/Serial . . . : F80/44-D5817 | Main storage . . : 384.0 M | Started . . . . 29 07 94 10:01:00 |
| Library . . : RSFPFRLIB | System name . . . : WIDGETS | Version/Release : 2/ 2.0 | Stopped . . . . 29 07 94 10:31:00 |

| | | | | | Cum | Sync Disk I/O Rqs/Tns | | | | | Async | | Short | Seize | | Cum |
Rank	Number Tns	Program Name	CPU /Tns	CPU Util	CPU Util	DB Read	DB Write	NDB Read	NDB Write	Sum	DIO /Tns	Rsp /Tns	Wait /Tns	Wait /Tns	Pct Tns	Pct Tns
1	2508	GMYZDSR	.122	8.5	8.5	8		2		10	4	.741	.104	.057	15.9	15.9
2	1498	GM1SDSR	.081	3.3	11.9	7				8	4	.595	.087	.029	9.5	25.4
3	830	GLF2DSR	.188	4.3	16.2	20	1	1	1	23	4	1.293	.183	.033	5.3	30.7
4	726	GMQIDSR	.057	1.1	17.4	9		1		10	2	.437	.030	.004	4.6	35.3
5	569	BTNMFXC	.109	1.7	19.1			6	1	8	2	.765	.175	.082	3.6	38.9
6	555	GLNBDSR	.140	2.1	21.2	13	1	1	1	16	3	1.005	.094	.123	3.5	42.4
7	414	GMPTYLR	.023	.2	21.5						1	.430	.270	.032	2.6	45.0
8	401	GM22YLR	.050	.5	22.0			1		2	1	.539	.266	.046	2.5	47.6
9	375	GMOYDSR	.081	.8	22.9	9		2		11	3	.739	.056	.179	2.4	50.0
10	370	QUIINMGR	.069	.7	23.6		1	11		12	2	.421	.010		2.3	52.3
11	328	GMITNKR	.043	.4	24.0	6		1		7	2	.300	.030	.003	2.1	54.4
12	284	GM7TYLR	.068	.5	24.5						2	.366	.182	.001	1.8	56.2
13	274	GMMUDSR	.151	1.1	25.7	4		3		8	3	.661	.148	.059	1.7	57.9
14	273	GLXA8BR	.165	1.2	26.9	4		2		7	1	.886	.119	.042	1.7	59.7
15	262	WAILYCR	.095	.7	27.6	2		3		6	1	.531	.083	.059	1.7	61.3
16	202	GM8SDSR	.091	.5	28.1	1		1		3	1	.616	.181	.112	1.3	62.6
17	192	GMAF8BR	.102	.5	28.7	1		1		2		.521	.163	.011	1.2	63.8
18	175	WAILJMP	.176	.8	29.5	2		6		10	1	.772	.027	.009	1.1	64.9
19	157	GMBA4PR	.116	.5	30.1	1		2	1	3		.533	.160		1.1	65.9
20	154	FQYAJMP	.210	.9	31.0	9		3		12	2	1.042	.212		1.0	66.9
21	151	HSMDCLP	.136	.5	31.5	1		7		9	2	.656	.111		1.0	67.9
22	149	GM2MDSR	.491	2.0	33.6	11	3	2	1	18	192	4.868	.133	.026	1.0	68.8
23	148	GLJA3NR	.115	.4	34.0	4	1	2		6	1	.599	.136	.053	.9	69.8
24	143	MPPS1QC	.101	.4	34.4	3		4		7	7	1.256	.662		.9	70.7
25	123	GMFXSLR	.160	.5	35.0	10		2		11	7	.796	.087	.021	.9	71.4
26	122	NOIGXLS	.079	.2	35.2	3	13	1	12	29	3	1.441	.004	.031	.8	72.2
27	117	MCLIYCP	.168	.5	35.8	2	3	5	1	12	10	.810	.067	.011	.8	73.0
28	112	GMJUDSR	.148	.4	36.2	56				56	2	1.553	.034		.7	73.7
29	112	GLGZNKR	.036	.1	36.4						3	.101	.020	.002	.7	74.4
30	110	NOIP1QP	.094	.3	36.6	5	13	9	13	40	11	1.949	.009	.009	.7	75.1
31	90	GM6SDSR	.963	2.4	39.0	8		2		10	4	1.722	.099		.6	75.7

Figure 8.9.   Job Summary Report: interactive program statistics section.

179

Job Summary Report
Interactive Transactions by 5 Minute Intervals
After Tuning Changes

Member . . . : FRI290794	Model/Serial . . . : F80/44-D5817	Main storage . . : 384.0 M	Started 29 07 94 10:01:00
Library . . : RSFFPRLIB	System name . . . : WIDGETS	Version/Release : 2/ 2.0	Stopped 29 07 94 10:31:00

Itv End	Active Jobs	Nbr Tns	Tns /Hour	--- Pct Of Tns --- --- Categories --- %VS* %S %M %X *%VX					Pct CPU By Categories %S %M %X			Nbr Sign offs	Nbr Sign ons	Sync DIO /Tns	Async DIO /Tns	Avg Rsp /Tns	Excp Wait /Tns	Pct Ex-Wt /Rsp	Seize Wait /Tns	Active K/T /Tns	Est Of AWS
***																				
10.05*	103	2127	25524	19*	20	4	76 *	5	2	1	89	4	5	10	7	.939	.309	33	.091	5.568	46
10.10	116	2734	32808	18*	19	6	75 *	4	2	1	127	8	12	12	9	.958	.255	27	.019	7.869	80
10.15	113	2453	29436	22*	23	6	71 *	5	2	1	110	4	8	10	8	.858	.270	31	.052	10.822	95
10.20	114	2686	32232	22*	23	5	72 *	4	2	1	99	3	2	9	4	.651	.196	30	.009	10.741	101
10.25	116	2684	32208	22*	24	3	73 *	5	2	1	106	9	9	10	4	1.014	.346	34	.078	10.001	98
10.30	114	2594	31128	24*	26	3	71 *	6	2	1	132	8	12	13	7	.886	.234	26	.008	9.822	92
10.35*	63	484	5808	20*	21	4	75 *	5	0	0	18	1	3	14	3	.570	.083	15		9.149	15

* Denotes Partial Interval Data

Figure 8.10. Job Summary Report: interactive transactions by 5-minute intervals.

```
                    Job Summary Report
              Individual Transaction Statistics
                     After Tuning Changes

Member . . . : FRI200794    Model/Serial . . . :  F80/44-D5817   Main storage . . :  384.0 M    Started  . . . .  29 07 94 10:01:00
Library  . . : RSPFFRLIB    System name  . . . :  WIDGETS        Version/Release :  2/ 2.0     Stopped  . . . .  29 07 94 10:31:00
```

TRANSACTIONS WITH LONGEST CPU SERVICE TIME

Rank	Value	Time	Program	Job Name	User Name	Number	Pool	Type	Priority
1	87.102	10.23.19.991	GM7KDSR	PCS328S1	FIELR	942412	08	I	20
2	14.611	10.07.16.039	GMWPDSR	PCS328S1	FIELR	942412	08	I	20
3	13.585	10.07.59.727	GM2MDSR	PCS363S1	MACHEC	942869	08	I	20
4	12.359	10.05.07.975	GM2MDSR	PCS363S1	MACHEC	942869	08	I	20
5	12.253	10.01.47.915	GM2MDSR	PCS363S1	MACHEC	942869	08	I	20
6	12.134	10.10.16.981	GM2MDSR	PCS363S1	MACHEC	942869	08	I	20
7	11.901	10.17.21.644	GM2MDSR	PCS363S1	MACHEC	942869	08	I	20
8	7.758	10.10.05.950	GMHFDSR	PCS328S1	FIELR	942412	08	I	20
9	7.521	10.19.36.852	GMHFDSR	PCS328S1	FIELR	942412	08	I	20
10	5.720	10.22.41.162	GMIPDOR	PCS087S1	WATKIP	942816	08	I	20

TRANSACTIONS WITH LARGEST TOTAL SYNCHRONOUS DISK I/O

Rank	Value	Time	Program	Job Name	User Name	Number	Pool	Type	Priority
1	1774	10.05.20.254	GLNBDSR	PCS190S1	MCCRER	942511	08	I	20
2	1219	10.30.34.293	QUIMGFLW	PCS100S1	WASSEB	942888	04	I	20
3	1052	10.26.51.100	GMMYDSR	PCL011S1	STEVEK	942719	08	I	20
4	963	10.13.18.278	GMMYDSR	PCLO25S1	CHEESR	942733	08	I	20
5	873	10.01.47.915	GM2MDSR	PCS363S1	MACHEC	942869	08	I	20
6	863	10.22.38.514	QUIINMGR	PCS100S1	WASSEB	942888	04	I	20
7	822	10.08.50.488	GLF2DSR	PCS087S1	WATKIP	942615	08	I	20
8	777	10.15.12.238	QUIINMGR	PCS100S1	WASSEB	942888	04	I	20
9	752	10.05.14.153	GLF2DSR	PCS059S1	HUTCHI	942641	08	I	20
10	688	10.29.39.147	GMJUDSR	PCS321S1	FYPER	942415	08	I	20

Figure 8.11. Job Summary Report: individual transaction statistics.

181

Job Summary Report
Longest Seize/Lock Conflicts
After Tuning Changes

Member . . . . : FRI290794   Model/Serial . . . . : F80/44-D5817   Main storage . . : 384.0 M   Started . . . . : 20 07 94 10:01:00
Library . . . : RSFPPRLIB   System name . . . . : WIDGETS   Version/Release : 2/ 2.0   Stopped . . . . : 29 07 94 10:31:00

Rank	Value	Time	Job Name	User Name	Job Number	Pl	Typ	Pty	S/L	Holder-Object-	Type-Library.. File.....	User Name..	Number	Pool	Type	Pty RRN......
1	17.017	10.24.12.302	PCS174S1	THORNB	942456	08	I	20	S	HOLDER-	PCS212S1	MERRIP	942910	08	I	20
										OBJECT-	JRN GMJRN	GMJ				000000024
2	16.461	10.01.06.607	PCS056S1	MCKEND	942584	08	I	20	S	HOLDER-	PCS317S1	FREUNN	942379	08	I	20
										OBJECT-	DS GMDTA	GMBERXP				000000013
3	16.054	10.24.13.266	PCS035S1	KINGM	942583	08	I	20	S	HOLDER-	PCS212S1	MERRIP	942910	08	I	20
										OBJECT-	JRN GMJRN	GMJ				000000024
4	16.015	10.01.07.052	PCS174S1	THORNB	942456	08	I	20	S	HOLDER-	PCS317S1	FREUNN	942379	08	I	20
										OBJECT-	DS GMDTA	GMBERXP				000000013
5	15.939	10.24.13.381	PCS191S1	DENNEM	942913	08	I	20	S	HOLDER-	PCS212S1	MERRIP	942910	08	I	20
										OBJECT-	JRN GMJRN	GMJ				000000024
6	15.764	10.24.13.555	PCS192S1	SMITHF	942299	08	I	20	S	HOLDER-	PCS212S1	MERRIP	942910	08	I	20
										OBJECT-	JRN GMJRN	GMJ				000000024
7	15.614	10.24.13.706	PCS083S1	NEWMAM	942391	08	I	20	S	HOLDER-	PCS212S1	MERRIP	942910	08	I	20
										OBJECT-	JRN GMJRN	GMJ				000000024
8	15.137	10.24.14.183	PCS414S1	ROUSEM	942830	08	I	20	S	HOLDER-	PCS212S1	MERRIP	942910	08	I	20
										OBJECT-	JRN GMJRN	GMJ				000000024
9	15.099	10.24.14.221	PCS066S1	HATTD	942580	08	I	20	S	HOLDER-	PCS212S1	MERRIP	942910	08	I	20
										OBJECT-	JRN GMJRN	GMJ				'000000024
10	14.822	10.24.14.498	PCS203S1	HAINEM	942603	08	I	20	S	HOLDER-	PCS212S1	MERRIP	942910	08	I	20
										OBJECT-	JRN GMJRN	GMJ				000000024
11	14.769	10.24.14.771	PCS401S1	DAUBEP	942796	05	I	20	S	HOLDER-	DSP01	REUBEN	942367	05	I	20
										OBJECT-	DS CPDTA	CPLHIST				000000024
12	14.305	10.01.08.762	PCS191S1	DENNEM	942427	08	I	20	S	HOLDER-	PCS317S1	FREUNN	942379	08	I	20
										OBJECT-	DS GMDTA	GMBERXP				000000013
13	14.042	10.01.09.026	PCS321S1	FYFER	942415	08	I	20	S	HOLDER-	PCS317S1	FREUNN	942379	08	I	20
										OBJECT-	DS GMDTA	GMBERXP				000000013
14	13.476	10.12.18.786	PCS067S1	SMITHJ	942831	08	I	20	S	HOLDER-	PCS189S1	EDMUNB	942480	08	I	20
										OBJECT-	DS GMDTA	GMBERXP				000000001
15	13.186	10.12.19.076	PCS204S1	HULMEK	942252	08	I	20	S	HOLDER-	PCS189S1	EDMUNB	942480	08	I	20
										OBJECT-	DS GMDTA	GMBERXP				000000001
16	13.109	10.01.09.958	PCS166S1	SANDEA	942595	08	I	20	S	HOLDER-	PCS317S1	FREUNN	942379	08	I	20
										OBJECT-	DS GMDTA	GMBERXP				000000013

Figure 8.12. Job Summary Report: longest seize/lock conflicts.

initiated lock (e.g. for access path maintenance) which leaves the delayed job in its activity level. A lock conflict (e.g. for record update) results in a long wait (the job makes an active-to-wait transition) in which the delayed job loses its activity level.

(d) Unusual problems and error recovery activity will be revealed by significant resource utilization in certain system jobs and tasks. Check the 'Job Summary' report (Fig. 8.8) for unusual system activity. Tasks are identified under heading 'Typ' as type 'L', and relevant system jobs as type 'S' or 'X'. Activity by the SCPF or QSYSARB jobs can be followed up by examining their job logs.

After a system power down these will be found on an output queue; if the jobs are still active use DSPJOBLOG to find out what they were doing. Problems may also be recorded in the history log. To check this use the following command for the period in question:

```
DSPLOG    PERIOD((start-time start-date) (end-time end-date))
```

Activity in the error log or VMC log tasks also suggests problems. The easiest way to follow this up is to print the error log for the period using the command:

```
PRTERRLOG  PERIOD((start-time start-date) (end-time end-date))
```

Table 8.3.   System values relating to performance

System value	Current setting	Default setting	Recommended change	Change date
QMODEL		N/A	N/A	N/A
QSRLNBR		N/A	N/A	N/A
QACTJOB		20		
QTOTJOB		30		
QADLACTJ		10		
QADLTOTJ		10		
QCTLSBSD		QBASE QSYS		
QMCHPOOL		1500		
QBASPOOL		500		
QBASACTLVL		6		
QMAXACTLVL		*NOMAX		
QTSEPOOL		*NONE		
QAUTOCFG		1		
QPFRADJ		2		
QINACTITV		*NONE		
QINACTMSGQ		*ENDJOB		
QDSCJOBITV		240		
QDEVRCYACN		*MSG		
QCMNRCYLMT		0 0		
QDBRCVYWT		0		
QRCLSPLSTG		8		

The function of other system tasks which may be highlighted by your scrutiny of the 'Job Summary' report can be clarified by consulting the Diagnostic Aids manual (see Bibliography).

8.4.4 Documentation of system values affecting performance

The current status of those system values which have performance implications should also be documented alongside the performance and workload data. Use the DSPSYSVAL command to display the values listed in Table 8.3 and record the current settings. A larger copy of the table is provided in Appendix 1. Additional columns can be used to record subsequent changes.

8.4.5 User perceptions of performance

However objective and convincing our performance data may be, there is little doubt that the object of the exercise is usually to improve users' perceptions of performance; and what users think of performance may not be transformed by the piece of paper in your hand proclaiming a 0.1 second improvement in average response time. User experience should be sought and documented as part of the tuning project.

This is partly because it will cover a wider span than the measured spot checks, but also to gain an understanding of what aspects of performance are significant to the job. Particular transaction responses or local printouts may be critical, while other longer-running functions are no problem. Tuning is allocation of resources between competing items of work, and if you don't know what users want you are not best placed to provide it.

A good time to collect user input is after the preliminary assessment of performance and before tuning changes are made. Armed with a general understanding of system performance plus knowledge of whatever individual problems and anomalies showed up during the measurement periods, we are in a good position to evaluate statements made. Any outstandingly implausible claims should be demonstrated and measured with a stopwatch.

Of course, there may not be a performance problem. Tuning may be done to optimize performance even if it is already satisfactory; perhaps as a preliminary to a capacity planning exercise that estimates the effects of future workload increases. Alternatively, there may be a well-understood problem that requires no further elucidation. In such cases interviewing users may be unnecessary, because it has effectively already taken place.

8.4.6 Gathering user input

In many cases, to discover the real nature of performance problems you will need to talk to representatives of the main groups of users, including those who are happy. The object is to observe problems at first hand, document your findings and get agreement about what most needs fixing. If there is a service level agreement in use as discussed in Chapter 7, you can note where levels are not met, or where changes in the agreement may be desirable.

The following questions may be useful as a starting point in your investigations:

1. What are the main jobs you do on the system?
2. Regarding interactive response times:
   - Are they fairly consistent?
   - Which responses take longest?
   - Are responses worse at particular times of the day? Or days of the week?
   - Have response times changed recently?
   - Do response times ever hold up your work? If so, what, when and how often?
3. Are reports that you request available when you want them?
4. Is information that you require from the system always available or are you sometimes asked to wait for access?
5. Does your workstation ever lose the link with the system for no apparent reason? If so, how do you get reconnected?

The dream outcome following your system tuning changes is that the users ring up unsolicited and overflowing with thanks, saying things like: 'Have you put a bigger machine in?' or 'It's going like greased lightning'.

Sometimes this happens before you have done anything—the well-known placebo effect. Realistically, though, you will have to chase up feedback after the event, and users will only grudgingly admit to any improvement. Hence the importance of documentation, and of establishing the objectives in advance.

8.4.7 Workstation connectivity

The Component report 'Local Work Stations—Response Time Buckets' section lists the devices attached to each of the local workstation controllers. It also shows the average utilization of each controller and counts of the number of transaction responses in the range 0–1 second, 1–2 seconds, 2–4 seconds, 4–8 seconds and greater than 8 seconds for each locally attached screen.

This allows us to check for even spread of activity and performance across the available controllers. The preceding section of the report ('IOP Utilizations') shows the split of activity across the communications processors. It does not list the names of remotely attached devices, which must be obtained from installation documentation.

8.5   Secondary performance indicators

Understanding as we do the factors that contribute to performance, it is often more revealing and convenient to observe the effects which tuning changes have on secondary indicators, which we know will feed through to external performance. A number of these useful indicators will now be discussed.

8.5.1   Page fault rates

In Sec. 3.4 we explained how main memory is used and how partitioning, activity level settings, purge attributes, the SETOBJACC command and use of the Expert Cache facility can all influence page fault rate. The page fault rate is part of the total disk I/O rate that the system must sustain, and we saw that page faults directly impact performance because they delay execution of the job that causes them.

The effectiveness of system tuning changes can be assessed by comparing page fault rates before and after the change. A way to view this interactively is via the WRKSYSSTS display, an example of which appears in Fig. 8.13.

As with WRKACTJOB, to get meaningful performance data we must press key F5 (Refresh) after about 5 minutes to average out transient effects. We then see database and non-database average page fault rates for each of the system pools over the elapsed period.

The columns headed 'Pages' can be ignored for tuning purposes, but a reduction in the total of the figures under the 'Fault' columns for a given workload indicates improved performance. Reduced faults in the machine pool (system pool 1) are

```
                      Work with System Status                 NBS400B
                                                    13/07/94   10:17:41
  % CPU used . . . . . . . :       37.0    Auxiliary storage:
  Elapsed time . . . . . . :    00:06:06     System ASP . . . . . . :      1712 M
  Jobs in system . . . . . :        187      % system ASP used  . . :   56.6144
  % addresses used:                          Total  . . . . . . . . :      1712 M
    Permanent   . . . . . . :      1.617     Current unprotect used :       463 M
    Temporary   . . . . . . :       .108     Maximum unprotect  . . :       464 M

  Type changes (if allowed), press Enter.

  System    Pool    Reserved    Max     -----DB-----   ---Non-DB---
  Pool    Size (K)  Size (K)   Active   Fault  Pages   Fault  Pages
    1        6303      4058      +++      .0     .0      .1     .3
    2        3572         0        6      .0     .0      .0     .3
    3         700         0        2      .0     .0      .0     .0
    4       22193         0       15      .0     .2      .5    3.5

                                                             Bottom
  Command
  ===>
  F3=Exit    F4=Prompt       F5=Refresh   F9=Retrieve   F10=Restart
  F11=Display transition data   F12=Cancel   F24=More keys
```

Figure 8.13.   WRKSYSSTS display: page fault rates.

particularly beneficial. In Sec. 9.7 we discuss guidelines for peak sustainable page fault rates. They are fully documented in the *Work Management Guide* (see Bibliography).

Once again a more convenient way to measure, view and store the performance data is by using the performance tools. Rows (n) and (o) of Table 8.1 contain the critical figures from the performance reports. The tools also allow us to check that we are comparing like workloads, as described above in Sec. 8.4.3.

8.5.2   Ineligible transition rates

We saw in Sec. 3.5 that WI (wait-to-ineligible) transitions occur when a transaction is ready to become active but all activity levels in the pool are occupied. If we can reduce the rate of WI transitions for a given throughput, then we will reduce the ineligible wait time component of the responses. Remember how the activity level setting for a pool controls the WI rate and gives us a potential tuning mechanism.

Remember also that a high activity level can eliminate WI transitions but increase page fault rates because of extra contention for memory, so this indicator cannot be used in isolation. Reduced WI rates are good providing the fault rates in the changed pools are not increased. On a busy well-tuned system with balanced resources the WI rate will normally be slightly above zero. A useful rule of thumb is that the WI rate can be up to 10 per cent of the AW (active-to-wait) rate without cause for concern.

The WRKSYSSTS transition data display (see Fig. 3.6 for an example) contains the necessary figures, and, as usual, the screen should be refreshed after at least 5 minutes to give meaningful information. The same figures are printed in the 'Storage Pool Utilization' report (Fig. 8.6).

8.5.3   Disk actuator utilization

This figure is a good index of interactive performance because it relates to two of the largest components of a typical interactive response time, namely disk queue time and disk I/O time. We saw in Sec. 4.3 how reducing utilization reduces queue time, and, of course, reduced utilization arises because fewer I/Os are being done. Probably this means that the average transaction demands less I/Os.

The previously referenced 'Disk Utilization' report (Fig. 8.7) contains the figure we want, and it should have been logged on line (p) of Table 8.1. Another check we need to make is that the activity is fairly evenly distributed over the actuators. If individual actuators are grossly over-utilized in relation to the average, we must consider tuning by redistribution of active objects across the auxiliary storage units (Sec. 9.8.2).

```
                              Work with Disk Status                   NBS400B
                                                           26/07/94  14:46:19
     Elapsed time:     00:05:33

                   Size    %    I/O   Request  Read  Write  Read  Write    %
     Unit   Type   (M)   Used   Rqs  Size (K)   Rqs   Rqs   (K)    (K)   Busy
       1    9335   427   57.0   3.1    1.5      .6    2.4   1.8    1.4     10
       1    9335   427   57.0   3.7    1.5     1.3    2.4   1.6    1.4     12
       2    9335   427   56.7   2.5    1.5      .4    2.0   2.3    1.3      8
       2    9335   427   56.7   3.0    1.6     1.0    1.9   2.1    1.4     10
       3    9335   427   56.7   3.1    1.5      .5    2.6   2.1    1.4     10
       3    9335   427   56.7   4.0    1.7     1.5    2.5   2.1    1.5     13
       5    9335   427   56.7   2.4    1.7      .3    2.0   2.4    1.6      8
       5    9335   427   56.7   3.1    1.9     1.1    1.9   2.3    1.6     10




                                                                     Bottom
     Command
     ===>
     F3=Exit    F5=Refresh    F12=Cancel    F24=More keys
```

Figure 8.14.   WRKDSKSTS display.

There may also be a reduction in the synchronous I/Os per transaction logged on line (r) after successful tuning. In this case make sure as described in Sec. 8.4.3 that the functional content of the workload has not changed.

For immediate inspection of disk activity enter the following command:

WRKDSKSTS

After at least 5 minutes press F5 (Refresh) and inspect the average ' per cent Busy' figures. A display similar to Fig. 8.14 will be seen. The figures are estimates based on the number of I/Os and are less reliable than those measured by the performance tools. You need to do some arithmetic to get an overall average.

8.5.4   CPU utilization

It is unlikely that system tuning changes alone will make much difference to the CPU utilization. A notable shift in this figure is more likely to signify a variation in the functional content or volume of the workload. Nevertheless a small reduction in CPU utilization should ensue from a decrease in disk I/Os. Because it is not often a sensitive indicator of performance changes we will generally not use it for this purpose.

The figure is obtained from the 'Resource Utilization Expansion' report illustrated in Fig. 8.5 and logged on line (m) of Table 8.1. An interactive approach would involve using WRKACTJOB as described in Sec. 8.4.1 and Fig. 8.1, and adding the elapsed CPU percentage numbers for the group of jobs being measured. The system overhead due to high-priority tasks active on behalf of user jobs will be missed by the latter method.

9
Improving system performance

This chapter is aimed directly at the AS/400 technician who has been given the task of improving system performance, or of validating how the system is tuned. If you are that person, simply work your way through the following 'to do' list. It is a 'how to do it' expansion of the outline presented in Sec. 8.2. It assumes that the basic initial documentation referred to in items 1(a) to 1(d) of the outline in Sec. 8.2 already exists. If not, you must follow the referenced topics in Chapter 8 to collect this information, before making any changes.

9.1 Documentation of initial memory usage

Record the information required by Fig. 9.1 using the WRKSYSSTS command. For each pool record the pool size and activity level which are shown in the central portion of the screen, columns 2 and 4. The pool name is found on the WRKSYSSTS display showing Pool Data. The name will be *MACHINE, *BASE, *INTERACT, *SPOOL, or *SHRPOOL1-10 for the shared pools, or will be the number of the subsystem pool for a private pool.

Also record the normally active subsystems, the pools that they use and the run-time attributes of their jobs. The WRKSBS command will give some of this information, and the remainder comes from displaying the subsystem descriptions. For completeness you should print the subsystem descriptions of all active subsystems and store the output safely. Remember that each subsystem can use multiple memory pools so your copy of Fig. 9.1 will need to show this.

9.2 Effect of automatic performance adjustment support

Set the QPFRADJ system value to '3' and thereby allow the system to adjust the sizes and activity levels of the shared pools.

```
CHGSYSVAL   QPFRADJ   3
```

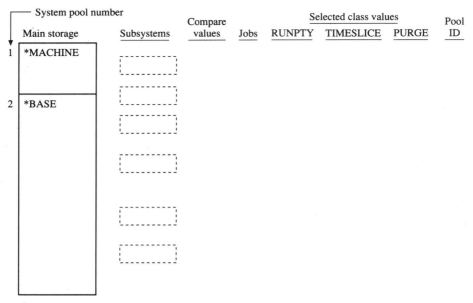

Figure 9.1   Memory partitioning and usage by subsystems.

During a typical peak period of activity record the resulting pool sizes and activity levels on a form similar to Fig. 9.1 and then switch off the automatic performance adjustment support before the workload subsides. Make sure that the full complement of jobs, including group jobs, are active during the peak period.

```
CHGSYSVAL   QPFRADJ   0
```

During automatic adjustment you can ask the system to journal the adjustments it makes. This is discussed in the *Work Management Guide* (see Bibliography).

9.2.1   What the performance adjustment support does

The automatic performance adjustment support is controlled by the setting of the system value QPFRADJ as follows:

- 0—no automatic performance adjustment
- 1—performance adjustment at IPL
- 2—performance adjustment at IPL and dynamically
- 3—performance adjustment dynamically, not at IPL.

The adjustment at IPL examines the machine configuration—number of devices configured, size of the system, and the controlling subsystem in use (value of system value QCTLSBSD). It can then make reasonably informed changes to the following:

1. The size of the machine pool (system pool 1). This will be reflected in a change to the system value QMCHPOOL.
2. The system pool used by pool 2 of subsystem QSPL in QGPL. This will become the shared pool *SPOOL. QSPL subsystem pool 2 is where spool writers run.
3. The size and activity level of *SPOOL.
4. The system pool used by pool 2 of subsystem QBASE in QGPL and QSYS. This will become shared pool *INTERACT. QBASE pool 2 is where interactive work using QBASE subsystem is run.
5. The system pool used by pool 2 of subsystem QINTER in QGPL and QSYS. This will become shared pool *INTERACT. QINTER pool 2 is where interactive work using QINTER subsystem runs.
6. The size and activity level of *INTERACT.
7. The activity level in *BASE. This will be reflected in the system value QBASACTLVL.

Note that changes 4, 5 and 7 are only made if the controlling subsystem is QBASE in QSYS or QGPL, or QCTL in QSYS or QGPL. This is because use of other controlling subsystems means that changes have been made to the default method of running, and the performance adjustment support is at a loss to know what will be running where.

The dynamic adjustment support monitors the use of storage in the shared system pools and attempts to move storage away from under-utilized pools to pools which might benefit from more storage. It also attempts to balance the activity levels with the storage in the pools. The page fault rate guidelines shown in the Work Management Guide, which we will be examining later in this chapter, are the basis for adjustment decisions. The following items may be changed:

- The size of the machine pool (system pool 1). This will be reflected in a change to the system value QMCHPOOL.
- The activity level in *BASE. This will be reflected in the system value QBASACTLVL.
- The size and activity level of *INTERACT pool.
- The size and activity level of *SPOOL pool.
- The sizes and activity levels of shared pools *SHRPOOL1-10.

9.3   Use of the Performance Tools/400 Advisor

Enter the command ANZPFRDTA and select for analysis the performance data member created as part of the initial workload documentation. You will be prompted with a list of the component sampling intervals. By selecting only a subset of these you can limit the analysis to a period where the interactive workload peaked, or when you know particular performance problems were experienced. Alternatively, just press F13 to select all the data.

When the analysis completes. a list of tuning conclusions and recommendations is displayed. Display the details of each item to understand the basis for the recommendations. Then press F9 to see a concise list of the proposed changes. At this point you should probably select option 1 to have the advisor implement the changes. If you wish to be selective about the changes, note down the ones you want implemented, exit from the recommendations screens and use appropriate commands to make the changes manually.

For documentation, use the command:

```
ANZPFRDTA  OUTPUT(*PRINT)
```

and keep the listing by you for reference as you complete the tuning process. Note that the advisor tends not to recommend massive changes in one go. Therefore if the system tuning is way out from optimum, multiple iterations of the measure, analyse and change process may be required. We can achieve the same result more directly by continuing through our action list.

9.4   Recommended changes to the performance system values

9.4.1   System value descriptions

Many of these system values have been defined in earlier chapters, particularly in Chapter 3. In Table 9.1 we give a brief description of each one followed by a section on how to check what settings are appropriate to your installation.

9.4.2   System value settings for your installation

Note down your recommendations for system values in Table 8.3 using the guidance provided in the remainder of this topic.

QACTJOB

This should be the usual maximum value shown in the field 'Active jobs' on the WRKACTJOB display at times of peak activity. A value too low results in table extension which is a heavy system task. A value too high increases the system overhead of referencing the table.

QTOTJOB

This should be the usual maximum value shown in the field 'total jobs in system' on the WRKSYSSTS display. Note that it is best to keep this value low by reducing the number of spool queue entries relating to old jobs. You can perform regular housekeeping on spool queues either by manually deleting or printing old output or by using Operational Assistant(*).

A value too low results in table extension which is a heavy system task. A value too high increases the system overhead of referencing the table.

Table 9.1. System value descriptions

System value	Description
QMODEL	The model of AS/400, e.g. B10, F45. Cannot be changed.
QSRLNBR	The unique serial number of your AS/400. Cannot be changed.
QACTJOB	The initial number of entries in the active jobs table.
QTOTJOB	The initial number of entries in the total jobs table.
QADLACTJ	The number of elements by which the active jobs table is extended when more jobs become active than are allowed by the current table size.
QADLTOTJ	The number of elements by which the total jobs table is extended when more jobs enter the system than are allowed by the current table size.
QCTLSBSD	The name of the controlling subsystem—the one that is started automatically at IPL.
QPFRADJ	Specifies whether or not you want the automatic performance adjustment to run, and how you want it to run.
QMCHPOOL	The size of the system machine pool in KB.
QBASPOOL	The minimum size of the system base pool in KB. The base pool contains all main storage not allocated to any other pool.
QBASACTLVL	The activity level setting of the base pool.
QMAXACTLVL	The maximum activity level of the whole system.
QTSEPOOL	Specifies whether or not interactive jobs which exceed their time slice should be moved to the base pool temporarily.
QAUTOCFG	Specifies whether or not devices added to the system or moved are automatically configured to the AS/400.
QINACTITV	The inactive job timeout value in minutes.
QINACTMSGQ	The action to be taken when a job is inactive for the QINACTITV value.
QDSCJOBITV	How long in minutes a job is disconnected before it is ended.
QDEVRCYACN	The action to be taken when an I/O error occurs on a workstation.
QCMNRCYLMT	Controls recovery attempts after a communications error.
QDBRCVYWT	Controls when recovery of database files created with the RECOVER(*AFTIPL) option is done during an unattended IPL after an abnormal system termination.
QRCLSPLSTG	How long in days empty spool members are retained for re-use.

QADLACTJ

If QACTJOB is set appropriately this increment value will probably not be used. A value too low could potentially result in multiple table extensions at peak times. Set it to 10 per cent of the QACTJOB value.

QADLTOTJ

If QTOTJOB is set appropriately this increment value should be rarely used. A value too low may result in multiple table extensions before the next housekeeping session occurs. A value too high may make the table unnecessarily large. Set it to 10 per cent of the QTOTJOB value.

QCTLSBSD

This should be QCTL in QSYS since this results in more flexibility for grouping together and controlling jobs of similar types.

QPFRADJ

If set on while you are doing your own system tuning it may overwrite your changes. If left off on a system where manual system tuning is not done you will lose the benefit of the automatic adjustments. We suggest you set it to 0. When you have finished tuning the system, if you wish to allow dynamic reconfiguration of pool sizes and activity levels in response to workload variation, set it to 3.

QMCHPOOL

The initial size should be set according to a formula described in Sec. 9.4.3. The automatic performance adjustment support will change the value dynamically if it is set on. A value too low means that the machine pool can become a bottleneck for all work on the system, with a potentially devastating effect on performance. A value too high means that some main storage may be wasted.

QBASPOOL

The initial value should be set as described in Sec. 9.4.4. A value too low means that the base pool could be allowed to go too low, and that it can become a bottleneck for all work on the system. A value too high means that some main storage may be wasted, since you will be prevented from removing storage from the base pool if that means that it would go lower than the value in QBASPOOL.

QBASACTLVL

The initial value should be set as described in Sec. 9.4.4. The automatic performance adjustment support will change this value dynamically if it is set on. A value too low will restrict the number of jobs allowed to occupy activity levels in the base pool to a number lower than the storage will support, thus wasting main storage. A value too high will allow more jobs to occupy activity levels in the base pool than the storage will support with the consequent risk of excessive page faulting.

QMAXACTLVL

This should be set to *NOMAX unless you have a specific reason for putting a limit on the total number of activity levels over the whole system. A value less than the sum of the activity levels of all the pools will restrict the number of jobs allowed to become active at any one time. A value too high should not have any effect since the number of jobs allowed active will be controlled by activity levels in individual storage pools.

QTSEPOOL

This should normally be set to *BASE since it can minimize the effect of CPU intensive interactive jobs on other jobs in the interactive pool.

QAUTOCFG

This should be 1 if you want automatic device configuration, 2 if you do not. Leaving automatic device configuration on for a long time in an environment where devices are frequently moved may leave you with many out-of-date device descriptions on your system. The number of device descriptions is used by the automatic performance adjustment support at IPL time. It will make inappropriate allocations if there are more device descriptions on your system than there are real devices.

QINACTITV

Inactive jobs do not present a significant workload to the system. They can, however, pose a security risk since an unauthorized person can use a vacant signed-on terminal with the absent user's user profile. With respect to performance, the shorter you make this interval, the more work you are asking the system to do since a job is more likely to hit its timeout value. This could become significant if the action to take at timeout is to end the job. If your security requirements do not dictate a shorter interval, a value of 15–30 minutes should be suitable to most installations.

QINACTMSGQ

The possible values are:

*DSCJOB—the job and associated secondary or group jobs are disconnected.
*ENDJOB—the job and associated secondary or group jobs are ended.
Message queue name—message queue to be notified of the job timeout. A program, waiting on this queue, could then take appropriate action.

A disconnected job is one that is not attached to a workstation but stays in the system in a suspended state until the original user signs on again at the same terminal. The suspended job will be ended automatically if it remains disconnected for the interval specified in system value QDSCJOBITV. If you expect interactive jobs to be inactive frequently where users will want to get back on to the system after timeout, *DSCJOB will be the best setting and will cause less system overhead than *ENDJOB.

QDSCJOBITV

The possible values are:

*NONE—disconnected jobs will stay around until reconnected, or until the next IPL.
5-1440—disconnected jobs are ended after this number of minutes

The best setting will depend upon how long you estimate before it is safe to assume that disconnected jobs will not require reconnection. Too short a value will result in jobs terminating unnecessarily with the associated abnormal termination of the application in use. The default value of 4 hours is probably reasonable.

Anyone who takes a lunch hour longer than this is unlikely to be coming back to work!

QDEVRCYACN

The possible values are:

*MSG—a message is sent to the application in use so that it can handle the problem
*DSCENDRQS—the job is disconnected. When the user signs back on, a cancel request function returns control to the last request level
*DSCMSG—the job is disconnected. When the user signs back on, a message is sent to the application in use.
*ENDJOB—the job is ended. A job log is produced.
*ENDJOBNOLIST—the job is ended. No job log is produced. A message is sent to the system history log.

I/O errors should not occur frequently as long as users are trained not to switch off their workstations without signing off or disconnecting their job. The best option is to set the value to *DSCMSG and for the applications to handle the recovery of the application when the user signs back on and requests reconnection to their interrupted job. In this case all applications must be able to handle the application recovery required. You should set the value QDSCJOBITV in order to avoid too many disconnected jobs hanging around holding files open and associated locks. If the default of *MSG is retained, all applications must be able to handle I/O errors without performing endless retries and producing large job logs with the associated performance overhead.

If your applications are not capable of handling the recovery or errors as above, you will need to set the value to *DSCENDRQS, *ENDJOB or *ENDJOBNOLIST. In a situation where workstation I/O errors are occurring frequently, for example because of a cabling problem, the *ENDJOB can cause significant performance overhead because of the production of job logs. Obviously such a problem must be tracked down and corrected, but while it persists you might choose to change the value to *ENDJOBNOLIST.

QCMNRCYLMT

This system value consists of two parts:

Count limit—0 or 1–99
Time interval—0 or 1–120

The correct setting for your system will depend upon how many communications errors you experience. A count limit of 0 will give no recovery whatever the setting of the time interval. This will potentially cause needless failures on communications with a loss of the link which will obviously affect performance for users at the other end of the link.

A non-zero value in count limit with a 0 value in time interval will give infinite recovery. If an unrecoverable error occurs, the system will use effort pointlessly trying to re-establish contact, with the associated performance overhead.

A reasonable starting point would be a count limit of 2 with a time interval of 5 (2 5). This means that when an error occurs and the line or control unit retry value has been exceeded, the system will try again twice within 5 minutes. If the error persists the system will cease recovery attempts and put the line or controller in the status 'recovery pending'. Operator action is then required.

QDBRCVYWT

The possible values are:

  0—IPL completes before all files are recovered
  1—IPL completes only after all files are recovered.

A setting of 1 will force all users to wait for full file recovery before they can access the system after an abnormal termination. A setting of 0 gives the system operator the option to allow certain users on to the system before all files are recovered. 0 is usually the better option although control must be exercised over users accessing the system after an abnormal termination.

QRCLSPLSTG

Possible values are:

  *NOMAX—empty spool members are not automatically deleted
  *NONE—empty spool members are deleted immediately
  1–366—empty spool members are deleted after this number of days.

If you have a lot of empty spool members on the system they occupy useful disk storage to no purpose. The correct setting is dependent upon how variable the production of printout is on your system. The default of 8 is satisfactory for most systems. The value *NONE can cause severe performance impact if your system generates and prints lots of spool files, especially to workstation printers. If you want to reclaim the disk space promptly, use 1 rather than *NONE.

9.4.3   Calculating the initial size of the machine pool (QMCHPOOL)

The initial machine pool size is the sum of four values:

- The minimum pool size, determined mainly by the main storage size of your AS/400
- The main storage required to support the number of jobs to be run at once
- The main storage required to support the amount of communications
- Additional main storage required to run miscellaneous functions such as 3270 emulation or OfficeVision/400.

Table 9.2. Sample initial machine pool sizes

System size	Machine pool size (KB)
8 MB/40 active jobs	2 000
24 MB/100 active jobs	4 000
48 MB/200 active jobs	7 000
96 MB/300 active jobs	12 500
160 MB/500 active jobs	18 500
256 MB/700 active jobs	28 000
512 MB/1500 active jobs	50 000
1024 MB/3000 active jobs	97 000

The *Work Management Guide* (see Bibliography) contains a section on machine pool sizing. This includes a number of large tables which show the amount of main storage required for the various elements of the workload. Rather than reproduce this section in this book, we refer you directly to the manual. We have provided in Table 9.2 a few sample systems and the initial machine pool size calculated according to the current version of the manual. A reasonable amount of communications for the size of system was assumed.

Be aware that the size of machine pool is vital to the healthy running of the system since all jobs use the machine pool. The value calculated from the manual is only an estimate and further monitoring and review will be required, as discussed later in this chapter.

9.4.4   Calculating values for QBASPOOL and QBASACTLVL

Once again, the *Work Management Guide* contains a table with suggested values for the base pool and its activity level. Rather than reproduce this table, we refer you directly to the manual for your version of OS/400. We have provided in Table 9.3 a few sample systems with base pool size and activity level taken from the current version of the manual.

Table 9.3. Sample minimum base pool size and activity level

Main storage size (MB)	Pool size (KB)/activity level
LE 12	500/2–1250/3
16–28	1500/4–2350/5
32–48	2700/5–4000/6
56–192	4625/5–14 000/7
208–272	15 000/8–18 600/9
288–384	19 500/9–23 100/10
416–512	24 000/15–27 900/15
512–768	27 900/15–37 500/20
768–1024	37 500/20–47 100/20
1024–1280	47 100/20–56 000/25
1280–1536	56 700/25–66 300/30

Note that an assumption underlying these figures is that batch job streams will run in the *BASE pool. Also remember that QBASPOOL does not set the size of the pool, but merely specifies the minimum allowable. To leave some scope for manual or automatic performance adjustment, set QBASPOOL to about two thirds of the estimated pool size.

As with the machine pool, the base pool is vital to the healthy running of the system, since all jobs use the base pool for some functions. The tabulated values are only estimates, and further monitoring and review will be required as discussed later in Sec. 9.7.

9.5   Estimation of spool and interactive pools

Create a new copy of Figure 9.1 to record the recommendations for pool sizes and activity levels.

9.5.1   Estimating spool pool size and activity level

The size of the spool pool required depends on the number of concurrently active print spool writers to be run, and whether they are feeding advanced function printers or not. The *Work Management Guide* provides sizing tables. Since they are small we have reproduced them here, but please refer to the manual for tables for your version of OS/400. Add together the values from Tables 9.4 and 9.5 to get the recommended spool pool size and activity level.

Table 9.4.   Spool pool sizes for advanced function printers

No of writers	Pool size (KB)	Activity level
1	1500	1
2	1700	2
3	1900	3
4	2100	4
GT 4	2300	5

Table 9.5.   Spool pool sizes for non-advanced function printers

No. of writers	Pool size (KB)	Activity level
1	80	1
2	160	2
3	225	3
4	290	4
GT 4	350	5

9.5.2   Estimating interactive pool size and activity level

The interactive pool size available is what is left from total main storage after you have taken out the calculated allocations for:

- The machine pool
- The minimum base pool
- The spool pool.

When you have calculated the amount of storage left for the interactive pool, *INTERACT, you must then calculate a suitable activity level. Another table in the *Work Management Guide* provides guidance on the amount of storage to allow per activity level. Refer to the manual for this information for your version of OS/400. For convenience, we have reproduced the current table from the manual in Table 9.6.

Table 9.6.   Estimated storage per activity level in *INTERACT

Main storage size (MB)	Estimated storage per activity level (KB)
LE 12	450
16–28	900
32–48	1600
64–192	2500
208–272	3000
288–384	3500
416–512	4000
512–768	4500
768–1024	5000
1024–1280	5500
1280–1536	6000

9.6   Making the tuning changes

The tuning changes could have been made as the recommendations were arrived at and recorded. At this point check, complete or carry out the changes as follows:

- Refer to Table 8.3 and modify all the system values which require change, recording the date of the change on the form. Be careful when changing the size of the machine pool and the minimum size of the base pool. If the calculated value is less than the current value by a considerable amount, check your arithmetic and check the figures for reasonableness against Tables 9.2 and 9.3 before making the change.
- Use the WRKSHRPOOL or CHGSBSD command to modify the sizes and activity levels of pools to match the values calculated in Sec. 9.5.
- Use WRKSYSSTS to assure yourself that the changes have taken effect.

9.7   Reassessment of system performance

Re-measure and record the workload and performance data as described in Sec. 8.4. We will now go on to assess the effectiveness of the changes by comparing the new data with the original measurements, and by checking the main performance indicators against published guidelines in the IBM manuals.

As explained in Sec. 8.4, the primary indication of success is a reduction in the average interactive response time for the same workload content and throughput. The measurement must be repeated until you are confident that like is being compared with like. The following indicators are more sensitive measures of performance which can be viewed as the causes of performance changes.

9.7.1   Checking the size of the machine pool

We have stressed how important is the correct sizing of the machine pool. The ideal indicator is the number of non-database page faults in the pool. Table 9.7 shows the guidelines from the current edition of the *Work Management Guide*. Check the table in the manual for your version of OS/400 and compare your 'before' and 'after' results in Table 8.1 with these.

If the results for the machine pool are in the good area, then you can assume that the size of the pool is at least big enough. We can leave it until something significant changes in the workload.

If the results are in the acceptable area, your action will depend upon the size of main memory available to you and on what we find when assessing the other pools. We recommend that you make the machine pool large enough so that the faults are in the good area, unless the other pools are overloaded. As you will see, the process of appropriately allocating storage is a balancing act: what you give to one pool must be taken from others.

If the results are in the poor area, we recommend that you allocate additional storage to the machine pool now. Take it from the interactive pool, since we do not want to reduce the base pool from the calculated initial value, unless the results show that it is oversized. Remember to adjust the activity level in *INTERACT to a value suitable for the reduced pool size.

The process of increasing the machine pool may have to be iterative. The amount of storage to add at each iteration will vary with the size of system you

Table 9.7.   Guidelines for non-database page faults in the machine pool

Good	Acceptable	Poor
LT 2	2–5	GT 5

have. Add 10 per cent of the current size each time and repeat until the results are in the acceptable to good range. Remember to record what you have done.

9.7.2   Checking the size and activity level of other pools

For each pool other than the machine pool, we are interested in the sum of the database and non-database page fault rates (remember faults not pages). Calculate these totals from your recorded results and use the table in the *Work Management Guide* to assess the effectiveness of storage and activity level allocation to each pool. The table in the manual is too large to reproduce here but we have provided a subset to give you an indication.

The first figure shown in Table 9.8 is for the combined page fault rates within the busiest pool (usually *INTERACT). The figures in parentheses are the total across all pools (as recorded in Table 8.1). Both of these thresholds need to be observed to achieve the level of performance described at the top of the column.

Table 9.8. Guidelines for total (DB and non-DB) faults

AS/400 model	Good	Acceptable	Poor
B10 B35 D04 E02	LT 10 (15)	10–15 (15–25)	GT 15 (25)
B40 F04 200/2030	LT 15 (25)	15–25 (25–40)	GT 25 (40)
F06 F50 300/2042	LT 25 (35)	25–50 (35–60)	GT 50 (60)
F60 30S/2412 320/2050	LT 50 (80)	50–100 (80–130)	GT 100 (130)
E90 E95 F80	LT 100 (180)	100–200 (180–300)	GT 200 (300)
F90 F97 320/2051/2052	LT 150 (250)	150–350 (250–440)	GT 350 (440)

We are also interested in the ratio of wait-to-ineligible (WI) transitions to active-to-wait (AW) transitions in the interactive pool(s). As you will recall, the WI transitions reflect the situation where a job is ready to become active and there is no activity level slot free for it to use. Divide the number of WI transitions by the number of AW transitions and compare your results to the values in the *Work Management Guide*. In Table 9.9 we show the values from the current manual.

Note that the page fault guidelines are much more important than the transition guidelines. If you have insufficient memory in the interactive pool you will have to reduce the activity level (or add memory) to meet the acceptable page fault guidelines. Reducing the activity level will increase the WI/AW ratio, and if it becomes unacceptable, so be it, until more memory becomes available.

Table 9.9.   Guidelines for WI transitions

	Good	Acceptable	Poor
Ratio WI/AW	GT 0 and LT 0.1	0.1–0.25	GT 0.25

Note also that if the WI rate is zero at peak times, the activity-level setting should be reduced until a very small WI value appears. A zero value could result from the activity level being very much too high, a potentially dangerous situation.

The best balance can only be achieved by trial and error. Repeat the process of redistributing memory and modifying activity levels until minimum page fault rates are achieved. During this iterative process you may prefer to use the more immediate system commands over a suitable elapsed time to give you the performance indicators rather than rerunning the performance monitor each time. The following comments may assist you in getting to the optimum position as quickly as possible.

Pool with fault rate too high

The activity level is likely to be too high for the storage allocated. If you get to a position in a pool where you cannot get the fault rate down to an acceptable level without pushing up the WI/AW ratio to an unacceptable level, there is not enough storage in the pool. You must then increase the storage (if available from elsewhere) and try again. Decrease activity level or add memory.

Pool with low fault rate and unacceptable WI to AW ratio

The activity level is set too low for the amount of work going through. Increase the activity level.

9.8   Reassessment of CPU and disk utilization

9.8.1   Reviewing CPU utilization

The high-priority CPU utilization figure was logged on Table 8.1, and as discussed in Sec. 8.5.4, is not a sensitive indicator of system tuning improvements. All we will do here is check that the machine is not overloaded. This is done by confirming that the utilization is below the threshold figure shown in Table 4.1 (80 per cent). If this is not the case we must presume that capacity planning is not among the installation management disciplines in use in your department. Our only options are to consider a faster CPU or review the applications to highlight inefficiencies in the design or coding of specific jobs. Investigation and modification of applications to improve performance is beyond the scope of this book, but use of BEST/1 to evaluate hardware changes is covered in Part IV.

There is one area of installation management policy which might allow us to reduce the CPU utilization without changing the workload. Check the authority lookup rate listed in the 'Exception Occurrence Summary and Interval Counts' section of the Component Report, and use the table in the *Performance Management 'Red Book'* (see Bibliography) to gauge the amount of CPU that

Table 9.10. Authority lookup exception CPU cost

Exceptions/s	F02	F04	F06	F10	F20	F25	F35	F45	F50	F60	F70	F80	F90	F95
10	2	2	1	1	1	1	1	0	0	0	0	0	0	0
25	6	5	3	3	3	2	2	2	1	0	0	0	0	0
50	13	10	7	7	6	5	5	4	2	1	1	0	0	0
100	27	20	15	15	12	10	10	8	5	3	2	1	1	1
200	54	41	31	31	25	21	21	17	10	7	5	3	2	2
300	81	61	46	46	38	32	32	26	16	11	8	4	3	3
400		82	62	62	51	43	43	34	21	15	10	6	4	4
500			77	77	64	54	54	43	27	18	13	7	5	5
1000								87	54	37	27	15	11	10
2000										75	54	30	23	20
3000											81	46	35	30
4000												61	46	40
5000												76	58	50
6000												92	70	60
7000													82	70
8000													93	80
9000														90

these exceptions are costing. Table 9.10 is a subset of the table in the manual. If the authority lookup exceptions are using a significant proportion of your CPU, say 8 per cent or more, you should review your security set-up as discussed in Sec. 9.15.2.

9.8.2 Reviewing disk utilization

The average actuator utilization was logged in Table 8.1, but you should also consult the source report (Disk Utilization) to check for even spread of activity across all actuators. If the machine is not overloaded we expect an average utilization figure of less than 40 per cent. An average of more than 40 per cent utilization when you are happy that your main storage and activity levels are appropriately allocated indicates that you do not have enough disk actuators on your system. Normally the figure will be acceptable and we are looking for a reduction caused by our tuning activity.

If only one or two actuators consistently exceed the 40 per cent guideline, this could be because a frequently required piece of data (most likely a data file or combination of data files) is stored on the heavily used actuators. This situation is quite rare since the system, by default, tries to spread objects across multiple actuators. In exceptional cases of markedly uneven activity, the thing to do is to identify the object(s) concerned and move them so that active data is more evenly spread.

Use the Performance Tools/400 Disk Activity report to identify the objects concerned. You can then move them by the process of saving, deleting and restoring. This should give a more even spread and lighten the load on the busy actuators. In order to obtain this report, you must specifically request it by following the instructions in the Performance Tools/400 Guide for analysing disk activity. Briefly, these are:

- Start disk data collection using command STRDSKCOL
- End disk data collection using ENDDSKCOL—do this 1 to 5 minutes after starting disk data collection
- Print the Disk Activity Report using PRTDSKRPT and selecting the disk units which are over-utilized.

Be aware that the process of data collection and ending it carry a high overhead and the collection should be run for as brief a time as possible.

In addition, you should review the utilization of the disk I/O processors in the Performance Tools/400 Component Report in the section on IOP Utilization. The overload threshold is 45 per cent or 70 per cent utilization depending on the IOP type. If one or two are over the guideline you should proceed as for over-utilized disk arms by viewing the Disk Activity Report for the actuators controlled by the busy IOP.

9.9   Assessment of time slice values

A measure of the number of transactions which exceed their time slice is the rate of AI transitions in the interactive pool. As discussed earlier in Sec. 3.5.3, the default is that a transaction exceeds its time slice if it uses more than 2 seconds of CPU time during one occupation of an activity level slot. When this happens it may cease to be active, and join the ineligible queue. If QTSEPOOL is set to *BASE, it is moved out of its own pool temporarily and finishes its transaction in the base pool.

The time-slice mechanism is designed to punish interactive jobs for being too greedy and to minimize the impact on concurrent well-behaved jobs. It is a good solution for occasional excessively complex transactions. Be aware, however, that jobs which exceed their time slice and get transferred into *BASE operate at their own priority and could interfere with lower-priority work.

You may well wish to modify the default time slice. On the faster models of AS/400 2 seconds is generally a very large CPU time slice to allow. A good starting point is to use three times the average CPU time per transaction logged in Table 8.1. On the other hand, you may have important transactions in your workload which often require more than this amount of CPU time to complete; possibly because you are running complex transactions on a relatively low-speed CPU. If so, use the Transaction Summary (Interactive Program Statistics section) report to gauge how much CPU time these transactions need.

You should be aware that, by extending the time slice, you are allowing long-running transactions to occupy activity levels more continuously, and this will potentially keep other transactions out and slow their response.

Changes to time slice are, of course, made by changing the value in the interactive class (CHGCLS command). Like all system tuning changes, the effects need to be assessed by repeating measurements.

9.10   Assessment of PURGE values

The effect of the PURGE parameter has been discussed in detail in Sec. 3.6. Please refer back to this topic for a full description. The decision we are faced with now is to decide whether or not we have enough room in an interactive pool to take advantage of setting the PURGE parameter on the class to *NO. Using PURGE(*NO) requires more memory for the same number of active jobs and the same workload.

If you can allow 350K for each job running in the pool you should try PURGE(*NO). Note that this guideline is for each job running in the pool, not for each activity level. So if you have a hundred interactive users concurrently signed on in a pool each running one interactive session, you will need something like 35 MB in the interactive pool before you should consider trying PURGE(*NO). The activity level of the pool should remain as discussed in Sec. 9.5.2.

Even if you have 35 MB as in the above example, this does not guarantee that PURGE(*NO) will work. Your applications may have a higher memory requirement. Thus, it is vital that you continue taking measurements after the change and review the effect. If the fault rate increases to an unacceptable level, you do not have enough memory in the pool. You can either go back to PURGE(*YES) or transfer memory from another pool.

9.11   Use of separate pools for batch

The default pool configuration consists of four pools: *INTERACT, *SPOOL, *BASE and *MACHINE. Batch jobs will run in *BASE along with:

● Certain system tasks required by any job on the system
● Subsystem monitors
● Communications jobs.

Some of the activities in *BASE have higher priority than batch jobs, and in a busy *BASE pool batch jobs will tend to lose their memory pages. When control eventually passes to the batch job it is unable to make progress until its active pages are brought in. While waiting for this a higher-priority job somewhere in the system is likely to become ready and take the CPU again.

Repetition of this cycle means that batch jobs make very slow progress and introduce non-productive paging into the *BASE pool which disrupts other users. It is clearly more efficient to run a batch job in its own pool, so that when it gets control the active pages are loaded and it is ready to execute immediately.

Table 9.11. Storage guidelines for batch pools (single stream)

Type of batch job	Storage range (KB)	Possible good start point (KB)
Short-running production	250–750	500
Long-running production	500–1000	750
Program compiles	1500–3000	2000
Reformat (sort)	1500–3000	2000
Queries	1500–4000	2000
Save/Restore	1000–3000	2000

Table 9.11 gives an indication of the storage requirements for typical kinds of batch work.

To make this change modify the pools parameter in the subsystem description(s) used for batch work. By default, this is QBATCH. Be sure to change the correct pool number. The pool number used by any particular job in the subsystem is specified on the routing entry used by the job.

You can specify an amount of storage which will give the batch work a private storage pool, or you can specify one of the shared pools. In the latter case, be sure to use the CHGSHRPOOL command to set up the storage for that pool. The advantage of a shared pool is that, if dynamic performance adjustment support is running, the storage will get allocated to other pools when it is not being used. Otherwise the storage will sit unused waiting for work.

If you need to cater for multiple concurrent batch streams it is usually best to provide a separate pool for each. With one job per pool there is no danger of memory-hungry jobs overwriting the active pages of other jobs. Multiple concurrent batch streams are often used for the following reasons:

- To maximize batch throughput
- To avoid queuing short-running urgent jobs behind long-running ones
- To provide asynchronous services through 'never-ending' jobs.

With multiple batch pools, it is particularly beneficial to use the dynamic performance adjustment support and shared pools. If the pools are not continuously active, and memory is in short supply elsewhere, memory will be automatically redistributed.

The easiest way to implement this approach is to create a new subsystem description and job queue for each additional batch stream, as follows:

1. Use the CRTDUPOBJ command to create a duplicate of subsystem description QBATCH, named, for example, QBATCH2.
2. Use the CRTDUPOBJ command to create a duplicate of job queue QBATCH, named, for example, QBATCH2.
3. Use the command CHGJOBQE to change the job queue entry in QBATCH2 subsystem to QBATCH2. This means that QBATCH2 subsystem will look for work from your new job queue, QBATCH2.

4. Alter the POOLS parameter in the subsystem QBATCH2 to route work into a private pool or one of the shared pools.

In order to use the new batch subsystem with its new pool, you must start the subsystem QBATCH2 with the STRSBS command and submit jobs to the new job queue QBATCH2. You can automate the start of the subsystem at IPL by placing the STRSBS command in your start-up program, if you use one. In the case of 'never-ending' server jobs it is usually more convenient to initiate the job as an autostart job, rather than having to submit it to the job queue each time the subsystem is started.

Note that the fault guidelines for *BASE change if batch has been removed. They are documented in the *Work Management Guide*. Of course, the effects of these changes need to be assessed in the normal way.

In addition, you may wish to allocate different run priorities to different batch jobs. For example, you may have a 'hot batch' stream (priority 48, say) which takes precedence over normal batch, and a server job performing time-critical asynchronous services for online users at higher priority still (46, say). This is achieved simply by providing new classes for the higher-priority subsystems, and changing the appropriate subsystem description routing entries to reference the new classes, e.g.

```
CRTCLS      QGPL/QBATCH2
            RUNPTY(48)
            TIMESLICE(5000)
            PURGE(*NO)
            DFTWAIT(120)
            TEXT('For hot batch')

CHGRTGE     QGPL/QBATCH2
            SEQNBR(9999)
            CLS(QGPL/QBATCH2)
```

One could, of course, provide multiple routing entries within one subsystem to select different classes and/or pools for jobs depending on their routing data, but routing via job queues as described above is easier to control.

9.12   Use of multiple pools for interactive work

Partitioning of interactive users into multiple pools is also advisable in some circumstances. A general principle is to minimize the fragmentation of main memory to make it easy for the system to optimize usage as workload components fluctuate in activity. However, separate pools should always be provided for users with different priority and/or purge attributes, to minimize unproductive paging.

For instance, a group of favoured users running at higher than normal priority (like our example in Chapter 3) would be given a dedicated pool. Such a user might be in the customer services or sales department, dealing with customers on the telephone and using the AS/400 to check product availability. A more negative example would be where you have development work on the production machine, and wish to restrict the share of system resources used by programmers. You might give them a priority of 30 and their own pool to run in. IBM have, in fact, foreseen this requirement and provided a spare subsystem (QPGMR) which can be used for the purpose.

To calculate the initial size and activity level of such a pool, follow the same rules as for setting the size of *INTERACT (Sec. 9.5.2). You will obviously need to decrease the size and activity level for *INTERACT to reflect the reduced workload in that pool.

To provide an additional pool and segregate users within an existing interactive subsystem, you have first to decide what is going to identify the users who will use the new pool. This could be their workstation name but it will generally be better to use their USER ID. In this case you want to modify QINTER subsystem so that it works like XYZ subsystem discussed in Chapter 3 (see Fig. 3.4). Here's one way you might achieve the desired effect:

- Create a job description called, for example, SPECIAL, similar to the job description QINTER but with RTGDTA specified as, for example, SPCL.
- Create a class called, for example, SPECIAL, with PURGE(*NO) and/or run priority higher or lower than normal interactive, e.g. 19 or 21.
- Change the POOLS parameter to add pool 3 in the subsystem QINTER and specify the calculated amount of storage and activity level (for a private pool) or one of the shared pools SHRPOOL1–10.
- If you have specified a shared pool, use the CHGSHRPOOL command to set up the pool specified as you have calculated that it should be.
- Add a routing entry to subsystem QINTER with CMPVAL(SPCL), POOLID(3), PGM(QCMD) and CLASS(SPECIAL). The routing entry must be higher in the list of routing entries than the one with CMPVAL(*ANY).
- In the user profile for each of these special users, specify the job description SPECIAL.

We have assumed that the workstation entry in the subsystem used by the user specifies that the job description should be picked up from the user profile. This is the default arrangement.

There are other ways to do the same job. One way is to create a new subsystem like QINTER, put workstation entries in for each workstation used by the special users, and remove those workstation entries from QINTER. This has disadvantages:

- You can no longer use workstation type entries (unless the special users are the only users who use a particular type of workstation; this is unlikely).
- Using workstation name entries gives you a maintenance problem, especially if you are allowing autoconfiguration. When workstations move about or are

added, the new names must be added to the correct subsystem. Use of a generic naming convention (all devices owned by a particular subsystem begin with the same characters) can circumvent the difficulty.

Perhaps a better way to use a new subsystem like QINTER is to make the work-station entries specify workstation allocation at entry (*ENTER) rather than at sign-on (*SIGNON). You can then modify the initial program for the special users so that they are transferred from QINTER into your new subsystem immediately after sign-on by using the TFRJOB command. The delivered QPGMR subsystem is set up like this.

9.13   Use of Expert Cache

The Expert Cache function was discussed in Sec. 3.6.5. It involves changing how the system handles data transfer from disk, allowing it to effectively block records based on the utilization of storage in the pool at the time. For this to benefit performance, the workload in the pool must include sequential processing. Hence it is more likely to be of use in a pool running batch-type jobs.

To set the Expert Cache support on in a pool use the CHGSHRPOOL command to specify the paging option *CALC rather than the default of *FIXED. Obviously, you should monitor the results to make sure that the change has been beneficial.

9.14   Additional tuning for System/36 Environment users

9.14.1   Minimize cost of common System/36 application techniques

There are techniques used in many applications migrated from S/36 which are not normally seen in native AS/400 applications. The main ones are:

- Multiple requester terminal (MRT) jobs. These are interactive jobs which can support more than one user.
- Evoked jobs. These are mini batch-type jobs which are created as needed to perform functions caused by the interactive job itself. A common example is a file update or a print job.

Although these were efficient ways of using the architecture of the S/36, the way they are used on AS/400 deserves some consideration. The overhead of job start-up and termination is higher on the AS/400 than on the System/36. On the AS/400, therefore, we wish to minimize the number of job starts and terminations, and the overhead of attaching new users to an existing MRT job.

Factors which we can control include:

- The length of time for which an MRT job will stay in the system while no users are attached to it

- The amount of authority checking required when a user attaches to an MRT job.

The methods of control are:

- Use the CHGS36A or WRKS36A command to change the MRTDLY parameter default for all MRT jobs in the S/36 Environment.
- Use the CHGS36PRCA, WRKS36PRCA or EDTS36PRCA command to change the MRTDLY parameter for a particular procedure.
- Use the CHGS36A or WRKS36A command with parameter MRTAUT (*FRSTUSR) to change the S/36 Environment such that authorities are checked only for the first user of an MRT rather than for each user which attaches to it.

These values can also be changed on S/36 Environment configuration screen formats.

In order to estimate the appropriate value for the MRTDLY parameter, you will need to understand how the MRT jobs are used. If they are used constantly throughout the day a value of 900 seconds (15 minutes) should ensure that the job remains active for most of the day but does not hang around too long at the end of the day before closing itself down. Be aware that this parameter refers only to MRT jobs which are not specified as never-ending programs (NEPs). MRT-NEPs will remain active regardless of whether or not users are attached.

Since multiple users attach to the MRT job, there will potentially be many more transactions than for a native job with one user. Therefore purging the PAG for every transaction may not be appropriate, and you should probably change the class used by these jobs to PURGE(*NO).

Evoked jobs are mini-batch jobs. In order to avoid the potential disruption of running them at interactive priority in the same pool as interactive jobs, you should ensure that evoked jobs run in a batch pool and at a batch priority. A word of warning, though—if the function of the evoked jobs is time-critical, the priority may have to be raised. For instance, if file updates queue for an unacceptable time, files will be out of date, which could adversely affect the operation of the business application.

In order to optimize the operation of evoked jobs the operational parameters should be changed as follows:

- Elect that evoked jobs bypass the job queue by setting the parameter EVKJOBINIT in the S/36 Environment to *IMMED.
- Use the CHGS36A or WRKS36A command to change the parameter EVKJOBPTY to a suitable batch priority, e.g. 50.
- Use the CHGS36A or WRKS36A command to change the parameter EVKJOBPOL to *BASE. This will cause evoked jobs to run in *BASE. If you would prefer them to run in a separate pool rather than in *BASE or the pool of the originating job, they will need to go via a job queue which is set up to

submit jobs into a subsystem using the separate pool. In this case EVKJOBI-NIT should be set to *JOBQ.

9.14.2 Limit logging of OCL statements

System/36 procedures contain Operations Control Language (OCL) statements. These perform similar functions to some CL statements and control the application. By default, these statements are logged to the job log and the job message queue. This logging is useful when debugging an application but for normal running the overhead should be avoided. Use the command CHGS36PRCA, WRKS36PRCA or EDTS36PRCA to change the LOG parameter to *NO for all S/36 procedures in use.

9.15   Operational procedures and practice

9.15.1 Reducing overhead of users signing on and off

The processes of signing on and off on the AS/400 carry significant overhead. Use of DSCJOB command will allow users to leave their workstation apparently signed off and secure, and will allow them to reconnect to their job by signing on again. DSCJOB can be keyed as a command or selected from an application menu option.

A disconnected job will leave files open and locks held, so the option should really only be available to users at safe points in the application. This means it is best to have the option under application control.

The process of signing on or off is controlled by the subsystem monitor. When many users sign on or off at the same time, they may have to wait while the subsystem monitor deals with the requests sequentially. If there is a large number of users who regularly sign on or off at the same time, the waiting can be reduced by using multiple subsystems and splitting the users across these subsystems. They can still share the same memory pool. The cost of an additional subsystem is minimal at 1 KB in the machine pool.

9.15.2 Reducing the overhead of security authorization checks

In order to use any object on the AS/400 the user must have the appropriate authorization by virtue of one of the following:

- The user has *ALLOBJ special authority
- The object is available to the public
- The user is specifically authorized to use the object, or is a member of a group so authorized

- The user has adopted the authority of one or more other users, and their combined rights are sufficient.

Specific or private authority searching is time consuming and, depending on the way access controls are implemented, may have to be carried out multiple times for each object access request. This can cause significant CPU overhead on a busy system with many private authorities to be checked. The way to calculate the actual impact on your system was described in Sec. 9.8.1.

We do not recommend that you render your business data and programs insecure in the interests of performance. We do suggest, however, that you take into account potential performance cost when setting your security strategy. The following are reasonable guidelines:

- Do not privately authorize 'low-grade' uncontroversial objects—make them publicly available. This includes frequently accessed IBM supplied objects such as message files and programs.
- Only define private authorities which permit a higher level of access than the public's authority to the object.
- Where access to objects is to be restricted, consider controlling this by means of private authorizations to the containing library. The contained objects could be publicly authorized, have no private authorizations, but remain inaccessible to users without rights to the library. This is a very simple access control system with good performance characteristics. It relies on grouping objects into libraries based on similar access requirements.

Use of authorization lists and group profiles provide a convenient, easily maintained method of implementing security for many installations. The points with respect to private authorizations still apply where these are used.

The system is only able to use the efficient method of providing object access to a user by virtue of the public authority if there are no private authorizations of a lesser level than the public authorization for that object. This fact is stored with the object. If there are private authorizations of a lesser level than public, relevant user profiles must be checked. This is different from the old System/38 implementation where public authority was accepted without further check. If there are no private authorities for an object, this fact is also stored with the object and the system checks only public authority.

If a user with private authority to an object is removed from the system, the object is not automatically reset to reflect whether or not private authorities exist for it. This is done the next time the object's authority is displayed or changed. The program QSYFIXAUT in QSYS will set all objects correctly and ensure that private authorities will be checked as little as necessary. QSYFIXAUT will take a very long time to run as it checks all objects on your system, and once running it must not be interrupted. Running it is only recommended if the number of authority lookups is significant, and you suspect that user profiles with unique private authorities have been removed from your system.

Use of security level 50 causes additional checking when programs are run on the system. This adds performance overhead and security level 50 should only be specified if you have need of the very high level of security which it provides. Level 30 or 40 is perfectly adequate for most environments. In addition, the options specified in the system value QAUDLVL should be carefully chosen. By the setting of QAUDLVL you can cause various activities on the system to be logged. Such logging will also have performance implications, so select logging only for essential activities.

9.15.3 Reducing the overhead of systems operator and programmer functions

Systems operators and programmers work mostly with OS/400 commands and system menus rather than through applications. They are capable of performing high overhead functions at high priority, which can degrade the performance of production work. The keys to preventing this are:

- Ensure these users accept that the real business users have a prior claim to all resources of the system.
- Ensure that these users understand the effect of high resource consumption commands and functions on the general performance of the system.
- Police the use of the system to highlight abuses.

Some examples of undesirable functions which would adversely affect other users are:

- Compiling a program interactively
- Running a save or restore interactively
- Heavy use of the system console at privileged priority
- Over-use of potentially high overhead system functions such as WRKACTJOB
- Running large queries, SQL requests or file copies interactively when testing applications.

If necessary, you can change any AS/400 command so that it can only be run in batch. Use the CHGCMD command for this purpose. The Job Summary report produced by the PRTTNSRPT command (see Sec. 8.4.2) is the best tool for policing abuses.

One way to partially isolate end users from the effects of programmer activity is to put the programmers into QPGMR subsystem, as discussed earlier in Sec. 9.12. When using QPGMR, by default, the programmers operate at priority 30, which is lower than normal interactive jobs. You should change the default *BASE pool used by QPGMR subsystem to an appropriately sized separate pool.

Of course, programmers are expensive people, and it is only sensible to give them an environment where they can develop software at their own speed, unhindered by slow response times and long compilations. Many organizations find it worth while to provide separate machine resource for them, such as another AS/400 or a PC with suitable tools so that they can do some of the development offline from the production system.

9.15.4 Reducing the overhead of job log production and CL logging

The job description used by a job controls whether or not CL commands are logged to the job log and under what circumstances a job log is produced when the job terminates. Both logging of CL and job log production can cause unnecessary overhead on a busy system. Suitable settings on production jobs are:

- LOG(4 0 *NOLIST)—job log will be produced if the job completes unsuccessfully
- LOGCLPGM(*NO).

9.15.5 Reducing the overhead of printing

If Advanced Function Printing is not being used, ensure that printer device descriptions are created with AFP(*NO). This reduces the overhead of the print driver job. If printing is destined for an IPDS printer, ensure that the printer file used has DEVTYPE(*IPDS) specified, either at creation time or by changing or overriding it. If not, the print data stream produced may default to *SCS and the data stream will be converted when it comes to print.

9.15.6 Reviewing frequency of IPLs

Certain housekeeping functions are performed automatically at IPL time, and cannot be done at any other time. These include the regeneration of permanent and temporary addresses and the rebuild of job structures. You should ensure that the system goes through the IPL process at least once every month, so that these important jobs are not overlooked.

Temporary addresses are used in many situations, including file open and close and query execution. If the machine runs out of addresses, *it stops*, and an IPL must be performed before work can continue. The current percentage usage of permanent and temporary addresses is shown only on the WRKSYSSTS screen (see Figs 3.6 and 8.13) and should be reviewed daily if you do not IPL daily. It could be the trigger which governs the frequency of IPL required by your system.

9.15.7   Allocating a separate subsystem for remote users

For operational reasons it can occasionally be necessary to perform ENDSBS and
STRSBS on a subsystem supporting remote users. This may be because of some
communications error. If the remote site is using the same subsystem as your other
users, they will all have to stop work as well. A separate subsystem for users on
each line will enable you to correct problems with remote sites without affecting
other users. The various subsystems can use the same pool, as long as it is a shared
pool.

9.15.8   Setting up an alternative environment for overnight or weekends

All the recommendations so far in this chapter have referred to the business day
with interactive users as the favoured users. It is also important to consider
performance and tuning for other times. The work is obviously likely to be of a
batch type and all the recommendations about batch in this chapter still hold true.
So there is nothing new.

However, you should give thought to how you leave the system after the
business day so that best use is made of resource and none is wasted. Interactive
subsystems must be stopped. You may need to implement an automatic procedure
which closes down these subsystems when all users have gone and another which
starts them up at the right time in the morning. This will leave the available storage
for use by whatever subsystems you require overnight. These can also be started
automatically.

9.15.9   Disk housekeeping

The amount of free disk storage does not normally affect performance until there is
very little storage left. The system will warn at IPL if the user-designated threshold
has been reached. It is a feature of the AS/400 that it can use a lot of disk storage on
items like job logs, journals and history logs which you do not want to keep forever
online. Operational Assistant is a very handy tool for preventing the disks
gradually becoming full without your noticing.

Be aware that if a threshold message is missed and the system continues until it
really is full, the resulting situation is not pleasant. Avoid it at all costs.

9.15.10 Reducing exceptional wait time

In Table 8.1 you will record how much exceptional wait time each transaction is
experiencing on average. Often this is a result of application design or running
some interactive work at a lower priority than others. However, there may be
something you can do about exceptional wait time caused by locks. If the lock

conflicts are between a batch function and an interactive function, alternative scheduling of batch may reduce the wait time.

9.15.11 Reducing IPL time after an abnormal termination

Prior to OS/400 Version 3.1, unless access path journalling had been implemented, the recovery of access paths after an abnormal termination could take a long time and cause significant downtime in some cases. From Version 3.1 System Managed Access Path Protection (SMAPP) is available to substantially reduce the time to recover access paths. The user sets the target recovery time to a value between 10 minutes and 24 hours. The SMAPP function then calculates to what level it needs to protect files in order to meet the target and will automatically implement the required protection.

In order to provide the protection SMAPP uses a function similar to access path journalling with less system overhead. The system overhead will vary with the number, size and volatility of files and also the target time specified. You may need to set the target time in light of the system overhead. If you are not using access path journalling you should consider using SMAPP.

9.16   Communications considerations

9.16.1 Balancing the load on communications facilities

The data transmission component of the response experienced by users attached to the AS/400 via communications lines is subject to the utilization of the communications line, the remote controller to which they are attached and the AS/400 communications adapter. The Performance Tools/400 Component Report gives information about the utilization of these resources which should be reviewed against the guidelines in Table 4.1.

Where you have over-utilization of a line, you should check the error statistics. High utilization could be caused by resulting retransmissions. The Performance Tools/400 Advisor produces very clear information on this subject.

When a communications line is over-utilized and it is the only one to the location concerned, your only courses of action are to increase the speed of the line or lower the traffic on the line. Where you have multiple lines running to the location with multiple remote workstation controllers and one is over-utilized, you have the option of attempting to balance the load across the lines and controllers. The following are reasonable objectives in this situation:

- Spread high-activity users across the lines and controllers
- Move printers onto their own line and controller if possible, away from users.

Where you have multiple controllers on one line (multi-point) you can attempt to balance the controller load in the same way. However, this will not help if the line itself is over-utilized.

The amount of line traffic generated by remote users is a function of how busy they are and the design of the applications. Good design should minimize line traffic by use of various techniques and avoidance of others. Such techniques are beyond the scope of this book but are discussed in the *Performance Management 'Red Book'* (see Bibliography).

9.16.2 Increasing remote print throughput

Since the advent of the 5394 workstation controller, it has been possible to take advantage of larger SNA buffers and SNA pacing values to increase remote printer throughput. This is more appropriate where printers are on a dedicated line and controller rather than sharing with interactive users. Increasing the printer throughput may degrade the interactive response of users sharing the line/ controller. However, you could experiment on a shared line and review the results. The following parameter changes should be tried:

- AS/400 line description—MAXFRAME size 521 or larger
- AS/400 controller description for the 5394 or 5494 controller—MAXFRAME size 521 or *LINKTYPE
- AS/400 printer device description—MAXLENRU(*CALC) and PACING between 3 and 7

This guideline applies specifically to the 5394 Release 2.2 and OS/400 Version 1.3 and later.

9.16.3 Minimizing recovery and retries

The principles of this were discussed in the Sec. 9.4.2 on the system value QCMNRCYLMT. We recommended a value of (2 5) for this system value in order to limit the number of retries after an error. AS/400 line and control unit descriptions have a parameter CMNRCYLMT. Ensure that this parameter contains sensible values, or defaults to the system value. Remember specifying (*n* 0) where *n* is non-zero, can cause infinite retries and associated overhead.

9.16.4 Reducing the polling of inactive controllers on a multi-point line

Where multiple control units are attached to a line and you expect that some of these will often be inactive (in a powered-off state) while others are communicating, it may be desirable to alter certain defaults to minimize the overhead of polling. The controllers could be varied off until they are actually needed, but this will require operator intervention.

Alternatively, you may specify values for the line description parameter CNNPOLLTMR and the control unit description parameter NDMPOLLTMR. The default for CNNPOLLTMR is 30 which means that when the system polls one of the inactive controllers it will wait for 3 seconds before continuing with other activity on the line. A setting of 5 (one half second) could be better in this situation.

In addition, you can limit the frequency of polling by specifying a large value for NDMPOLLTMR such as 900. This means the controller will only be polled every 90 seconds. Be aware that this will mean a potentially long delay between turning on the controller and receiving a sign on screen. The Performance Tools Advisor and the Resource Interval report will tell you how much time is being wasted in this area. Be aware also that a change in OS/400 implementation at some future stage may render the above recommendation unnecessary.

9.16.5 Optimizing the sharing of a multi-point line by remote workstation controllers

By default, where there are remote workstation controllers sharing a multi-point line, the system will send seven frames to a controller, expect an acknowledgement and then move on to the next controller. This is normally fine except where the seven frames are not enough to hold all the data outstanding for the controller. In this case a possible symptom is that some users will sit for an extended period with their screens only partly painted and the input inhibited indicator on. If this does occur, you can change the OUTLIMIT parameter from the default of 0 to 1 or 2. With 1, 14 frames can be sent before the system moves on to the next controller and with 2, 21.

Use this with care. For instance, setting one controller to a higher value will penalise the other controllers on the line.

9.16.6 Optimizing SDLC line throughput via line and control u it parameters

With SDLC communications there are certain parameters which allow you to change:

- The size of the SDLC frame (MAXFRAME)
- The number of frames which can be sent without requiring acknowledgement (MAXOUT).

Note that the maximum allowed in MAXOUT on the line description depends on the MODULUS parameter setting on that line description.

The degree of control at the AS/400 end depends upon the type of communication and the system/controller with which the AS/400 is communicating. On a point-to-point line which has few errors, the objective for batch data transfer is to use the largest frames possible, and to transmit the largest possible number of frames before an acknowledgement is required. Once again the largest possible will depend on what you are talking to and how.

On a line prone to errors, specifying high values for these parameters could be counterproductive since errors will cause retransmission of more data. If a private line is giving errors, the cause should be tracked down and corrected. On a switched line you can often expect a fair amount of errors although modern communications equipment can help.

Be aware that increasing throughput by using high values in the above parameters will normally only make substantial improvements where large amounts of data are being transferred, e.g. with batch data transfer or printing. Where batch and interactive are mixed on a single line, raising these parameters is likely to improve batch throughput but degrade interactive response times. You should use this advice with care and always monitor closely after any change. Using larger frame sizes and fewer acknowledgements also reduces the CPU overhead.

9.16.7 Optimizing line throughput via SNA device and session parameters

In addition to the optimization of throughput at the system to controller level (Sec. 9.16.6) there are parameters which can be specified at the device level:

- The Response Mode
- The size of the Request/Response Unit (MAXLENRU)
- The number of RUs that can be sent before an acknowledgement is required (pacing).

It is not within the scope of this book to discuss the various layers of SNA. The RU size and pacing are roughly equivalent to the frame size and number of frames as discussed in Sec. 9.16.6 but operate at a different level. The RU size is the amount of data sent as a single entity. The pacing value is the number of RUs which can be sent without requiring an acknowledgement.

On the link one RU may cover several SDLC frames or form only part of one frame. When setting the RU size, you should take into account the frame size. Use an RU size which is slightly smaller than a multiple of the frame size. This will allow the RUs and the header information to be sent in a the minimum number of frames rather than requiring an extra frame to send a last small part of the RU.

As with frame sizes, in order to improve batch throughput we are looking to make RUs large and to send a large number before an acknowledgement is required. Once again there is more scope for control of these parameters with Advanced Peer-to-Peer Communications(*) (APPC) programming than with remote workstations. Increasing the parameter values is not advised where batch and interactive workloads are sharing the line.

Using larger RUs and fewer acknowledgements also reduces the CPU overhead. When the AS/400 is communicating with an IBM mainframe or equivalent host, most of the control over such parameters is within the host configuration rather than the AS/400.

The Response Mode can be set at either definite or exception. Definite response mode requires negative and positive acknowledgements whereas exception response mode requires only negative acknowledgements.

In Advanced Peer-to-Peer Networking(*) (APPN) communications there is also the option to specify high, medium and low priority in the Class of Service (TMSPTY parameter). APPN supports adaptive pacing, which can minimize the effect batch transfer has on higher-priority work such as interactive, and still allow batch to operate with high values when interactive is absent. This assumes that the classes of service are set appropriately, i.e. with batch at low priority, interactive at high priority, RU length of *CALC and 7 for pacing.

9.16.8 Optimizing token ring LAN throughput via line and control unit parameters

The principle here is very much the same as in Sec. 9.16.6. You should use the largest frame size available to you via the MAXFRAME parameter on the AS/400 line description. The largest available will depend on the speed of the LAN and the maximum supported by any machines or equipment on the LAN.

The frequency of sending acknowledgements is controlled by the LANACKFRQ parameter. When to expect acknowledgement is controlled by the LANMAXOUT parameter. Both of these are on the control unit description.

LANACKFRQ should never have a larger value on a system than the value of LANMAXOUT on the other system. A reasonable guideline is to set LANACKFRQ to half the value of LANMAXOUT and to set them the same on sending and receiving systems. For interactive environments the value of *CALC for both can often be the optimum. Where large amounts of data are transferred, other settings may be more appropriate such as LANACKFRQ 2, LANMAXOUT 4.

9.16.9 Options for batch data transfer

If you have a requirement to exchange data with another system via a communications link there are many options available to you on the AS/400. These will obviously be limited by the type of system at the other end, and by the software you use to execute the exchange. If the link is to another AS/400 the main choices are APPC programming, Distributed Data Management(DDM), Object Distribution Facility(*) (ODF) and the File Transfer Subroutine(*) (FTS).

The best performance can be provided by user written APPC programs if they are written correctly. Therefore, if you have a very critical requirement and access to an AS/400 communications programmer, you may choose this course.

ODF sends data efficiently across the link but the data must be placed on a distribution queue at the sending end, and received from the network file into the AS/400 database at the receiving end. This increases the start to end time. Using file copy (CPYF) with DDM will normally provide a higher transfer rate than ODF. If choosing between DDM and ODF, you would probably choose DDM for speed. However, ODF is very simple to use and allows transfer of many types of objects as well as data files. You would probably not select FTS from a performance viewpoint except where a slow communications line is used and the data benefits well from data compression.

9.16.10 Using pre-start jobs to speed program start requests from remote systems

In an environment where program to program communications are used it is common for a remote program to request the evocation of a program on a communicating system. When this occurs the remote program has to wait for a full job start on the target system. This is time consuming.

Pre-start jobs are initiated prior to any request arriving, and are ready to communicate with the remote program. They are controlled by pre-start job entries in the associated subsystem. For a full description of how to implement them, refer to the relevant chapter in the *Work Management Guide*.

9.16.11 Consider use of data compression

Data compression is a method of reducing the number of characters sent across a link (or held on tape) by using algorithms which do such things as remove repeated characters. The algorithms are reversed at the far end to recreate the original data stream. The indicators which point to improved throughput from data compression are:

- The nature of the data is such that compression yields a significantly shorter data stream. For instance, compressed text tends to be much shorter than uncompressed text owing to blank compression, whereas binary data does not benefit so much.
- The speed of the link is comparatively slow, so that the time for the CPU to perform data compression is more than compensated for by the reduced line time.

With APPC communications you can request compression via the DTACPR network attribute, and via the DTACPR parameter in a mode description.

9.16.12 Disclaimer

Before we leave the topic on tuning in a communications environment, it would be wise to point out that we have been able to give only a limited insight into controlling the performance of communications. An expert in this area would see gaps, and possibly some over-simplification. For instance, we have concentrated on SNA communications. We have not discussed TCP/IP(*) or Binary Synchronous communications. Neither have we discussed anything specific to the X.25 Packet Switched Service(*). For further information relating to performance with communications you should refer to the *Communications Management Guide* manual and the *Performance Management Red Book*. In addition, this is an area in which we can expect to see changes in new releases of software. If you have critical communications which you wish to tune to the optimum, you may be well advised to employ the services of a communications specialist.

9.17   Considerations for PCs attached to the AS/400

PCs attached to the AS/400 can operate in many different ways and some of the most common are:

* Using 5250 type workstation emulators to access interactive AS/400 applications without using PC Support or Client Access/400
* Using WSF or workstation emulators like Rumba/400(*) to access interactive AS/400 applications using PC Support or Client Access/400
* Using the file transfer function of PC Support or Client Access/400 to transfer data files to and from the PC
* Making AS/400 act as a PC file server by using shared folders
* Using client/server type applications with cooperating components on the PC and the AS/400 which use techniques such as remote command, DRDA(*), ODBC(*), APPC, Remote SQL, data queues, EHLLAPI(*), etc—the list is endless (see Glossary)
* As printers where the AS/400 sends spooled output to the PC for printing on a locally attached PC printer
* Using virtual printing where the AS/400 acts as a set of print servers.

   When using non-PC Support 5250 emulation the load on the AS/400 is the same as for a non-intelligent terminal. Operating PC Support workstation emulation the load on the AS/400 is only slightly greater than that of a non-intelligent workstation performing similar functions. When operating as printers they represent a workload similar to an attached printer.

   When using file transfer the workload on the AS/400 can be high if many users are transferring large numbers of records at the same time. The effect is that of multiple batch jobs running at once and tuning action should be similar to that for multiple batch jobs (see Sec. 9.11).

When using shared folders to make the AS/400 act as a file server the performance will be noticeably inferior to a true PC-based server. However, this situation has improved in OS/400 V3.1 for LAN-based PCs with the introduction of the File Server Input Output Processor (FSIOP). This AS/400 LAN attachment card with its onboard PC provides access to AS/400 disk at speeds consistent with standalone PC servers.

For client/server applications the load on the AS/400 will vary greatly depending upon the amount of data traffic and upon the efficiency of the mechanisms used for the connection. The AS/400 Server Series are specifically optimized for this environment. Where you are attaching a large number of PCs predominantly to run client/server type applications to an AS/400 you may wish to consider the option of a separate Server Series model.

9.17.1 Communications subsystem

If your system supports a large number of attached PCs you should consider running the associated communications jobs in a separate pool. As shipped the default is that these jobs run in the QCMN subsystem which runs in the base pool. When PC Support/400 or Client Access/400 is started on a PC there is heavy activity until the connection process is complete. If the base pool is also being used for batch work at a time when many PCs are trying to connect, the system may be overloaded.

Remember that the base pool is the default for many subsystems and also for 'bad boy' jobs which get shifted there if they exceed their time slice when you specify *BASE for the QTSEPOOL system value. It is also used frequently by system routines such as file open/close, evoked by jobs in other pools. The loading will also be increased on a irregular basis if you have specified that the PC performs automatic download of PTF's or in-house applications. So if starting a PC on your system seems slow, check if the base pool is overloaded and make appropriate adjustments.

9.17.2 Shared folders

If you are using the Basic DOS option of PC Support use Shared Folders Type 2 if possible. Extended DOS users do not have to make a choice. This will reduce CPU utilization compared with previous types. Be aware that type 2 folders take up more PC storage and also can affect the performance of other users on the AS/400 since Shared Folder type 2 file transfer runs at priority 0.

A subsystem on the AS/400 called QXFPCS handles Basic DOS type 2 and Extended DOS shared folder access requests. This subsystem gets started automatically when the first PC connects and assigns a drive to a shared folder. You can speed up the first PC's drive assignment time by putting the STRSBS

QIWS/QXFPCS command in the system start-up program. You can manage this subsystem like any other and affect its performance by adjusting its pool size.

Shared folder performance can also be controlled by the size of memory cache on the PC. If you use PC applications that continuously access specific files in a shared folder (e.g. an application that uses a PC file as a database as opposed to intermittently loading programs or copying files from the shared folder) then you should set up your memory cache carefully as documented in the DOS/OS2 installation guides.

Another factor to improve the shared folder's performance is the size of the communications buffer. The size of this buffer can be set between 1K and 64K bytes in conventional or expanded memory. Increasing the buffer size generally improves shared folder performance at a cost of losing the use of the memory. However, do not assume that by using a 64K buffer you will get the best performance. You should experiment with your particular configuration to determine the optimum figure for your installation. Both the memory cache size and the communications buffer size are set by using the Shared Folders option of the PC Support Configuration Program or equivalent.

9.17.3   Integrated File System (IFS)

The Integrated File System(*) (IFS) announced with OS/400 Version 3.1 provides potential performance improvement over shared folders.

9.17.4   Further information

For further information on performance where PCs are attached, refer to *PC Support/400 Implementation and Performance* manual (see Bibliography).

9.18   Tuning a newly installed AS/400

In this section we discuss the tuning of a new system that is not yet supporting a regular workload. As soon as you do have a regular workload you can proceed as for an installed system as discussed in the major part of this chapter. If workload is implemented over a number of phases, you will need to review the tuning at each phase.

9.18.1   Action list

1. Record recommendations for setting of system values affecting performance. (see Sec. 9.4). You will need to make estimates for certain values which depend upon the workload. The important ones to consider at this stage are:

QMCHPOOL
QBASPOOL
QBASACTLVL
QCTLSBSD
QPFRADJ

2. Perform an initial estimate of desirable subsystem/storage pool allocation. (see Sec. 9.5).
3. Make initial tuning changes (see Sec. 9.6).

10
Discriminating between applications

10.1   Class distinction and other systems of privilege

Up to this point we have concerned ourselves mainly with optimizing overall system performance. An underlying democratic assumption has been made which could be summarized as 'fair shares for all' or 'all interactive users are created equal'. We have dealt with average performance figures and system-wide performance criteria, with little regard for differing individual needs.

This is not to say that a class hierarchy does not exist. Sec. 3.5 on work management explained how the task despatcher operates a rigid priority scheme for CPU access, and how jobs get their priority by association with a *class* object. Normally system tasks take precedence, the console is the king of user jobs, spool writers are the aristocracy, interactive users are middle class and batch jobs are looked down on by everybody else (Fig. 10.1).

When it comes to sharing out memory, the normal arrangement is to make it available on an 'as required' basis. This means that residency is determined partly by activity, and the priority hierarchy again tends to dominate, although we have seen how partitioning of main memory can be used to positively discriminate in favour of underprivileged or other groups of users.

We have also seen that data is spread over disk actuators in a way that tends to even out the average activity, and by default takes no account of individual job requirements; nor even of job class. The disk activity is determined by the requirements of the most active jobs, which again is controlled by run priority.

None of the default arrangements between the main classes of work (e.g. interactive, batch and spool) have to be accepted. Even if we do decide to accept them as a basis for operations, we can still identify individual jobs or groups within a class which are to receive different treatment from their peers. The purpose of this chapter is to summarize how we can 'separate the sheep from the goats' in our flock of users. Most of the methods have been discussed previously in a different context, and require little further explanation.

In addition to tailoring the default access priorities as between different components of the workload, the apparent complexity of parts of the workload

Console	Spool	Interactive	Batch
(royal class)	(aristocratic class)	(business class)	(working class)
RUNPTY = 10	RUNPTY = 15	RUNPTY = 20	RUNPTY = 50

Figure 10.1.   Class distinction.

may also be modified. We will limit ourselves to techniques which do not require application redesign or recoding.

10.2   Enhancing execution priority for selected jobs

In the previous section we referred to the overriding importance of run priority in gaining access to system resources, and hence controlling performance. If we wish to promote a job or group of jobs the primary mechanism must be priority adjustment.

In Sec. 3.3.4 a general method is described whereby a group of users is given a different priority from the norm by virtue of their use of a special job description. The job description contains special routing data which links to a special class during job initiation. The actions needed to achieve this result are listed in Sec. 9.12. We recommend this approach for interactive users because it avoids the maintenance difficulty associated with multiple interactive subsystems.

Batch jobs can be controlled most simply by having one subsystem per batch stream, as described in Sec. 9.11. The same section illustrates how different classes can be used in the subsystems to differentiate the priorities of the batch streams.

If the priority required is not constant throughout the life of the job, the job might adjust its own priority, most simply by executing the CL command:

```
CHGJOB    RUNPTY(nn)
```

as required, or less directly through use of the RRTJOB command. The CHGJOB command can also be issued externally, say by an operator, to vary the priority of a job.

We have previously (Chapter 3) described various circumstances in which the system will automatically make temporary adjustments to job priority. These include seize or lock contention, and I/O-intensive situations.

Great care must be used in selecting the jobs which are given privileged priorities. Extra benefits for the few will be paid for by the many, and although this may be exactly what you want in general, promotion of long-running CPU intensive jobs carries this principle to extremes. One such job could take over the system (unless you have multiple main processors) and bring all other jobs to a halt.

The default priorities give precedence to spool and interactive jobs, which normally spend most of their life in long wait states interspersed with brief spurts of activity. It is exactly these characteristics which enable a job to profit from enhanced priority without undue impact on other users.

10.3   Providing an exclusive pool for selected jobs

If a job or jobs have been promoted by improving the run priority, it follows from the general tuning principles of Chapter 9 that a separate pool should also be provided. Where granting such a significant distinction as a better priority is considered too generous, we can still give some advantage to a subset of users by giving them exclusive use of a main storage pool.

To be of much use there should be sufficient memory in the pool to allow users to operate with the PURGE(*NO) paging algorithm, as explained in Sec. 9.10. The way to do this is described in Sec. 9.12 except that the class should specify normal execution priority.

10.4   Providing exclusive disk units for selected jobs

In a normal interactive plus batch environment a large number of concurrently active jobs access database records and other objects in a more or less random way, and it is not possible to predict the sequence of I/O requests that will arise. Overall performance is optimized by achieving an even spread of I/O activity across the actuators, and experience shows that the algorithm used by OS/400 storage management to allocate space for objects generally achieves this end without user intervention.

We have already discussed (Sec. 9.8) what to do if the default storage allocation algorithm doesn't get it right first time. Another option we have is to remove one or more actuators from the system auxiliary storage pool (ASP) and manage the contents of this user ASP ourselves. A total of 15 user ASPs can be defined in addition to the system ASP, and their primary function is to improve system availability by reducing the need to restore backup following a catastrophic disk failure.

The responsibility of keeping track of free space in multiple ASPs, and the potential negative effect on system performance due to uneven activity, count against user ASPs. However, in some circumstances performance benefits can be obtained which more than compensate, even without accounting for improved availability.

Consider a batch job which processes two large input files sequentially and produces a new output file. If the data is sorted and the three files are placed in three separate user ASPs shared with no other concurrently referenced data, there will be no contention for the actuators. Physical reads and writes will occur with no actuator movement other than a periodic one-track seek. If batch run times are your main concern, it would be difficult to devise a more favourable set-up.

A similar but much more commonly practised strategy is to place each active journal receiver in a dedicated ASP. Writing entries to the receiver is somewhat akin to the database file output function in the job described above, and the same considerations apply. In a system which uses commitment control and involves much database update and add activity, writing to the journal receiver generates synchronous I/Os which can significantly add to response times. A dedicated actuator will then substantially benefit multiple jobs.

An additional functional benefit also accrues because if the system ASP is lost, the receiver is intact, and contains all database changes up to the time of the crash (for journalled files).

Both the foregoing examples could be implemented successfully using relatively slow disks, since seeks are minimized. If the configuration includes a mix of disk types, the older, less sprightly, hardware could be employed. The inverse argument also applies. Suppose that some critical applications perform lots of direct record access by key. If the relevent files are placed on the fastest units, significant performance benefits can be obtained.

Here, admittedly, we are suggesting more supervision and adjustment of disk space and activity than most AS/400 installation managers would contemplate. A far simpler solution would be to replace the slower disk units so that the whole configuration is equally fast. A further justification for this approach comes from the superior reliability of new disk technology.

10.5   Reducing physical I/Os for selected jobs

The importance of minimizing the number of physical I/Os, and the system tuning
techniques for doing it, have been emphasized and explained at various points in
this book. Where system resources are insufficient to apply a technique on a
system-wide basis, we may, of course, be able to apply it selectively to our most
critical jobs. The following list refers to sections where the relevent methods are
described:

1. *Revision.* For revision of physical versus logical I/Os, synchronous versus
   asynchronous I/Os and a description of the effect of reducing disk I/Os see Secs
   1.3.1, 1.3.2 and 1.3.7.
2. *Add memory to the exclusive pool and use PURGE(*NO).* See Secs 3.6.1, 3.6.2
   and 9.10.
3. *Use the SETOBJACC command to control the loading of small files and programs into an exclusive pool.* See Sec. 3.6.4. Explicit placement of entire active
   files and programs into a specially reserved pool with no paging activity can
   dramatically improve the performance of multiple jobs. The key is to identify
   files and programs which are very active, and files which are small enough to
   justify the memory expenditure.One example might be a small file which is
   accessed by a large number of different keys, so many that it is necessary to
   build the access paths on the fly at run time. The access path build, though still
   a heavy task, will be faster if no disk accesses are required for database records.
   Another example might be a program which is used by a large number of users.

    As usual when we redistribute resources, the effects will be both positive and
   negative. Preloading files and programs will be a matter of trial and error, and
   the net benefit needs to be assessed by performance measurement. The following procedure implements the technique. After testing, the commands used
   would presumably be incorporated into a CL program.

   (a) Define a private memory pool in a subsystem, large enough to hold the
   objects in question, and do not route any jobs into the pool. A private pool
   is used to avoid the storage being stolen by the dynamic performance
   adjustment support.

   (b) Clear the pool of all existing objects:

```
CLRPOOL     POOL(subsystem-name pool-id)
```

   Note that the run time for this function depends on the number of changed
   pages in the pool and can be lengthy. Each changed page is written to disk
   synchronously, one at a time. Assuming about 20 ms per write, in a 100
   MB pool 20 per cent populated with changed pages (40 000 pages), the disk
   time would be roughly $40 \times 20 = 800$ seconds. In a 25 MB pool with only
   10 per cent changed pages the disk time would reduce proportionately to

about 100 seconds. The CLRPOOL command is uninterruptable; once issued it will complete.

(c) Place each object required into the pool:

```
SETOBJACC   OBJ(library-name/object-name)
            OBJTYPE(*FILE or *PGM)
            POOL(subsystem-name pool-id)
            MBR(*FIRST or member-name)
            MBRDATA(*BOTH or *ACCPTH or *DATA)
```

This command loads the object using large blocking factors and parallel overlapped I/Os. It also clears any parts of the object from other storage pools.

(d) Remove each object from main storage when it is no longer required:

```
SETOBJACC   OBJ(library-name/object-name)
            OBJTYPE(*FILE or *PGM)
            POOL(*PURGE)
```

Note that record updates and additions will result in normal disk output activity.

4. *Block data transfers to and from disk.*   See Secs 1.3.7, 3.6.5 and 9.13. Where a significant amount of sequential file processing is done, we have seen that blocking data transfers can make a big difference to performance by reducing the number of physical I/Os required. This is most often done with batch jobs, but is also appropriate for interactive jobs which use sequential processing within limits to search the database. The following procedure can be used to implement this technique:

(a) Sort the files concerned periodically, so that the physical record sequence reflects the processing sequence and deleted records are dropped. If this is not done, blocking may well be counter-productive: each block will contain many unwanted records which will be overwritten on the next logical read.

```
RGZPFM   FILE(name) MBR(name or *FIRST)
         KEYFILE(*FILE or name)
```

Added records are normally inserted at the physical end of the data, and updates which change the key remain at the same relative record number position in the file. Therefore the benefits of blocking will be gradually eroded, and after a period of time depending on the frequency of such additions and updates the files need to be reorganized.

Note that an alternative method of sorting files is provided by the FMTDTA command which is directed by sort specification source statements. This is a more comprehensive function sort utility which can merge up to eight input files into a single sorted output file.

(b) Execute the following database override command as part of each selected job, for every sequentially processed file. This must be done before the files are opened by the job.

```
OVRDBF   FILE(name) NBRRCDS(number)
```

The number of records per block can be adjusted for optimum performance, which will depend on the availability of memory in the pool. The number of records multiplied by the record length should currently be less than or equal to 32KB. *Note.* If the selected jobs are running as the only jobs in a shared pool we could simply activate the Expert Cache function for this pool, and avoid having to insert the override statements in the jobs. The question is whether the system overhead used to monitor the pool and dynamically change the blocking is a price worth paying. If the number of jobs involved is small, it is worth doing the job yourself.

10.6   Special batch considerations

In addition to the general techniques covered above, which apply to batch and interactive jobs alike, there are some particular methods that are more appropriate to the batch environment.

1. *Run multiple independent batch streams.*   See Secs 1.2.4, 1.2.5 and 9.11. In a normally tuned system, batch jobs are the lowest-priority user jobs, and are expected to use whatever CPU time is not taken up by other work. The number of concurrent batch job streams is selectable and has implications for performance as well as operational convenience. If the number of concurrent batch streams is too small, the batch work is unable to use all the available CPU cycles and the wasted capacity results in lower overall batch throughput. If the number is too large, one or more streams will occupy memory unproductively. The optimum number depends on the CPU usage by higher-priority jobs, and the character of the batch jobs themselves, all of which are likely to vary from minute to minute.
   The relative costs of providing CPU power and main storage space suggest that we should err on the side of too many batch streams to ensure that the CPU operates at peak capacity for as much time as possible. Requirements for serial execution of batch jobs and possibilities of contention between concurrent batch jobs may limit our ability to carry out this plan.
2. *Split long-running batch jobs.*   A special case of the multi-programming recommendation given above occurs when a dedicated batch stream is used, because the jobs must be run in sequence. If the run time is too long, and one or more long-running jobs cause low CPU utilization, the possibility of splitting these jobs should be investigated.
   Low CPU utilization usually correlates with high synchronous disk I/O activity. However, low CPU utilization will result even without such activity on an *n*-way processor model, unless the job can be split. On a four-way processor such as an F97 or a 320-2052 four concurrent jobs are required to avoid leaving processors (each representing 25 per cent of the system capacity) completely idle.

Often the processing carried out by a job can be divided between two or more jobs running in parallel. The CPU is thereby kept busier and the processing completes sooner. Run times can often be reduced to a small fraction of the original values in this way. For best results the original CPU utilization should be low, and the configuration should be able to support the resulting much higher I/O rate. Strictly speaking, this approach involves application changes and falls outside the scope of the book. However, the changes are minor in relation to the benefits, and you should be well placed to identify the potential and press for implementation.

3. *Drop or defer unnecessary processing.* Perhaps surprisingly we have several times encountered situations where batch streams include jobs which perform no useful function. This can happen when a package solution is used, and it is inadequately tailored to a specific user's needs. Lengthy reporting jobs whose output is never printed because it is irrelevant to the way your business works are not that uncommon, particularly if the package was developed in another country.

Sometimes unnecessary programs are removed, but unnecessary files and access paths remain. These can cause significant maintenance overhead both for batch and interactive work. An audit of file and access path usage is recommended. This will also pick up the logical file you created six months ago for a one-off demonstration, and forgot to delete. A sequence of jobs with a critical completion time window may contain steps which could be taken out and run later.

10.7   Printing considerations

Spooled output is placed on the designated output queue, and by default becomes available for printing by an associated print writer when the job closes the printer file. This is normally the best option, since multiple jobs will be feeding output concurrently to the queue. When the spool file is complete the writer can print it at close to the printer's rated speed without fear of being delayed by the job producing the report.

In a situation where a user or a small group have their own dedicated workstation printer a different option may give a better perception of performance. The SCHEDULE parameter of the spool file can be given the value '*IMMED'. In this case the print writer starts printing when there is a block of output ready to send to the device, and continues in parallel with the print job.

The attribute can be changed 'permanently' in the printer file used by the user(s), or by executing an OVRPRTF command within the job(s). It can also be changed interactively while reviewing the output queue.

11
Case notes

The purpose of this chapter is to help you understand the most common causes of systems not performing to their full capability. We will try to do this by describing a few typical situations in which the authors were involved. Although no company names are revealed and only the most salient details in each case are presented, they are drawn from real life. They may also provide a little light relief.

We have quoted only cases where poor performance was at least in part caused by inappropriate system tuning. In something like 70 per cent of cases of poor performance, the cause lies in the design and implementation of the applications involved. The remainder are almost entirely due to overloaded machines i.e. lack of effective capacity planning. It is rare to find situations where system tuning alone can transform the performance of the machine.

One or two exceptions to this rule are quoted here to encourage you to keep looking. In those cases, the situation before tuning could best be described as wilful abuse of the system, or wilful neglect of application requirements. On the other hand, very few installations are tuned optimally, and in most cases of poor performance, bad system tuning is a contributory factor.

In almost all cases the values of QTOTJOB and QACTJOB were incorrectly set and quite often QDEVRCYACN was also set inappropriately. See Sec. 9.4 for recommendations. You will notice that in most cases the average response time before tuning looks acceptable. However, the average often hides a multitude of poor responses which are only apparent from the PRTCPTRPT or PRTTNSRPT output.

The recommendations on memory allocation were always only a starting point. Further adjustments could be beneficial, and use of automatic performance adjustment could optimize storage allocation in a more dynamic way as workloads fluctuate.

11.1   Situation 1—Divided we fall

11.1.1   Background

- System installed—AS/400 B60 with 48 MB of main memory
- Number of users—200
- Performance just acceptable at perceived average response time of 4 seconds
- Some system tuning carried out in-house
- Requirement—advice on further tuning

11.1.2   Observations

Performance indicator	Observed	Comments
Average response time	1.2 s	Better than perceived
Interactive and system CPU utilization	Near 65%	System near maximum at peak load
Total CPU utilization	96%	OK
Disk actuator utilization	LT 40%	OK
Page faults per second all pools	30 +	High, examine memory allocation
Authority lookups	Up to 125/s	Cost 14% of B60 CPU, indicates many private authorities
Users signing on/off	Frequent	Costly

Memory allocation

Pool number	Storage	Activity level	Use
1	9 193	N/A	Machine pool
2	7 259	8	QCTL/batch/SNADS
3	5 000	40!	Interactive
4	2 500	40!!	Interactive
5	1 500	3	
6	1 700	20	Communications
7	1 200	1	
8	4 800	6	Programmers—interactive and batch!!
9	750	7	Spool
10	250	15	
11	15 000	25	Interactive

11.1.3   Recommendations

Combine the priority 20 interactive pools and reduce the total activity level. Separate batch from *BASE and the interative pools.

1. Alternate initial memory allocation

Pool number	Storage	Activity level	Use
1	9 000	N/A	Machine pool
2	3 000	5	QCTL/SNADS/communications
3	400	1	Dynamically allocated/de-allocated
4	1 500	5	Communications
5	1 200	3	
6	800	2	Batch
7	800	2	Programmers' batch
8	4 800	8	Programmers (priority 30)
9	500	7	Spool
10	26 000	40	Interactive

2. Prevent access to job queues in the interactive subsystems.
3. Reconsider practice of users signing on and off so frequently. Consider use of DSCJOB instead.
4. Reconsider current implementation of security. Reduce private authorizations if possible.

11.1.4 Results

Customer reported much reduced page fault rates, and a significant reduction in average response time down to 0.98 s. Revision of access control strategy reduced CPU overhead to 5 per cent.

11.2 Situation 2—Don't lose your memory

11.2.1 Background

- System installed—AS/400 B70 with 64 MB of main memory
- Number of users—150
- Interactive throughput—10 000 transactions per hour at peak load
- Performance not highly rated normally but perceived poor at month-end peak interactive load concurrent with payroll processing
- Requirement—improvement in interactive and batch performance

11.2.2 Observations

Performance indicator	Observed	Comments
Average response time	1.6 s	
Interactive and system CPU utilization	Near 65%	System near maximum at peak load
Total CPU utilization	99%	OK
Disk actuator utilization	10%	OK
Page faults per second all pools	Up to 50	High—examine memory allocation
Authority lookups	Up to 160/s	Cost 13% of B70 CPU, indicates many private authorities
Busiest communications IOPs	48%/44%	Costly
Interactive job at priority 10	Occasionally	Affects priority 20 users
Average transaction	0.17 CPU s/20 physical disk I/Os	Moderate to complex
Exceptional wait/transaction	0.2 s (peak 0.6 s)	0.6 s significant

Memory allocation

Pool number	Storage	Activity level	Use
1	11 000	N/A	Machine pool
2	14 036	15	QCTL/SNADS/communications
3	7 000	5	Batch
4	22 000	175	Interactive
5	4 000	3	Programmers' batch
6	3 000	2	Unused (in reserve)
7	3 000	2	Unused (in reserve)
8	1 500	10	Spool

11.2.3 Recommendations

1. Alternate initial memory allocation

Pool number	Storage	Activity level	Use
1	11 000	N/A	Machine pool
2	5 000	5	QCTL/SNADS/communications
3	4 000	5	Batch
4	39 536	20	Interactive
5	2 000	10	Spool
6	3 000	2	Programmers' batch
7	1 000	1	Batch

2. Of five communications IOPs, two were utilized over the guideline of 35 per cent. Redistribution of lines over the IOPs could give more equal utilization within the guideline figure on all IOPs.

3. Ask operations staff not to run complex transactions (e.g. WRKACTJOB) at the system console as this runs at priority 10. The one high exceptional wait time coincided with misuse of the system console.

4. Use PURGE(*NO) in the interactive pool.

5. Reconsider current implementation of security. Reduce private authorizations if possible.

6. Consider use of blocking for batch jobs as discussed in Sec. 10.5.

7. Occasional excessively heavy transactions were observed. Set QTSEPOOL to *BASE to minimize the effect of these on other users.

11.2.4 Results

Customer reported reduced page fault rates and an unspecified improvement in response times. Security implementation review under way but changes not yet made.

11.3   Situation 3—Don't lock up your files

11.3.1 Background

- System installed—AS/400 D45 with 64 MB of main memory
- Number of users—100 (many remotely connected)
- Peak interactive throughput—6000 transactions per hour at peak load
- Performance acceptable for some of the time but often poor at higher than usual interactive load. Sometimes extremely bad, apparently when a packaged report writer was used.
- Increase in workload expected.
- Requirement—improvement in performance if possible, pending upgrade

11.3.2 Observations

Performance indicator	Observed	Comments
Average response time	8.8 s periodically 2.0 s normally	
Interactive and system CPU utilization	Average 72%	High, system overloaded at peak periods
Total CPU utilization	Near 100%	
Disk actuator utilization	Always under 35%	OK
Page fault per second all pools	25	OK
Busiest local workstation IOP	Up to 40%	Includes low-priority activity but greater than twice other workstation controllers
Very complex interactive job at priority 10	Frequent	Affects priority 20 users
Private pools	Under-utilized	Memory wasted
Exceptional wait/transaction	Very high during worst periods (approx 7 s)	Seize/lock contention (not associated with suspect package)
Average transaction	0.36 CPU s/22 physical disk I/Os	Fairly complex but should merit about 2 s response

Memory allocation

Pool number	Storage	Activity level	Use
1	11 000	N/A	Machine pool
2	13 436	8	QCTL/communications/batch/interactive
3	500	6	Spool
4	24 000	15	Interactive
5	4 800	3	Interactive
6	4 800	3	Interactive
7	2 500	1	Batch
8	2 500	1	Batch
9	1 000	1	Batch
10	1 000	1	Programmers' batch

11.3.3 Recommendations

1. Alternate initial memory allocation. There were ten separate pools allocated. Use *INTERACT for all interactive users running at priority 20. Specify all other user pools as shared pools and set QPFRADJ to 2 or 3 to allow for adjustment and re-allocation of idle memory.

Pool number	Storage	Activity level	Use
1	9 000	N/A	Machine pool
2	3 436	4	QCTL/communications
3	45 600	20	Interactive
4	500	5	Spool
5	2 500	1	Batch
6	2 500	1	Batch
7	1 000	1	Batch
8	1 000	1	Programmers' batch

2. Consider recabling workstations to even the load on the local workstation controller IOPs.
3. Ask operations staff not to run complex transactions (e.g. WRKACTJOB) at the system console as this runs at priority 10. Submit very complex work such as file copies to batch.
4. The significant exceptional wait was caused mainly by seize contention. A batch job took a lock on a library required by interactive users. The problem was extended because after the batch job obtained the lock, it lost control of the CPU owing to its low priority and was unable to release the lock for some time (V1R1.0 software). An operating system change at the next release would relieve the problem. Therefore install the next release as soon as possible, and meanwhile schedule the batch job to run out of hours.
5. Perform capacity planning with view to an upgrade.

11.3.4 Results

Exceptional performance troughs eliminated. Normal performance marginally improved. Work load monitoring and regular capacity reviews instigated.

11.4 Situation 4—Don't thrash about

11.4.1 Background

- System installed—S/38 M700 with 16 MB of main memory
- Number of users—36 (14 remotely connected)
- Peak interactive throughput—3500 transactions per hour
- Interactive performance perceived not to have improved since upgrade from significantly less powerful system
- Requirement—improvement in performance if possible
- Additional requirements—give priority to order entry department over all other interactive, give lower priority to three developers than all other interactive

Although this is a System/38, the situation is such a good example of where a few minutes spent on system tuning produced a vast improvement in performance that we make no apology for including it. The principles hold true for the AS/400.

11.4.2 Observations

Performance indicator	Observed	Comments
Average response time	2.3 s	
Interactive and system CPU utilization	Always well under 70%	
Disk actuator utilization	Average under 40% but occasional high utilization on some actuators	
Page fault per second all pools	38 (54 at peak)	Very high, examine memory allocation!
Machine pool NDB page fault rates	24 (45 at peak)	Very high, examine memory allocation!!
Average transaction	0.18 CPU s/38 physical disk I/Os	Moderate to complex

Memory allocation

Pool number	Storage	Activity level	Use
1	1 314	N/A	Machine pool
2	9 184	30	QCTL/communications/interactive/ batch/programmers at priority 30
3	1 400	11	Order entry at priority 19
4	200	2	Spool
5	300	2	Batch
6	300	2	Programmers' batch
7	3 000	11	Remote users at priority 20

11.4.3 Recommendations

Alternate initial memory allocation. Inadequate machine pool size is clearly crippling the system through excess page faults. Interactive users in *BASE were running with different priorities. Memory allocation to other pools was not related to activity. Route the three programmers with their priority of 30 into a separate pool, and route the four remote users at priority 20 into the base pool with other priority 20 users. Set all interactive users to PURGE(*NO).

Pool number	Storage	Activity level	Use
1	2 000	N/A	Machine pool
2	11 184	20	QCTL/communications/interactive/ remote users
3	2 000	7	Order entry at priority 19
4	200	3	Spool
5	300	2	Batch
6	300	1	Programmers' batch
7	1 000	3	Programmers at priority 30

11.4.4 Results

Performance indicator	Observed	Comments
Average response time	0.5 s	
Disk actuator utilization	18%	OK
Page fault rates per second	15	OK
Machine pool NDB page fault rates	0.5	OK
Average transaction	0.16 CPU s/eight physical disk I/Os	Moderate

The dramatic improvement in fault rates was achieved by allocating memory where it was needed and by reducing activity levels. This, coupled with the use of PURGE(*NO), reduced the disk utilization. The change in the average transaction resulted from avoidance of unnecessary disk I/Os.

11.5 Keep your brain active

11.5.1 Background

- 'Overnight' batch run of five consecutive steps took 19 hours 17 minutes to complete on a test system.
- Customer required batch run to finish in 3 hours on AS/400 hardware.
- Test system was D80 with 9336 disks. This was close to the top of the range hardware (E90) at the time.

11.5.2 Observations

- CPU utilization averaged 10–13 per cent during the various steps, offering plenty of scope for multiprogramming where appropriate to the processing logic.
- The disk actuator utilization averaged 5 per cent and the total disk I/O rate averaged 88 per second, again leaving plenty of slack to be taken up by concurrent activity.

11.5.3   Recommendations

- Drop step 2 (3 hours 20 minutes duration) which could be run out of sequence and was not essential within the 3-hour window.
- Split step 3 into six parallel jobs to be run concurrently over different portions of the input transaction file. Similarly, split steps 4 and 5 into ten concurrent jobs.
- Load six small frequently used files permanently into a reserved memory pool using a technique equivalent to SETOBJACC.
- Reorganize the larger physical files, sequencing data according to the most important process sequences, and block data transfers from disk up to 32 KB where appropriate.
- Inspect all dependent logical files and reduce the number of maintained access paths if possible. Also check that dynamic select is used in appropriate cases and not in others.

11.5.4   Results

- Run completed in 2 hours 45 minutes on D80.
- CPU utilization averaged 80 per cent for long periods.
- Disk actuator utilization averaged 28 per cent and I/O rate averaged 350 per second.
- Total synchronous I/Os reduced from about 3 million to about 495 000.

Part IV
AS/400 capacity planning

12
Performance and workload monitoring

12.1 Introduction to capacity planning and workload monitoring

Capacity planning is making sure that your installed machine continues to support future workloads while delivering agreed service levels to the users. It is all about keeping users happy (or at least satisfied) with the performance of the system in spite of changes which might threaten this state. The specific underlying objectives of capacity planning are easily summarized, but less easily achieved:

- Identify potential performance resource bottlenecks in the installed machine before user satisfaction is impacted.
- Estimate the configuration changes required to support planned workloads, and the consequent hardware costs.

System throughput capacity results primarily from the CPU power, the number and speed of disk actuators, the main storage size and the number and speed of communications facilities. Planning for adequate performance involves predicting when these resources will reach critical utilization thresholds, and deciding what evasive action to take. Normally the response will be hardware upgrades, but alternatives theoretically include application changes, and restricting/scheduling access to applications.

If you find yourself asking the following sorts of questions, and have difficulty in answering them, you need to establish capacity-planning disciplines within your installation:

- Will performance still be satisfactory when the extra users of one of our applications are connected, or when the new application is installed?
- How much general growth in volumes is supportable by the current configuration, and what are our expected volumes next year?
- Is the current configuration balanced, or are some resources under-utilized due to a bottleneck elsewhere?

- What upgrade would support the proposed workload increments, or provide the required performance improvement, in the most cost-effective way?

There are two essential processes plus one commonly required additional task needed to do the job:

1. Workload and performance monitoring is an on-going and undemanding activity. It can normally be satisfied by filing the output from one or more automatically scheduled weekly performance measurements. A few critical figures should be extracted and plotted to highlight trends. Advice on exactly how to organize this job follows later in the chapter.

2. At regular intervals, say half-yearly, plus whenever significant workload changes are planned, a capacity review should be carried out. This involves examining the workload/performance data over the last period, assessing the impact of business plans on the future workload, and modelling the effects of the changes on the installed machine. Advice on how to do this is the subject of Chapter 13. The output will be an update to the capacity plan in the form of anticipated workload over the next period (say, 12 months) and any consequent changes required to the machine configuration. This job typically takes up to half a day, but additional time may be needed to collect information about business plans, and to produce a report.

3. If your workload is stable or falling, the third process is not required. However, workload volumes seem to increase year by year almost as a rule of nature, in which case the machine hardware will need to be upgraded periodically. The business case for additional hardware arises naturally out of the capacity plan, and should come as no surprise to recipients who have been kept up to date with the capacity situation. Advice on preparing a business case is given in Chapter 14.

The capacity planning tool used to perform the modelling part of the job is, of course, BEST/1, which we used for sizing purposes in Chapter 6. The tool itself is well established, and the reliability of the results will depend almost entirely on the accuracy of the workload estimates. An exercise is provided as an opportunity for further familiarization with the product and some of its additional functions. BEST/1 needs to be thoroughly understood, and there is quite a lot of it for a new user to find out about.

12.2   When to collect the data

Before monitoring the workload on the AS/400 for input to capacity planning, you should ensure that the system is well tuned (see Chapter 9). The mechanics of performance data collection are much the same as described in Chapter 8 except that in most cases they can be initiated automatically. What may require some initial research is identifying *when* to collect the data.

If they are to be suitable for capacity planning, the collection periods must be carefully chosen. For example, if we take a snapshot of the workload when the throughput is low, or when frequently used complex functions are not active, or when abnormal activities are distorting performance, the data will be accurate but unrepresentative. Similarly, an all-day measurement of a fluctuating workload provides average figures which may well include all major workload components, but hides throughput peaks on which we need to base our capacity plan.

The old computer maxim GIGO (garbage in, garbage out) applies here. The model cannot compensate for unspecified inadequacies in the data; it can only reformat and extrapolate from the input it receives. If the data lies, the capacity plan will be a work of fiction.

What is needed is measurement of a normal peak period of interactive activity lasting half an hour to an hour at most, which can be repeated regularly, possibly weekly. The selected periods should meet the following criteria:

- The workload should be representative of a typical mix of functions with no abnormal activity. The best way to confirm this is to collect trace data as well as sample data.
- The workload should be at a peak, and the machine should be coping without exceeding its performance resource utilization thresholds.

Since we need to collect trace data, which uses a significant amount of system resource and produces voluminous output, the collection period should not exceed one hour. Half an hour or 40 minutes is a reasonable standard to adopt. To kick off the data collection we must either wait for a peak to appear and then start the data collection job, or be able to predict when suitable peaks will arise. The latter is often possible, and will allow us to automate the data collection.

12.2.1 Identifying regular workload peaks

If you are unsure how the workload changes from hour to hour and day to day it must be monitored for a week or more to see if a pattern emerges. The following procedure is recommended:

1. Sample workload and performance data throughout the interactive day for at least a week. Do this as follows:
   (a) Check if automatic performance collection is already specified, and temporarily hold any conflicts with the proposed measurements. This is because only one performance collection job can be active at any time.

```
WRKPFRCOL   /* Use option 3 if necessary */
```

(b) Add a collection entry to schedule the data collection.

```
ADDPFRCOL   PFRCOL(name)
            COLDAYS(*MON *TUE *WED *THU *FRI)
            COLSTART(0900)
         INTERVAL(30)
         HOUR(9)
         /* Other parameters take default values */
```

(c) Start the QPFRCOL batch job if it is not already running in the controlling subsystem.

```
STRPFRCOL
```

2. Print the Component Report from each day's data. This command submits a batch job for one report, and can be run any time after the relevant collection period finishes (after 6 pm in this example).

```
PRTCPTRPT   MBR(name)
            /* Other parameters take default values */
```

3. Scan the 'Component Interval Activity' section of the report and note the times when the interactive CPU utilization peaks. Secondary indicators of loading, which are likely to suggest the same peaks, are the total disk I/Os per second and the pool faults per second, both in the same report. The tr/h figure may well not peak at the same times, unless the functional content of the workload is remarkably homogeneous through the day. Note that similar information can be obtained interactively by using the command DSPPFRDTA and selecting the member from the list presented. However, the information is dispersed over a number of screens, and some navigational and arithmetic work is needed to get it together.

4. Repeat steps 1 to 3 over a period of several weeks and review the daily load variations (perhaps with the aid of graphical charts) until you are convinced that one of the following is true:

(a) A fixed half to one hour period during the week normally gives a representative peak interactive workload (e.g. Monday morning between 10:30 am and 11:00 am).

(b) Workload peaks do not occur regularly.

5. Reset the schedule of performance data collections.

12.3   Collecting the data for capacity planning

12.3.1 Regular workload monitoring

If workload fluctuations are predictable, use the automatic collection facilities as follows:

1. Hold or remove conflicting data collection entries.

```
WRKPFRCOL   /* Use option 3 or 4 */
```

2. Add one or more entries to schedule collection of sample and trace data for the identified period(s).

```
ADDPFRCOL   PFRCOL(name)
            COLDAYS(*MON) /* or other day */
            COLSTART(1000)/* or other time */
            INTERVAL(5)
            HOUR(0)        /* or 1 */
            MINUTE(30)      /* or 40 or 0 or other duration */
            TRACE(*ALL)
            /* Other parameters take default values */
```

3. Make a note of the QPFRADJ system value and set it to '0' before the start of each data collection period. Reset it afterwards.

12.3.2 Impromptu workload monitoring

If peaks do not appear regularly they must be identified in some other way. At worst, you may be reduced to sitting at a screen and monitoring the workload manually until a peak arrives. More likely, your previous analysis will have revealed that although peaks are not regular, they coincide with the occurrence of business deadlines or other irregular but predictable events. It is usually possible at least to define periods when peaks are likely.

The most convenient way to watch for peaks is to enter the following command, and then press F19, when the screen similar to Fig. 12.1 appears.

```
WRKSYSACT INTERVAL(20)
```

```
                        Work with System Activity
    Automatic refresh in seconds . . . . . . . . . . . . . . . .    20
    Elapsed time . . . . :    00:00:20      Overall CPU util . . :   8.0


    Type options, press Enter.
      1=Monitor job    5=Work with job
                                             Total  Total
        Job or                          CPU  Sync   Async   PAG     EAO
    Opt  Task      User      Number  Pty Util  I/O    I/O   Fault   Excp
         PSTRNF02D  MAGGIE    173005   20  2.5   0      0      0       0
         PSTRNF09A  FREDA     173011   20  2.3   0      0      0       0
         PSTRNF03F  ADTEAM01  173002   20  1.1   0      0      0       0
         PSTRNF07L  QSYSOPR   172999   20   .8   0      0      0       0
         PSTRNF05J  QSECOFR   173004    1   .5   0      0      0       0
         MPMGR2                        0   .0   1      0      0       0
         MPMGR5                        0   .0   1      0      0       0
         MPMGR3                        0   .0   1      0      0       0
         MPMGR4                        0   .0   1      0      0       0
         MPMGR1                        0   .0   1      0      0       0
                                                               More...
                                                               Bottom
    F3=Exit   F10=Update list   F11=View 2   F12=Cancel   F19=Automatic refresh
    F24=More keys
```

Figure 12.1.   WRKSYSACT display.

The displayed data will then be automatically refreshed every 20 seconds. It lists active jobs by CPU utilization during the previous 20 seconds. Subtracting any low-priority batch utilization from the overall utilization shown at the top gives a series of snapshots of high-priority workload activity.

To terminate automatic refresh mode press the Attention key, or use the System Request key and option '2' to exit from WRKSYSACT altogether. If you have spotted the likely onset of a peak period, proceed as in Sec. 8.4.2, action 1, to measure it.

12.3.3   Selecting data for capacity planning

However the data was arrived at, it cannot be used until it has been carefully screened for suitability. The first step is to print the System, Component and Job Summary reports for each candidate peak period, and extract key workload and performance parameters. This process was described in Sec. 8.4.2, actions 2 to 4.

Next we have to reject data which is unrepresentative, distorted by parallel abnormal events, or collected while the machine was overloaded. An example of an unrepresentative set of data might be where the figures fail to reach anywhere near the level of previous measurements. Another might be if the application mix was very unusual. This can be checked by looking at the 'Job Summary' and 'Interactive Program Statistics' sections of the Job Summary Report.

Abnormal conditions can be identified as described in Sec. 8.4.3, action 5, and overload situations are easily detected by comparing the figures in rows m to p of Table 8.1 with the corresponding thresholds. CPU and disk actuator 'no-go area' thresholds are documented in Table 4.1, while page fault guidelines for good or acceptable performance are presented in Tables 9.7 and 9.8, and more fully in the *Work Management Guide*.

It is essential that data that fails these screening tests is not used for capacity planning. In the case of less than peak volumes or abnormal conditions, clearly the data is unrepresentative and therefore irrelevant. Where overload has occurred the workload characteristics will be skewed, and the data is equally unsuitable for planning. It is too late for planning anyway; what is the point of working out how to shut the stable door, when the horse has already bolted?

The solution here is to examine subpeak workload periods for suitability, and use this data to project the upgrade required for current peak volumes. The process is exactly the same as that described in Chapter 13 for capacity planning, but the end product will indicate what hardware you should have already installed, rather than what you will need in a year's time.

We hesitate before mentioning this possibility, but for cost reasons you could conceivably choose to tolerate a degree of overload during short peak periods, if performance is not critical at these times. In effect, you select a minor peak for capacity planning purposes, and allow performance to suffer badly when the absolute peaks arise. This means that you will work closer to the edge all the time,

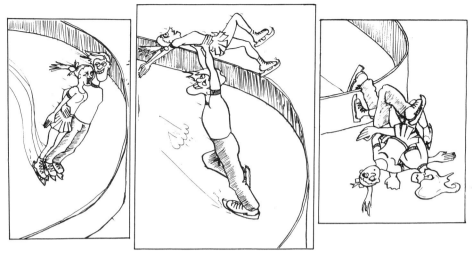

Figure 12.2.   Working near the edge.

as well as occasionally over it. Hence it is not a recipe for a long and happy life, but it is an option if you are desperate, and feel lucky (Fig. 12.2).

Note that if a high exceptional wait time is consistently shown in a number of measurement periods, this does not invalidate the data. It will not affect the predicted resource utilizations on which capacity-planning decisions are made. However, it will influence the predicted response times, so rely on these even less than usual. High exceptional wait time is usually connected with application design features, which may be modifiable but are beyond the scope of this book.

12.4   Trend analysis

The regular or irregular peak period data left in Table 8.1 after unsuitable columns have been scratched is a valuable historical record of activity and resource utilization. Over a period of time variability and trends will be evident, and the selection of data which best reflects the current position should be straightforward. Trends will also help in the estimation of future workloads, which is part of the planning process.

It is very helpful to display significant items from the data in graphical form, along a time axis. If guideline values are also shown, you have an immediate visual check on spare capacity, how long a particular resource will cope if present trends continue, and what resource will run out first. The most important figures to track are:

- High-priority CPU utilization (against 70 per cent guideline)
- Disk actuator utilization (against 40 per cent guideline)
- Total faults per second (against appropriate guideline: see Chapter 9)

- Transactions per hour (against service level agreement figure)
- Average response time (against service level agreement figure).

You might usefully add disk space utilization to the above list. It is reported in the System Report and could be added to Table 8.1.

The best presentation of the data is probably obtained by keying it into a spreadsheet or PC graphics package. Alternatively, if the data remains on the system, you may choose to use the Performance Tools graphing functions. These allow screen display, printing or plotted output. Also supported is output to a graphics data format file which can be input to the Business Graphics Utility product.

The procedure for producing a graph is discussed in the *Work Management Guide*. To display a historical graph, the following steps are necessary:

1. Create a graph format using the command CRTGPHFMT, or select an IBM supplied graph format.
2. Create historical data from your collected data using the CRTHSTDTA command.
3. Display the graph using the DSPHSTGPH comand.

The graphs should be updated monthly and inspected at these times with the following questions in mind:

1. Are any of the performance indicators getting close to the guidelines?
2. Can we continue to honour the service level agreement until the next capacity planning review?

13
Producing a capacity plan

Capacity planning is similar to sizing in that both are concerned with assessing the hardware configuration required to support an estimated future workload. In cookery terms, sizing is like buying the ingredients for a cake when you are not too sure how many people will turn up for the party. Tuning is sharing out the cake, with slightly larger slices for favoured guests, and capacity planning is learning from your experience of giving a series of parties, when its time to provide a larger cake (Fig. 13.1).

Figure 13.1.   The slices are getting a bit thin.

The advantages that we have in a planning situation when compared with a sizing exercise generally allow a much higher degree of confidence in the accuracy of the predictions:

● The basis for our projections is the current workload on the current machine, which we have monitored for a considerable time. The measurements provide a calibration check on the accuracy of the model's predictions.

● We understand the workload fluctuations which occur during business cycles and can easily select representative measurements.

● The estimated workload increments over the next period are generally a moderate percentage of the current values. Therefore the model does not have to project too far from the established real data.

Of course, when large numbers of new users have to be catered for, and perhaps a new application's performance profile is not available or suspect, the confidence level is correspondingly reduced, and a safety margin should be built in as when sizing.

13.1   Selection of input data

Most of the this work has already been done during the monitoring and screening process described in Chapter 12. It remains only to select a recent measurement to represent the current workload. Abnormal measurements and measurements taken when the machine was overloaded have already been excluded, or at least identified as unsuitable for capacity planning.

The chosen measurement will be the basis for projections and therefore you must be satisfied that the workload character and volume correctly exemplify the current status. Although all the other data will not be used by the model, it will have served its purpose by guiding the selection of the representative measurement.

The volume figures are simply the total interactive throughput we logged in Table 8.1 and subsequently displayed graphically. The workload character is described by the demand for the main performance resources of its average transaction. These are the CPU seconds and synchronous disk I/Os per transaction. The combination of these volume and average demand figures largely determine the hardware requirement.

Where the workload character is consistent, there is no problem in choosing a typical set of figures. If the average transaction characteristics vary greatly from period to period it means that different sorts of work are being performed, or the relative volumes of different components of the work mix are changing. An explanation of this variation can be found by examining the 'Job Summary' and 'Interactive Program Statistics' reports (Figs 8.8 and 8.9).

Provided that the workload character is not extremely unusual, and therefore ruled out as abnormal, we then simply select one of the measurements which generates a peak demand and contains important business functions. This will be regarded as representative for planning purposes. Notice that lack of variation in workload character does not guarantee consistent workload content. Any number of combinations of user functions could result in the same average transaction.

We may be tempted just to ignore the possible effects of such hidden variations, and in some cases this is the correct approach. However, if different workload components with significantly different characteristics will experience differential growth rates over the planning period, we should satisfy ourselves that the measured job mix is indeed representative. This is done by comparing the reports mentioned above for a set of possible model input measurements.

13.2   Estimation of future workload

The first ingredient in this estimate is the trend analysis done as part of the workload monitoring process. This gives an overall indication of the pattern of change (usually growth). At best, this is a baseline only; we cannot assume that past trends will continue, but must consider possible discontinuities.

The other essential ingredients are an awareness of business plans and user requirements. If you are not certain that you already have at least a twelve-month horizon on these through your normal business contacts, you will need to consult higher management and user department management in this phase of the work. As a minimum, review and approval of your assumptions should be sought before proceeding. Sources of increased workload include:

1. Growth in business volumes for existing applications. This may result from an increase in market size and/or market share. Additions to the product line may cause predictable increases in activity.
2. Extension of terminal facilities to additional users.
3. New applications planned to go live during the period under review. Package applications may be implemented within a fairly short lead time.
4. Employment of additional staff or contract workers.
5. Latent demand. This term covers user requirements that are not currently scheduled, but will surface and need to be satisfied during the planning period.

13.2.1   Grouping applications

In assessing the changes, we are likely to have to consider more than just overall volumes. Changes to the character of the average transaction may also occur. Suppose our workload comprises two component functions described roughly as 'moderate' and 'complex' respectively in their demand for resources. If the volume of the moderate workload stays the same while that of the complex workload doubles, the average transaction profile will move towards that of the complex component. Similarly, a new simple application will have an effect in the opposite direction, while still increasing the overall volume and total resource demand.

For simplicity, we will link together jobs where the volume is expected to change by roughly the same proportion. In the simplest case this will be the complete workload. The smaller the number of separate workload groups we have to handle, the easier the planning process becomes, but this is determined by the number of different growth scenarios. For each group we should specify the expected percentage growth over each of the next three six-month review periods. The characterization of the various workload groups will be done for us by BEST/1 from the measured data. All we have to do here is work out how to assign jobs to the workload groups.

Usually this can be done by user profile name or workstation name, working from the Job Summary Report. If the function being performed, or at least the workload to which it should be assigned is ambiguous, we will have to print a transition detail report for each active unidentified job. As can be seen in Fig. 13.2, the report includes the names of programs in use at transition points during job execution. The application developers will be able to identify the functions from this listing.

In the majority of cases, transition detail reports should not be required to classify jobs. A few uncertainties can be lumped into a catch-all default workload. If required, the report is developed from the measured (trace) data by a batch job submitted as a result of the following command:

```
PRTTNSRPT   MBR(name)
            LIB(performance data library name)
            RPTTYPE(*TRSIT)
            SLTJOB(job number) /* from job summary */
            /* Other parameters take default values */
```

The transition detail report can be quite long, even for a single job over a half-hour measurement period. If the activity being performed was consistent, you could limit the reported time interval by using the PERIOD parameter of the above command.

13.2.2 New workload components

For new applications, the workload profile and transaction throughput information should be provided by the software supplier, as when sizing. You will shortly see how a workload derived from measured data can be saved, copied and re-used in another model. This is exactly what you require from the supplier. If the application is still in development and is not yet ready for testing, your two options are again similar to the sizing situation:

1. Assume that the characteristics of the new application will be similar to those of an existing component of your workload. Adopt the measured profile of the existing application to represent the expected new workload.
2. Compare the expected application with the available predefined applications built into BEST/1 and select one of these to represent the new workload.

```
                                      Transition Report                                    10/08/94 13:39:33
                                                                                                  Page 0002

Member . . . : FRI290794   Model/Serial     F80/44-D5879   Main storage . . : 384.0 M   Started . . . . : :29 07 94 10:03:00
Library . . . : RSFPFRLIB  System name      WIDGETS        Version/Release  : 2/ 2.0     Stopped . . . . : :29 07 94 10:05:00

Job name . . . : PCS363S1  User name . . .  MACHEC         Job number . . . : 942869     TDE/Pl/Pty/Prg . : 764E/08/20/
Job type . . . : I         Elapsed Time -- Seconds         Sync/Async Phy I/O           -MPL-
                                                          ------------------------      C  I  n       Last 4 Programs in Invocation Stack
               State  Wait   Long    Active  Inel   CPU   DB   DB  NDB  NDB             u  n  1
Time           W A I  Code   Wait    /Rsp*   Wait   Sec  Read Wrt Read Wrt  Tot         r  1      Last      Second     Third      Fourth
---------      ------ -----  ------  ------  -----  ----  ---- --- ---- --- ----        -  -  -   ----      ------     -----      ------
10.04.24.969   A      TSE
10.04.24.976   W                     .008           .003                               6          QQQIMPLE  QQQQUERY   QQQOPNQF   GM4PADR
10.04.25.033   A                     .057           .030                               6          QT3REQIO  QWSDSMSG   QMHSNSTA   QQQIMPLE
10.04.25.117   W                     .084                       2                       6          QT3REQIO  QWSDSMSG   QMHSNSTA   QQQQUERY
10.04.25.203   A                     .086                                               5          QWSSPEND  QWSPUT     GM2MDSR
10.04.25.462   W                     .258           .048  2     7                       6          QT3REQIO  PAG= 4     PWrt= 0    Bin= 0    Flp= 0
                                                                                                   EAO= 5    XSum= 0    Dec= 5
-------------
10.04.25.552   A                     .090           .015                               7          PCS363S1  GM2MDSR#   GM2MDSR
10.04.25.566          EOR1           .014                                               7          PCS363S1  GM2MDSR#
10.04.25.566          EOT1                                                              7          QT3REQIO  QWSGET     GM2MDSR    GMEFXLR
10.04.25.576   W<-                   .011           .003  2     9                       6          PAG= 5    XSum= 0    PWrt= 0    Bin= 0    Flp= 0
GM2MDSR                              .608*          .099              0    11*                      EAO= 7    Dec= 7

*****   YES Is The New Purge Attribute.
10.04.32.445   ->A    SOT1  6.869    .006           .006  2                             7          PCS363S1  CSM2DFR#   QWSPUT     GMAF8BR
10.04.32.446          SOT1           .001           .001  2     2                       7          HULMEK    942252     PWrt= 0
10.04.32.509          SZWT   */      .174/*                     HOLDER-- PCS204S1                  GMDTA     GM3GRXP    Bin= 0     Flp= 0
                                                               OBJECT-  DS
-------------
10.04.32.863   W                     .416           .121  1     3                       7          QT3REQIO  QWSSPEND   QWSPUT     GMAF8BR
                                                                                                   PAG= 3    XSum= 3    PWrt= 0
                                                                                                   EAO= 2    Dec= 2     Bin= 0     Flp= 0
-------------
10.04.32.978   A                     .115           .001                               8          PCS363S1  GMAF8BR#
10.04.32.997          EOR1           .020           .014                               8          PCS363S1  GMAF8BR#
10.04.33.002   W<-                   .005           .005  0     5                       7          QT3REQIO  QWSGET     CSFAE1R    GWM9XFR
GMAF8BR                              .563*          .148  1           0    5*                       PAG= 4    XSum= 0    PWrt= 0    Bin= 0    Flp= 0
                                                                                                   EAO= 2    Dec= 2
-------------
10.04.46.615   ->A    SOT1 13.613    .001           .001  0     0    5    0    5        1          PCS363S1  GMAF8BR#
10.04.46.615                                             1     1    0    0    1                    QT3REQIO  QWSCLOSE   QDMCLOSE   GMAF8BR
10.04.46.911   W                     .296           .046                               5          PCS363S1  GMAF8BR#
10.04.46.960   A                     .049           .027                               5          QT3REQIO  QWSRST     QWSPUT     GM2MDSR
10.04.47.030   W                     .070                                               5
-------------
10.04.47.190   A      EOR1           .159           .001                               6          PCS363S1  GM2MDSR#
10.04.47.196          EOT1           .006           .006                               6          PCS363S1  GM2MDSR#
10.04.47.196
```

Figure 13.2. Transition details report.

259

13.3   Use of BEST/1 for capacity planning

In this exercise we will introduce further BEST/1 features relevant to capacity planning. It is intended to follow on from the exercise in Sec. 6.3, which covered a number of basic facilities. For illustrative purposes we will work from some measured data collected on a busy F80. If you want to follow a parallel path at the terminal you must also have some performance data to work with. Clearly our results won't match, but the process will be much the same.

For the purpose of the exercise we will assume that an identified group of users is expected to double in number and another group will increase by 50 per cent, while the remainder should be unchanged in number and activity during the coming year. How do we determine the hardware upgrade requirements (if any)?

13.3.1 Building a model from measured data

1. Assuming that model data and results are to be kept in our MODELS library, and that the performance data has been collected in a library called RSFPFRDTA, enter the following commands:

```
CHGCURLIB    MODELS
STRBEST      PFRDTALIB(RSFPFRDTA)
```

2. Press *Enter* when the disclaimer screen appears.
3. The initial BEST/1 menu appears. (Fig. 13.3). Key selection '*1*' and press *Enter*.

```
                         BEST/1 for the AS/400

  Select one of the following:

      1. Work with BEST/1 models

      10. Work with results

      50. About BEST/1
      51. Moving from MDLSYS to BEST/1

      60. More BEST/1 options




  Selection or command
  ===> 1

  F3=Exit    F4=Prompt    F9=Retrieve    F12=Cancel
```

Figure 13.3.   Initial BEST/1 menu: select work with models.

```
                      Work with BEST/1 Models

   Library . . . . .   MODELS        Name

   Type options, press Enter.
     1=Create   3=Copy   4=Delete   5=Work with   6=Print   7=Rename

   Opt  Model     Text                                Date      Time
    1   MDL2
        MDL1        Sizing Exercise Output             10/08/94  12:15:14




                                                              Bottom
   Command
   ===>
   F3=Exit   F4=Prompt   F5=Refresh        F9=Retrieve   F12=Cancel
   F15=Sort by model    F16=Sort by text   F19=Sort by date and time
```

Figure 13.4.   Work with BEST/1 Models: create MDL2.

4. The 'Work with BEST/1 Models' screen appears. (Fig. 13.4). MDL1 is listed from the previous exercise.
   Key option '*1*' against the input field and give the name '*MDL2*' to our new capacity-planning model.
5. The 'Create BEST/1 Model' screen appears. (Fig. 13.5). This time we will be working from measured performance data. Key selection '*1*' and press *Enter*.
6. The 'Create Model from Performance Data' screen appears. (Fig13.6). Key some descriptive text to identify the model.

```
                        Create BEST/1 Model

   Select one of the following:

       1. Create from performance data
       2. Create from predefined and user-defined workloads













   Selection
       1

   F3=Exit   F12=Cancel
```

Figure 13.5.   Select create BEST/1 model from performance data.

```
                    Create Model from Performance Data

  Model . . . . . . . . . . . . . . :    MDL2

  Type choices, press Enter.

    Text  . . . . . . . . . . . . .   Capacity Planning Exercise
    Performance member  . . . . . . .              Name, F4 for list
      Library . . . . . . . . . . .    RSFPFRDTA   Name

      Start time  . . . . . . . . .    *FIRST      Time, *FIRST, *SELECT
      Start date  . . . . . . . . .    *FIRST      Date, *FIRST

      Stop time . . . . . . . . . .    *LAST       Time, *LAST
      Stop date . . . . . . . . . .    *LAST       Date, *LAST




  F3=Exit    F4=Prompt    F12=Cancel
```

Figure 13.6.   Create model parameters: press F4 for performance member list.

Then place the cursor in the 'Performance member' field and press *F4* to get a list of performance data members held on the system in RSFPFRDTA library.

7. The 'Select Performance Member' screen appears. (Fig. 13.7). Key option '*1*' against a member, in this example it is FRI290794, to select a set of workload and performance measurements. Press *Enter*.

8. You return to the 'Create Model from Performance Data' screen. The selected member is shown. Only the sample data will be used, so trace data need not be

```
                      Select Performance Member

  Library  . . . .    RSFPFRDTA    Name

  Type option, press Enter.
    1=Select

  Opt  Member    Text                              Date       Time
       XPD0406A  Data collected 130494 at 1000     13/07/94   15:09:14
       Q941361523                                  13/07/94   15:07:25
   1   FRI290794 Data collected 290794 at 0930     20/07/94   14:07:17




                                                              Bottom
  F3=Exit    F5=Refresh    F12=Cancel    F15=Sort by member    F16=Sort by text
  F19=Sort by date and time
```

Figure 13.7.   Select performance member.

```
                         Select Time Interval

  Library  . . . . . . . :    RSFPFRDTA    Performance member . . :    FRI290794

  Type option, press Enter.  Select first and last interval.
    1=Select

                          ---Transaction---    --CPU Util---    I/Os per Sec
  Opt   Date      Time     Count  Rsp Time    Total   Inter    Sync    Async
        29/07/94  09:36:50  2369    1.0         87      63      182      80
        29/07/94  09:41:49  2403     .9         60      50       96      32
        29/07/94  09:46:49  2701     .8         78      59      135      71
        29/07/94  09:51:48  2566     .7         75      48      104      58
        29/07/94  09:56:48  2366     .6         88      48       88      47
        29/07/94  10:01:46  2378     .8         88      54      103      43
    1   29/07/94  10:06:46  2682     .8         93      61      121      82
        29/07/94  10:11:46  2615    1.0         88      66      119     120
        29/07/94  10:16:45  2407     .8         68      49      136      50
        29/07/94  10:21:44  2785     .7         69      58      101      64
        29/07/94  10:26:43  2504    1.0         77      60      124      56
                                                                    More...
  F3=Exit    F12=Cancel    F15=Sort by interval       F16=Sort by count
  F17=Sort by rsp time   F18=Sort by total CPU util   F19=Sort by total I/Os
```

Figure 13.8.   Select time interval: first period.

present (although it *will* be required at the earlier stage where the data is screened for suitability).

Note that a measured workload/performance profile can be created from the data by the PRTSYSRPT command but this is not used by BEST/1. BEST/1 works directly from the collected data.

Specify '*SELECT*' against the 'Start time' field to use only a subset of the sampled data intervals, and press *Enter*.

9. When the 'Select Time interval' screen appears (Fig. 13.8) choose an adjacent group of intervals to represent the capacity plan input. Here we have selected a 35 minute period when the workload was at a peak. Assume that we have already screened the reports to confirm the suitability of this data.

    Key '*1*' against the *first and last* selected intervals (Fig. 13.9) paging up if necessary. Note that the time listed is the time the interval ended. Use the help key to confirm this information. Press *Enter*.

10. The 'Classify Jobs' screen appears (Fig. 13.10). Selection '1' would be the simplest and should be used when possible. It splits the workload into standard components based on job type (e.g. interactive, PC Support, passthrough). We need to be more selective Key selection '*2*' and press *Enter*.

11. The 'Specify Job Classification Category' screen appears (Fig. 13.11). This allows us to split our workload according to any one of ten criteria, including (predefined) functional areas, which we could have set up to correspond with the various departments which use the machine.

    In our case assume we have not had the foresight to define these areas, and are working from a Job Summary Report which identifies the job number of all the jobs we are intersted in. Key choice '*5*' and press *Enter*.

```
                          Select Time Interval

   Library  . . . . . . . :   RSFPFRDTA     Performance member . . :    FRI290794

   Type option, press Enter.  Select first and last interval.
     1=Select

                             ---Transaction---   --CPU Util---    I/Os per Sec
   Opt   Date      Time      Count   Rsp Time    Total   Inter    Sync   Async
         29/07/94  10:31:43   2511      .8         70      58      136     48
    1    29/07/94  10:36:42   2456      .6         66      47      110     62
         29/07/94  10:41:42   2321      .6         57      47       98     55
         29/07/94  10:46:41   2163      .7         66      46      118     44
         29/07/94  10:51:40   2451      .8         71      53      123     54
         29/07/94  10:56:39   2676      .6         94      52      121     49
         29/07/94  11:01:39   2355      .8         98      49      111     51
         29/07/94  11:06:38   2026      .9         97      45      104     61
         29/07/94  11:11:37   2550      .6         84      47      116     74
         29/07/94  11:16:37   2640      .8         91      48      130     63
         29/07/94  11:21:37   2533      .8         90      49      138     67
                                                                         More...
   F3=Exit    F12=Cancel    F15=Sort by interval      F16=Sort by count
   F17=Sort by rsp time    F18=Sort by total CPU util   F19=Sort by total I/Os
```

Figure 13.9.   Select time interval: last period.

12. The 'Edit Job Classification' screen appears, with input fields to define the
    workload categories (Fig. 13.12). We could simply key our input here, but to
    illustrate a more general approach which is often convenient, we will ask
    BEST/1 to prompt us with relevant values from the measured data. Press *F9*.
13. The 'Assign Jobs to Workloads' screen appears (Fig. 13.13). Depending on
    the classification category we selected, this screen presents user ids, job names,
    pools etc. extracted from the data. In our case just a string of job numbers

```
                          Classify Jobs

   Select one of the following:

        1. Use default job classification
        2. Classify jobs into workloads
        3. Use existing job classifications












   Selection
       2

   F3=Exit    F12=Cancel
```

Figure 13.10.   Select manual classification of jobs.

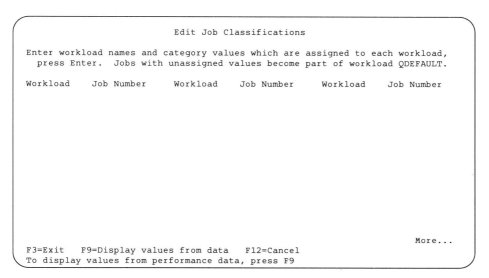

```
                    Specify Job Classification Category

Type choice, press Enter.

     Category . . . . . . . . . . .    5          1=User ID
                                                  2=Job type
                                                  3=Job name
                                                  4=Account code
                                                  5=Job number
                                                  6=Subsystem
                                                  7=Pool
                                                  8=Control unit
                                                  9=Comm line
                                                  10=Functional area




  F3=Exit    F12=Cancel
```

Figure 13.11.   Specify job classification by job number.

which we can relate to the Job Summary Report previously used to help select
this data for capacity planning.

Key '*WRKLD1*' to identify the group of users whose workload will double,
and assign job numbers to this workload by keying option '*1*'. After paging
through a number of screens to complete this assignment, press *Enter*.

14. The screen reappears with the workload name against the selected jobs (Fig.
    13.14).

```
                        Edit Job Classifications

  Enter workload names and category values which are assigned to each workload,
    press Enter.  Jobs with unassigned values become part of workload QDEFAULT.

  Workload    Job Number    Workload    Job Number    Workload    Job Number








                                                               More...
  F3=Exit    F9=Display values from data    F12=Cancel
  To display values from performance data, press F9
```

Figure 13.12.   Edit job classifications screen: press F9.

```
                        Assign Jobs to Workloads

   Workload . . . . . . . . . . . . . . . .     WRKLD1

   Type options, press Enter.  Unassigned jobs become part of workload QDEFAULT.
     1=Assign to above workload    2=Unassign

                               Number of       CPU         I/O
   Opt   Workload    Job Number Transactions   Seconds     Count
                      942286         0          .000         0
                      942290         0          .000         0
     1                942294        66         6.070        588
                      942296         0          .000         0
                      942298         0          .000         0
     1                942299       109        15.580       2016
     1                942300       154        25.624       2810
                      942304         0          .000         0
                      942307         0          .000         0
     1                942308        24         4.736        936
     1                942309        82        15.425       1882
                                                               More...
   F3=Exit    F12=Cancel       F15=Sort by workload      F16=Sort by job number
   F17=Sort by transactions    F18=Sort by CPU seconds    F19=Sort by I/O count
```

Figure 13.13.   Assign selected jobs to WRKLD1.

15. Repeat the process for *WRKLD2*. This represents the group of jobs which is expected to grow by 50 per cent over the planning period (Fig. 13.15). All the remaining unselected jobs will be bundled into a catch-all workload called QDEFAULT.

Note that system overhead is allocated to the selected jobs in a plausible way and included in the workloads. The residue is in QDEFAULT. Press *Enter*.

```
                        Assign Jobs to Workloads

   Workload . . . . . . . . . . . . . . . .

   Type options, press Enter.  Unassigned jobs become part of workload QDEFAULT.
     1=Assign to above workload    2=Unassign

                               Number of       CPU         I/O
   Opt   Workload    Job Number Transactions   Seconds     Count
                      942286         0          .000         0
                      942290         0          .000         0
         WRKLD1       942294        66         6.070        588
                      942296         0          .000         0
                      942298         0          .000         0
         WRKLD1       942299       109        15.580       2016
         WRKLD1       942300       154        25.624       2810
                      942304         0          .000         0
                      942307         0          .000         0
         WRKLD1       942308        24         4.736        936
         WRKLD1       942309        82        15.425       1882
                                                               More...
   F3=Exit    F12=Cancel       F15=Sort by workload      F16=Sort by job number
   F17=Sort by transactions    F18=Sort by CPU seconds    F19=Sort by I/O count
```

Figure 13.14.   Assign selected jobs to WRKLD1: after Enter.

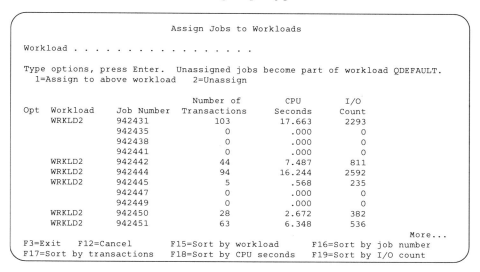

```
                        Assign Jobs to Workloads

  Workload . . . . . . . . . . . . . . . . .

  Type options, press Enter.  Unassigned jobs become part of workload QDEFAULT.
     1=Assign to above workload    2=Unassign

                             Number of        CPU          I/O
  Opt   Workload    Job Number  Transactions    Seconds      Count
        WRKLD2      942431         103          17.663        2293
                    942435           0           .000            0
                    942438           0           .000            0
                    942441           0           .000            0
        WRKLD2      942442          44           7.487         811
        WRKLD2      942444          94          16.244        2592
        WRKLD2      942445           5           .568          235
                    942447           0           .000            0
                    942449           0           .000            0
        WRKLD2      942450          28           2.672         382
        WRKLD2      942451          63           6.348         536
                                                                    More...
  F3=Exit    F12=Cancel      F15=Sort by workload    F16=Sort by job number
  F17=Sort by transactions   F18=Sort by CPU seconds  F19=Sort by I/O count
```

Figure 13.15.   Assign other jobs to WRKLD2 and press F3.

16. The 'Specify Paging Behaviors' screen appears (Fig. 13.16). It is best to accept the default paging behaviour. Press *Enter*.

17. The 'Define Non-Interactive Transactions' screen appears (Fig. 13.17). We have no way of relating this to an externally meaningful entity, so will stick with the defaults. Press *Enter*.

18. We are prompted to save the job classification we have just defined in a permanent member (Fig. 13.18). This can then be re-invoked (using option 3 of Fig. 13.10) for future capacity planning models.

```
                        Specify Paging Behaviors

  Type choices, press Enter.

                    Paging Behavior
  Workload           (F4 for list)
  QDEFAULT             *GENERIC
  WRKLD2               *GENERIC
  WRKLD1               *GENERIC




                                                                 Bottom
  F3=Exit    F4=Prompt    F12=Cancel
```

Figure 13.16.   Accept default paging behaviour: press Enter.

```
                      Define Non-Interactive Transactions

    Job classification category  . . . . . . :   Job Number


    Type choices, press Enter.

                   ---Activity Counted as Transaction---    Total Transactions
    Workload           Type                 Quantity         when Type = *NONE
    QDEFAULT          *LGLIO                 100.0                   0
    WRKLD2            *LGLIO                 100.0                   0
    WRKLD1            *LGLIO                 100.0                   0




                                                                   Bottom
    Type:  *LGLIO, *CMNIO, *CPUSEC, *PRINT, *NONE

    F3=Exit    F12=Cancel
```

Figure 13.17.   Accept default definitions of non-interactive transactions: press Enter.

A classification based on job number is never going to be any use outside this particular model, so we use a standard name which overwrites the last unrequired job classification. Key member name '*XXX*', replace '*Y*' and press *Enter*.

19. The 'Confirm Creation of BEST/1 Model' screen appears (Fig. 13.19). Model creation can be done interactively, by changing the job description name to *NONE, but this is a heavy resource-consuming process and we will use the

```
                        Save Job Classification Member

    Change values if desired, press Enter.

        Member . . . . . . . . . . . .   XXX            Name
          Library  . . . . . . . . . .   MODELS         Name

        Text . . . . . . . . . . . . .

        Replace  . . . . . . . . . . .   Y              Y=Yes, N=No






    F12=Cancel
```

Figure 13.18.   Save job classification member.

```
                    Confirm Creation of BEST/1 Model

 Type choices, press Enter.

    Model . . . . . . . . . . . .    MDL2          Name
       Library . . . . . . . . . .      MODELS     Name

    Text . . . . . . . . . . . . .   Capacity Planning Exercise

    Replace . . . . . . . . . . .    N             Y=Yes, N=No

    Job name . . . . . . . . . . .   CRTBESTMDL    Name, *JOBD
    Job description . . . . . . .    QPFRJOBD      Name, *NONE, *USRPRF
       Library . . . . . . . . . .      QPFR       Name, *LIBL, *CURLIB




 F12=Cancel
 Member XXX has been saved
```

Figure 13.19.   Confirm creation of BEST/1 model.

default batch environment. Key descriptive text to describe the model if not
already done, and press *Enter*.

13.3.2   *Validating the Model*

20. We are returned to the 'Work with BEST/1 Models' screen (Fig. 13.20). When
the new model has been created, *F5* (Refresh) will show it at the top of the list.

```
                     Work with BEST/1 Models

 Library . . . .    MODELS       Name

 Type options, press Enter.
   1=Create   3=Copy   4=Delete   5=Work with   6=Print   7=Rename

 Opt  Model      Text                         Date       Time

      MDL1       Sizing Exercise Output       10/08/94   12:15:14




                                                            Bottom
 Command
 ===>
 F3=Exit   F4=Prompt   F5=Refresh        F9=Retrieve   F12=Cancel
 F15=Sort by model     F16=Sort by text   F19=Sort by date and time
 Job CRTBESTMDL has been submitted to batch
```

Figure 13.20.   Work with BEST/1 models: note message.

```
                         Work with BEST/1 Models

    Library . . . . .   MODELS        Name

    Type options, press Enter.
      1=Create   3=Copy   4=Delete   5=Work with   6=Print   7=Rename

    Opt  Model      Text                              Date      Time

     5   MDL2       Capacity Planning Exercise        10/08/94  14:35:17
         MDL1       Sizing Exercise Output            10/08/94  12:15:14




                                                                  Bottom
    Command
    ===>
    F3=Exit    F4=Prompt    F5=Refresh        F9=Retrieve   F12=Cancel
    F15=Sort by model      F16=Sort by text   F19=Sort by date and time
```

Figure 13.21.   Work with BEST/1 models: after batch job completion and refresh (F5).

Our next job is to analyse and validate the model so that we are confident about using it for sizing.

21. Key option '5' against the MDL2 model and press *Enter* (Fig. 13.21).
22. The 'Work with BEST/1 Model' Screen appears (Fig. 13.22). Our main job is to examine the model for reasonableness. No changes will be made. We either accept or reject the model as it stands. Key selection '1' and press *Enter*.
23. The 'Work with Workloads' screen appears (Fig. 13.23). We will first carry

```
                         Work with BEST/1 Model

    Performance data . . . :
    Model/Text . . . . . . :   MDL2        Capacity Planning Exercise


    Select one of the following:

         1. Work with workloads
         2. Specify objectives and active jobs

         5. Analyze current model
         6. Analyze current model and give recommendations
         7. Specify workload growth and analyze model

        10. Configuration menu
        11. Work with results

                                                            More...
    Selection or command
    ===> 1
    F3=Exit   F4=Prompt   F9=Retrieve   F12=Cancel   F15=Save current model
    F17=Analyze using ANZBESTMDL   F20=More BEST/1 options   F22=Calibrate model
    Model MDL2 has been read
```

Figure 13.22.   Work with MDL2 model.

```
                        Work with Workloads

  Model/Text:    MDL2        Capacity Planning Exercise

  Type options, press Enter.
   1=Create    2=Change    3=Copy   4=Delete    5=Display   6=Print    7=Rename
   8=Save workload to workload member           9=Edit transactions

  Opt     Workload        Text

   7      QDEFAULT        Measured from RSFPFRDTA (FRI290794)
          WRKLD1          Measured from RSFPFRDTA (FRI290794)
          WRKLD2          Measured from RSFPFRDTA (FRI290794)




                                                                        Bottom
  F3=Exit    F6=Add saved workload    F9=Add predefined workload    F12=Cancel
  F13=Combine workloads
```

Figure 13.23.   Rename option for QDEFAULT workload.

out some housekeeping functions with our workloads. Key option '*7*' (rename) against the QDEFAULT workload and press *Enter*. When the prompt appears give the workload another name. We have called it *THEREST*.

24. Next we will save the workloads in turn so that we can reuse them in other models (Fig. 13.24). Key option '*8*' against WRKLD1 and press *Enter*.

25. You would normally change the text at this point so that you will recognize the workload on another occasion when you see it in a list. A mnemonic name

```
                        Work with Workloads

  Model/Text:    MDL2        Capacity Planning Exercise

  Type options, press Enter.
   1=Create    2=Change    3=Copy   4=Delete    5=Display   6=Print    7=Rename
   8=Save workload to workload member           9=Edit transactions

  Opt     Workload        Text

          THEREST         Measured from RSFPFRDTA (FRI290794)
   8      WRKLD1          Measured from RSFPFRDTA (FRI290794)
          WRKLD2          Measured from RSFPFRDTA (FRI290794)




                                                                        Bottom
  F3=Exit    F6=Add saved workload    F9=Add predefined workload    F12=Cancel
  F13=Combine workloads
  QDEFAULT has been renamed
```

Figure 13.24.   Save WRKLD1 option.

```
                    Save Workload to Workload Member

Change values if desired, press Enter.

    Member . . . . . . . . . . .    WRKLD1       Name
      Library  . . . . . . . . . .    MODELS       Name

    Text . . . . . . . . . . . .    Measured from RSFPFRDTA (FRI290794)

    Replace  . . . . . . . . . .    N            Y=Yes, N=No











  F12=Cancel
```

Figure 13.25.   Save to workload member prompt.

would also be useful (Fig. 13.25). Press *Enter* and then repeat the last two
steps for other workloads you may wish to re-use.

26. Return to the 'Work with BEST/1 Model' screen by pressing *F12*, and then
    take selection '*10*' to reach the 'Configuration' menu (Fig. 13.26). This is
    where we could manually edit the hardware configuration to try a 'what if'
    experiment at a later stage in the process. Just now we will save the configura-
    tion to make it available outside the model for other work. Press *F15*.


```
                         Configuration

CPU Model . . . . . . . . . :   F80       Main stor (MB) . . . . . . :   384
                                          Main stor pools . . . . . :   7
Disk IOPs . . . . . . . . . :   8
Disk ctls . . . . . . . . . :   10        Comm IOPs . . . . . . . . . :   8
Disk arms . . . . . . . . . :   46        Comm lines  . . . . . . . :   7
ASPs  . . . . . . . . . . . :   1         Local WS ctls . . . . . . . :   7
                                          LAN ctls  . . . . . . . . . :   121
                                          WAN WS ctls . . . . . . . . :   5


Select one of the following:

     1. Change CPU and other resource values
     2. Work with disk resources
     3. Edit ASPs
     4. Edit main storage pools
     5. Work with communications resources

Selection or command
===>
F14=Replace with saved configuration   F15=Save current configuration
F20=More BEST/1 options    F24=More keys
```

Figure 13.26.   Configuration screen: save current configuration (F15).

```
                    Save Current Configuration
Change values if desired, press Enter.

   Member . . . . . . . . . . .    XYZCFG        Name
     Library  . . . . . . . . .      MODELS      Name

   Text . . . . . . . . . . . .    Current configuration: 20/Sep/94

   Replace . . . . . . . . . .     N             Y=Yes, N=No




F12=Cancel
```

Figure 13.27.   Save current configuration prompt.

27. The 'Save Current Configuration' prompt appears (Fig. 13.27). Name the configuration and provide some text to promote future recognition. Key a name and text and press *Enter*.

28. Return to the 'Work with BEST/1 Model' screen (Fig. 13.28). We are now ready to see what the model makes of our data. Key selection '*6*' and press *Enter*.

29. When the analysis completes, we are presented with the Results menu, and can view the output by keying option '*5*' against desired reports. We will look

```
                    Work with BEST/1 Model
 Performance data . . . :
 Model/Text . . . . . . :    MDL2        Capacity Planning Exercise


 Select one of the following:

    1. Work with workloads
    2. Specify objectives and active jobs

    5. Analyze current model
    6. Analyze current model and give recommendations
    7. Specify workload growth and analyze model

   10. Configuration menu
   11. Work with results

                                                          More...
 Selection or command
 ===> 6
 F3=Exit    F4=Prompt    F9=Retrieve    F12=Cancel    F15=Save current model
 F17=Analyze using ANZBESTMDL    F20=More BEST/1 options    F22=Calibrate model
```

Figure 13.28.   Work with BEST/1 model: selection '6'.

```
                        Display Analysis Summary

   CPU Model . . . . . . . . :    F80
   Main Storage  . . . . . . :    384    MB

                                       Quantity    Predicted Util
   CPU  . . . . . . . . . . . . . . . :    2           80.5
   Disk IOPs  . . . . . . . . . . . :      8           10.8
   Disk ctls  . . . . . . . . . . . :     10            9.1
   Disk arms  . . . . . . . . . . . :     46           13.6
   Local WS ctls  . . . . . . . . . :      7            .0

                                                              More...
                                         Interactive   Non-interactive
   CPU utilization %  . . . . . . . . . . . . . . :    61.8         18.7
   Transactions per Hour  . . . . . . . . . . . :    33562         1129
   Local response time (seconds) . . . . . . . :      .0           .0
   LAN response time (seconds) . . . . . . . . :      .9          10.4
   WAN response time (seconds) . . . . . . . . :     1.8          10.9

   Performance estimates -- Press help to see disclaimer.
     F3=Exit   F10=Re-analyze      F12=Cancel    F15=Configuration menu
     F17=Analyze multiple points   F18=Specify objectives   F24=More keys
```

Figure 13.29.   Analysis summary screen.

at just three displays for the moment, starting with the Analysis Summary (Fig. 13.29). This shows the CPU working hard, but not overloaded, and giving good average response times to a heavy interactive workload.

30. The recommendations show a familiar message that we met previously in the sizing exercise (Fig. 13.30). Even though the installed machine is handling the measured workload well, the synchronous reads guideline prevents the model from handling this situation.

```
                        Display Recommendations

   *****  Analysis Exceptions  *****
   Sync reads per second exceeded for pools other than pool 1 (*MACH)
   Unable to find configuration that met all specified objectives










                                                              Bottom
   Performance estimates -- Press help to see disclaimer.
     F3=Exit   F12=Cancel     F15=Configuration menu   F17=Analyze multiple points
     F18=Specify objectives   F19=Work with workloads
```

Figure 13.30.   Recommendations display.

```
                    Display Main Storage Pool Report

Period:     Analysis
Pool    Act     Size    Ineligible   -----Avg Number-----   Sync Reads
 ID     Lvl     (KB)    Wait (sec)   Active    Ineligible    per Sec
  1      0     42000       .0          .9          .0           .9
  2      6     33716       .0          .9          .0          2.6
  3      3      6500       .0          .4          .0          7.4
  4      4      8000       .0          .2          .0          4.6
  5      4     15000       .0          .5          .0          6.8
  6      3     18000       .7         1.2          .1          4.0
  8     16    270000       .0         4.7          .2         88.7




                                                         Bottom
Performance estimates -- Press help to see disclaimer.
F3=Exit   F10=Re-analyze      F12=Cancel   F15=Configuration menu
F17=Analyze multiple points   F18=Specify objectives   F24=More keys
```

Figure 13.31.   Main storage pool report: current situation.

31. The main storage pool report shows the level of synchronous reads currently
    being sustained by the system (115 per second) (Fig. 13.31). Clearly we need to
    edit the guidelines, but this time we can do it rather more scientifically. Return
    to the 'Work with BEST/1 Models' screen and enter the command
    WRKSPLF.

32. Display the spool file 'CRTBESTMDL' (Fig. 13.32) and page through until
    you reach the part where the ratio of synchronous reads to page faults in the
    various pools is documented. In this example the overall average is 1.79. We

```
                       Display Spooled File
File . . . . . :    CRTBESTMDL              Page/Line   4/30
Control . . . .                             Columns     1 - 78
Find . . . . . .
*...+....1....+....2....+....3....+....4....+....5....+....6....+....7....+...
*BATCHJOB PCS367 100.0%
*BATCHJOB PCS414 100.0%
*BATCHJOB PCS474 100.0%
*BATCHJOB PCS167 100.0%
WAN inter jobs found but no WAN transactions for trans f2_104. Set to 1 per ho
No transactions seen for non-interactive transaction f4_202. Set to 1 per minu
No transactions seen for non-interactive transaction f3_202. Set to 1 per minu
Ratio of sync reads to pool faults = 1.10 for pool 1
Ratio of sync reads to pool faults = 1.46 for pool 2
Ratio of sync reads to pool faults = 1.06 for pool 3
Ratio of sync reads to pool faults = 1.36 for pool 4
Ratio of sync reads to pool faults = 1.50 for pool 5
Ratio of sync reads to pool faults = 1.30 for pool 6
Ratio of sync reads to pool faults = 2.08 for pool 8
Ratio of sync reads to pool faults = 1.79 for all pools other than pool 1
```

Figure 13.32.   Spool file from CRTBESTMDL job.

```
                    Edit Sync Reads Guidelines

Type changes, press Enter.  Values are used for Analysis recommendations.

    Max sync reads . . . . . . . . . .    *THRESH   *GUIDE, *THRESH, *NONE

                                          ------Pool 1 (*MACH)------
    CPU relative performance              Guideline        Threshold
    2.0 or less . . . . . . . . . . . .   2                5
    Greater than 2.0 . . . . . . . . .    1                3

                                          -----All Other Pools------
    CPU relative performance              Guideline        Threshold
    2.0 or less . . . . . . . . . . . . . 15               25
    3.0 or less . . . . . . . . . . . .   25               40
    10.0 or less . . . . . . . . . . . .  35               60
    30.0 or less . . . . . . . . . . . .  80               130
    50.0 or less . . . . . . . . . . . .  180              300
    100.0 or less . . . . . . . . . . .   250              440
    Greater than 100.0 . . . . . . . . .  300              500

                                                                    Bottom

F3=Exit    F12=Cancel
Relative performance of current CPU (F80) is 33.50
```

Figure 13.33.   Reinstatement of new synchronous reads guidelines.

will use this to modify the guidelines. Return to the 'Work with BEST/1 Model' screen and press *F20*.

33. Enter '*11*' on the 'More BEST/1 Options' menu to reach the 'Analysis Parameters' screen. If you previously saved the modified guidelines, restore them now by using *F14*. Then key '*2*' and press *Enter* to get to the edit guidelines screen. Figure 13.33 shows the V3R1 figures with the *GUIDE value changed to *THRESH, as used in the sizing exercise.

```
                    Edit Sync Reads Guidelines

    Type changes, press Enter.  Values are used for Analysis recommendations.

        Max sync reads . . . . . . . . . .    *GUIDE   *GUIDE, *THRESH, *NONE

                                              ------Pool 1 (*MACH)------
        CPU relative performance              Guideline        Threshold
        2.0 or less . . . . . . . . . . . .   2                5
        Greater than 2.0 . . . . . . . . .    1                3

                                              -----All Other Pools------
        CPU relative performance              Guideline        Threshold
        2.0 or less . . . . . . . . . . . .   27               45
        3.0 or less . . . . . . . . . . . .   45               72
        10.0 or less . . . . . . . . . . . .  63               108
        30.0 or less . . . . . . . . . . . .  144              233
        50.0 or less . . . . . . . . . . . .  323              537
        100.0 or less . . . . . . . . . . .   448              788
        Greater than 100.0 . . . . . . . . .  537              895

                                                                    Bottom

    F3=Exit    F12=Cancel
    Relative performance of current CPU (F80) is 33.50
```

Figure 13.34.   Modification of guidelines using CRTBESTMDL ratio.

```
                    Compare Against Measured Values

                                       Measured       Predicted
Total CPU util . . . . . . . . . . . :    76.3          76.2
Disk IOP util  . . . . . . . . . . . :    10.2          10.0
Disk arm util  . . . . . . . . . . . :    12.7          12.6
Disk IOs per second  . . . . . . . . :   289.1         287.9

LAN IOP util . . . . . . . . . . . . :     8.9           4.4
LAN line util  . . . . . . . . . . . :     2.5           1.3
WAN IOP util . . . . . . . . . . . . :    17.5          13.6
WAN line util  . . . . . . . . . . . :     5.1           3.1

Interactive:
  CPU util . . . . . . . . . . . . . :    57.8          57.8
  Int rsp time (seconds) . . . . . . :      .8            .5
  Transactions per hour  . . . . . . :   30893         30893
Non-interactive thruput  . . . . . . :    1114          1114



F3=Exit    F6=Print    F9=Work with spooled files    F12=Cancel
F17=Calibrate response time
```

Figure 13.35.   Comparing measured and predicted values.

34. We can now be a little more precise. Apply the ratio (*1.79*) noted from the CRTBESTMDL spool output to the page fault guidelines and thresholds, giving the synchronous reads shown in Fig. 13.34. Also change the *THRESH value back to *GUIDE* and press *Enter*.

35. Return to the 'Work with BEST/1 Model' screen and select '*6*' to re-analyse the model. When the Results menu appears confirm that the Recommendations say 'All the specified objectives have been met'. Also look at the Analysis Summary and press *F11* to compare measured and predicted results (Fig. 13.35). The two sets of values should agree fairly closely. Resource utilization figures for CPU, diskarm and disk IOP should be within 10 per cent of the measured values. Predicted response times should be within 20 per cent or 0.5 sec of the measured value.

    If the predicted response is outside acceptable limits this is almost certainly due to the occurrence of exceptional waits in the measured transactions. These are explained fully in Chapter 8 but include e.g. lock contention delays. They do not affect the accuracy of the resource utilization predictions, which are the usual basis of sizing decisions. To calibrate the response time (i.e. add exceptional wait time to the transactions to equalise predicted and measured responses) we can press F17 and then return (F12) to the 'Display Analysis Summary' screen and re-analyse via F10. Nothing else changes.

13.3.3 Modelling asymmetric workload growth

36. We should save or print all the results at this stage, to document the current position. This is done from the 'Results' menu. Then return to the 'Work with BEST/1 Model' screen and key selection '*2*' to get to the screen shown in Fig.

```
                    Specify Objectives and Active Jobs

    Model/Text:    MDL2

    Type changes, press Enter.

                          Workload     Active   ----Interactive-----   Non-inter
    Workload   Connect    Type         Jobs    Rsp Time    Thruput     Thruput
    THEREST    *LAN       *NORMAL      73.1      .0           0          0
    THEREST    *WAN       *NORMAL       9.2      .0           0          0
    WRKLD1     *LAN       *NORMAL      23.4      .0           0          0
    WRKLD1     *WAN       *NORMAL       2.0      .0           0          0
    WRKLD2     *LAN       *NORMAL      30.0      .0           0          0
    WRKLD2     *WAN       *NORMAL       1.9      .0           0          0




                                                                   Bottom
    F3=Exit    F11=Show all quantities    F12=Cancel    F15=Sort by connect type
    F19=Work with workloads
```

Figure 13.36.   Specify active jobs screen.

13.36. The 'Active Jobs' column shows the average number of jobs active during the measurement interval in each workload and connection category.

37. We can now specify the required workload increases by editing the 'Active Jobs' numbers. Apply the factor *2* to the number of WRKLD1 jobs and the factor *1.5* to the WRKLD2 jobs, giving the results shown iin Fig. 13.37. This represents our objective. Press *Enter*.

38. Take selection '*6*' from 'Work with BEST/1 Model' to re-analyse, and when the results appear display the recommendations again. Now we see a series of

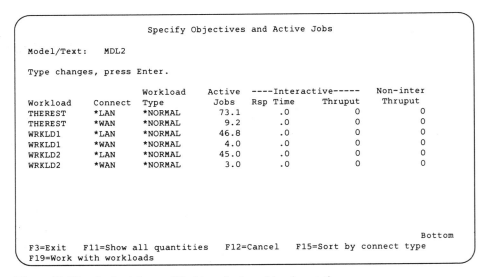

```
                    Specify Objectives and Active Jobs

    Model/Text:    MDL2

    Type changes, press Enter.

                          Workload     Active   ----Interactive-----   Non-inter
    Workload   Connect    Type         Jobs    Rsp Time    Thruput     Thruput
    THEREST    *LAN       *NORMAL      73.1      .0           0          0
    THEREST    *WAN       *NORMAL       9.2      .0           0          0
    WRKLD1     *LAN       *NORMAL      46.8      .0           0          0
    WRKLD1     *WAN       *NORMAL       4.0      .0           0          0
    WRKLD2     *LAN       *NORMAL      45.0      .0           0          0
    WRKLD2     *WAN       *NORMAL       3.0      .0           0          0




                                                                   Bottom
    F3=Exit    F11=Show all quantities    F12=Cancel    F15=Sort by connect type
    F19=Work with workloads
```

Figure 13.37.   Active jobs modified to reflect workload growth.

```
                        Display Recommendations

*****  Analysis Exceptions  *****
CPU utilization of 83.13 for priority 20 and higher exceeds objective of 70.00

*****  Analysis Recommendations  *****
Change CPU model to 2051
Delete 1 2615 IOP(s)
Create 1 9152 IOP(s)
Delete 1 6112 IOP(s)
Create 1 6502 IOP(s)
Create 4 6602 arm(s)
Delete 4 2800 disk ctl(s)
Create 4 6602 disk ctl(s)
Remove 4 6130 communications IOP(s)
Create 4 2623 communications IOP(s)
Remove 1 613L communications IOP(s)
Create 3 2618 communications IOP(s)
Remove 2 2619 communications IOP(s)
                                                              More...
Performance estimates -- Press help to see disclaimer.
F3=Exit    F10=Change to recommended configuration and re-analyze    F12=Cancel
F15=Configuration menu    F17=Analyze multiple points    F24=More keys
```

Figure 13.38.   Recommendations following upgrade analysis (Part I).

upgrade recommendations for CPU, disk and communications hardware (Fig. 13.38).

39. Line recommendations continue on the following screen (Fig. 13.39). The results should be saved and printed at this stage also, to show the impact of the planned growth on the present configuration. Then all we have to do is press *F10* to accept the recommendations and re-analyse.

```
                        Display Recommendations

Change line speed of line resource ABLNKLIN to 100000.000
Change line speed of line resource TRNA01 to 100000.000




                                                              Bottom
Performance estimates -- Press help to see disclaimer.
F3=Exit    F10=Change to recommended configuration and re-analyze    F12=Cancel
F15=Configuration menu    F17=Analyze multiple points    F24=More keys
```

Figure 13.39.   Recommendations following upgrade analysis (Part II).

```
                       Display Analysis Summary

CPU Model . . . . . . . . :   2051
Main Storage  . . . . . . :   384    MB

                                     Quantity    Predicted Util
CPU  . . . . . . . . . . . . . . . :    2           77.5
Disk IOPs  . . . . . . . . . . . . :    8           12.6
Disk ctls  . . . . . . . . . . . . :   10           10.7
Disk arms  . . . . . . . . . . . . :   46           15.6
Local WS ctls  . . . . . . . . . . :    7            .0

                                                             More...
                                     Interactive    Non-interactive
CPU utilization % . . . . . . . . . . . . . . . :    61.2          16.3
Transactions per Hour . . . . . . . . . . . . :    40331          1215
Local response time (seconds) . . . . . . . :     .0             .0
LAN response time (seconds) . . . . . . . . :     .9            8.4
WAN response time (seconds) . . . . . . . . :    1.9            8.7

Performance estimates -- Press help to see disclaimer.
F3=Exit   F10=Re-analyze      F12=Cancel   F15=Configuration menu
F17=Analyze multiple points   F18=Specify objectives   F24=More keys
```

Figure 13.40.   Analysis summary following upgrade.

40. The 'Analysis Summary' shows that a 2051 processor supports the increased workload (Fig. 13.40).
41. The 'Recommendations' show that no guidelines are exceeded with the proposed configuration (Fig. 13.41).
42. The 'Workload Report' gives a breakdown by component workload and type (Fig. 13.42). No problems here.

```
                       Display Recommendations

*****  Analysis Exceptions  *****
All the specified objectives have been met




                                                              Bottom
Performance estimates -- Press help to see disclaimer.
F3=Exit   F12=Cancel      F15=Configuration menu    F17=Analyze multiple points
F18=Specify objectives    F19=Work with workloads
```

Figure 13.41.   Recommendations following upgrade.

```
                      Display Workload Report

Period:    Analysis
                    CPU    Thruput  -------Response Times (Secs)-------
Workload   Type    Util   per Hour  Internal   Local    LAN     WAN
THEREST      1     26.4    18160       .5       .0      .8      1.9
WRKLD1       1     19.5    11009       .6       .0     1.0      2.2
WRKLD2       1     15.2    11162       .5       .0      .8      1.7
THEREST      2     12.7      858      9.4       .0     9.4      9.4
WRKLD1       2      1.9        0      5.1       .0     5.1      5.1
WRKLD2       2      1.7        0      5.8       .0     5.8      5.8




                                                             Bottom
Type: 1=Interactive, 2=Non-interactive, 3=*BATCHJOB
Performance estimates -- Press help to see disclaimer.
F3=Exit    F10=Re-analyze    F11=Response time detail    F12=Cancel
F15=Configuration menu       F17=Analyze multiple points  F24=More keys
```

Figure 13.42.   Workload report following upgrade.

43. The disk arm and IOP utilizations are well within guidelines (Fig. 13.43).
44. The synchronous reads per second are up compared with the original machine and workload (Fig. 13.44). This is reasonable considering that the main storage size is unchanged. We might well consider trying the effect of a main storage upgrade by changing this value from the 'Configuration' menu. It

```
                   Display Disk IOP and Arm Report

Period:    Analysis
                                 --------Disk Arm Averages---------
                   I/Os    IOP      Pct    I/Os     Msecs    Queue
IOP       Arms   per Sec   Util    Busy   per Sec   per I/O  Length
CMB01       4     31.7     8.3     10.4     7.9      16.4      .1
SI04        7     55.5    15.6     16.2     7.9      26.3      .2
SI05        7     55.5    15.4     16.4     7.9      26.6      .2
SI06        7     55.5    15.5     16.0     7.9      26.0      .2
SI07        7     55.5    15.4     15.6     7.9      25.3      .2
SI08        7     55.5    15.6     16.5     7.9      26.8      .2
SI09        7     55.5    15.5     15.9     7.9      25.8      .2




                                                             Bottom
Performance estimates -- Press help to see disclaimer.
F3=Exit    F10=Re-analyze    F11=Display ASP and Disk Arm report   F12=Cancel
F15=Configuration menu       F17=Analyze multiple points   F24=More keys
```

Figure 13.43.   Disk IOP and arm report following upgrade.

```
                    Display Main Storage Pool Report

 Period:    Analysis
 Pool    Act     Size     Ineligible    -----Avg Number-----    Sync Reads
  ID     Lvl     (KB)     Wait (sec)    Active    Ineligible     per Sec
   1      0      42000        .0         1.0         .0             .9
   2      6      33716        .0          .7         .0            2.9
   3      3       6500        .0          .3         .0            7.3
   4      4       8000        .0          .2         .0            5.7
   5      4      15000        .0          .6         .0            9.1
   6      3      18000        .3          .9         .1            4.0
   8     16     270000        .0         5.1         .3          105.7




                                                              Bottom
 Performance estimates -- Press help to see disclaimer.
 F3=Exit    F10=Re-analyze      F12=Cancel    F15=Configuration menu
 F17=Analyze multiple points    F18=Specify objectives    F24=More keys
```

Figure 13.44.   Main storage pool report following upgrade.

could reduce faulting, disk I/O rates and utilizations, and response times. However, these all appear to be satisfactory.

45. Communications resource utilizations are also predicted to be OK (Fig. 13.45). We can print off or save the final set of results, to support our case for additional hardware, and then exit from BEST/1.

Congratulations on finishing the capacity planning exercise.

```
                    Display Comm Resources Report

 Period:    Analysis
                              Overhead    Rsp Time per    Nbr of    Line Speed
 Resource            Util       Util      Trans (Sec)     Lines     (Kbit/sec)
 CC01                20.7
   ES1                4.3        .1           .15           1          64.0
 CC02                  .0
 CC03                 4.0
   ABLNKLIN            .0        .0           .00           1       100000.0
 CC04                45.0
   MANCHESTER          8.5       .2          1.04           1          19.2
   WEMBLEY             8.5       .2          2.08           1           9.6
   HOL1                4.2       .1           .15           1          64.0
   HOL2                4.2       .1           .15           1          64.0
 CC05                  .0
 CC06                  .0
 CC07                 2.9
   TRNA01              .1        .0           .00           1       100000.0

                                                                  Bottom
 F3=Exit    F10=Re-analyze      F12=Cancel    F15=Configuration menu
 F17=Analyze multiple points    F18=Specify objectives    F24=More keys
```

Figure 13.45.   Comm resources report following upgrade.

13.3.4 Postscript

Space constraints prevent us from helping you to explore any other facilities of BEST/1, but you are well placed now to use the manual or to find your own way with occasional use of the help key through the uncharted areas. It is likely that the externals of the model will develop and change slightly with time. This is part of the normal process of enhancing function and ease of use, and is not a good excuse for failing to learn how to use the product now. Spending time familiarizing will pay dividends when you are called on to use this tool in a real situation. It will also help to improve general understanding of performance issues.

14
Preparing a business case for additional hardware

Once you know what additional hardware is needed, in most organizations you will have to make a case to higher management for the required funds. Convincing management of the need for expenditure is rarely easy. Traditionally a number of people in top management positions have been unable or unwilling to understand even the simplest technical arguments with respect to computers. You may need therefore to put your case in very simple terms. It may also be subject to review by computer-literate auditors. Clearly there is a potential demand for two sets of documentation:

- A management summary with only the minimum of technical detail
- Full technical documentation.

In this chapter we deal with both of these requirements. Whatever the audience, it is essential that the report presents the argument clearly, fairly and without unnecessary technicalities. Any amount of skilled and painstaking work can be wasted if the report is misleading or misunderstood.

14.1   The detailed business case

This need not be a large document, nor should producing it be an onerous task. All the input, apart from costs, has been created during the capacity planning process. The main areas to cover are:

1. Current workload
2. Expected growth
3. Capacity plan
4. Hardware required and costs
5. Recommendations
6. Disclaimers.

14.1.1 *Current workload*

The contents of this section can be broken down as follows:

1.   Description of overall current workload

This will be based on the data you recorded in Tables 8.1 and 8.2 for your selected peak workload. Give data for a number of periods (say, three or four). This will show the degree of consistency in the workload.

2.   Workload profiles

This should consist of documentation of the profiles selected for input to the capacity planning tool.

3.   Integrity of data input to the capacity plan

Describe the steps you took in identifying the peak workload as discussed in Chapter 12. Point out that the data satisfies the guidelines for good input to a capacity plan and that system tuning was checked to ensure optimum use of current resources before embarking on the capacity plan.

4.   Comments about the peak workload

Comment on the main performance resource utilizations and on how close they are to recommended guidelines for maximum utilization. In addition, state the situation with respect to the amount of disk storage used and available.

As well as data produced by the computer, provide information on the users' perception of performance. Where possible, support any adverse user comments by quoting specific data collected by the performance tools. For instance, if one particular application gives a consistently longer response than average, give evidence of this.

Provide data on any trends you have noticed over past months. The historical graphs produced from the workload-monitoring process can be invaluable here.

5.   Basis for the size of the current system

State the basis for the size of the current system. This may be a previous capacity plan or the original sizing of the system. Where possible, document the associated workload and predicted response times and resource utilizations. Point out significant differences beween the documented assumptions and the current situation.

14.1.2 *Expected growth*

1.   Growth in current workload

State the expected growth.You may need to break this down into specific areas of the workload, where the expected growth is different for the different areas. The growth can be expressed as a percentage increase or as a number of additional users. You may categorize the additional users according to whether they are expected to be busy, steady or casual. If you do, you may wish to show examples of the average transactions per hour for similar existing users. Do not forget to include any growth in required data storage. State the anticipated time scales for the growth.

2.   Addition of new workloads

Where you plan to add new workloads to your system, provide performance profiles for these and state the number of expected active workstations and transactions per hour for each workload. Say where the performance profiles came from, any assumptions made and your reasons for presuming them to be valid. Point out the limitations of such profiles. In the case of a package, even if the profiles are taken from a user similar to your organization, there is no absolute guarantee that your organization will use the package in exactly the same way.

3.   Justification of expected growth

Give a business justification for the expected growth in each area. Quote the heads of user departments and their stated reasons for the anticipated growth. Add your own comments about allowing a contingency factor for growth in the medium term, if you feel this to be appropriate.

4.   Summary

Sum up this section with a comparison chart of the estimated peak number of active workstations and transactions per hour in each area and in total, compared with the current situation.

14.1.3 *Capacity plan*

The contents of this section can be broken down as follows:

1.   Capacity planning method

Record how you performed the capacity plan, stating the tools you used and why you used them.

2.   Results of the capacity plan

Use the reports produced by BEST/1 and any graphs you feel are relevant to show what the tool predicts. If BEST/1 predicts that the workload can be supported by a number of different upgraded configurations, e.g. either by additional DASD or by additional memory, provide the information for all options which you feel are appropriate. Do not forget to show what the model predicts for the anticipated workload on the current AS/400 configuration.

3.   Comments on the results

Point out the salient figures in the model such as transactions per hour, average response times (by user group where appropriate) and the resource utilizations, and how close these are to thresholds. Do this for the upgraded configurations and for the new workload on the current configuration.

It may be necessary to include a paragraph outlining the concept of resource utilization thresholds in relation to acceptable queuing times and stable performance. Do point out the dangers of relying on predicted response times as absolutes, particularly when working close to the threshold utilizations. Suggest that they are used only to compare alternative options.

4.   Requirement for additional data storage

Explain where data storage needs decree more DASD than the capacity planner suggests. Conversely, do not highlight low space occupancy arising from the primary necessity for sufficient actuators to support the I/O rate. It is irrelevant and may prompt resistance.

14.1.4   Hardware required and costs

Costs of additional hardware and upgrades have been traditionally supplied by IBM and its agents or business partners. Provide the costs of all alternative upgrades and justify your preferred option. One option may be cheaper in the short term but less so when you take into account a potential upgrade further in the future.

14.1.5   Recommendations

Use this section to summarize the case for the upgrade. Draw attention to the dangers of trying to run the increased workload on the current system if the upgrade is not in place in time.

14.1.6   Disclaimers

Point out that, although you have followed a logical approach in creating the capacity plan, you are essentially trying to predict the future. The accuracy of the prediction depends mainly on the following assumptions:

- Correct anticipated growth
- Accurate performance profiles and volumes for new workloads
- No major surprises, e.g. unexpected acquisitions.

In addition, review the disclaimer documentation in BEST/1; there may be some points here that you wish to include.

14.2   The management summary

Obviously, only you can decide how much of the technically detailed case it will be sensible to present to your management. Some will want to see everything and others will want only the briefest of documents. In either case you should add a one- or two-page management summary which contains the following:

1. Current workload in terms of transactions per hour, number of workstations and average response time
2. Predicted future workload described in the same terms as the current workload with business reasons for the growth in each area
3. Predicted average response time and main resource utilizations on the current hardware configuration compared to recommended guidelines
4. Predicted average response time and main resource utilizations on the upgraded configurations derived from BEST/1
5. Your recommendations where alternative courses of action are possible
6. Disclaimers.

14.3   The never-ending cycle

When your report is accepted and the new hardware finally arrives, you have reached the end of the performance management journey. Perhaps it would be truer to say the end of the first lap. Progress now consists of repeating the tuning, monitoring and capacity planning processes all over again, with perhaps the occasional sizing of an additional machine as a diversion.

In our experience there are always more than enough variations to prevent this cycle from becoming repetitious, or too much like the fate of the 'Flying Dutchman', condemned to circumnavigate the world for ever. We trust this guide will continue to help you sail through whatever performance management squalls blow up.

Bibliography

Title	IBM publication reference number
AS/400 System Handbook	GA19-5486
IBM Application System/400 Technology	SA21-9540
IBM Application System/400 Technology Journal (Version 2)	S325-6020
AS/400 Programming: Work Management Guide	SC41-8078
AS/400 Programming: Work Management Guide (V3R1)	SC41-3306
AS/400 Performance Management 'Red Book' (IBM ITSC Rochester)	GG24-3723
AS/400 Performance Tools/400 Guide	SC41-8084
AS/400 Performance Tools/400 Guide (V3R1)	SC41-3340
AS/400 New Products Planning Information for Version 3 Release 1	SA41-3100
AS/400 Advanced Backup and Recovery Guide	SC41-8079
AS/400 BEST/1 Capacity Planning Tool Guide	SC41-0139
AS/400 BEST/1 Capacity Planning Tool Guide (V3R1)	SC41-3341
AS/400 Diagnostic Aids	LY44-0597/8
AS/400 Communications: Management Guide	SC41-0024
PC Support/400 Implementation and Performance 'Red Book'	GG24-3636

Appendix 1
Useful forms

This appendix contains full-page versions of some tables and figures from the main text which can be copied and used.

Workload and performance summary data

Date[a]				
Start time[b]				
Average response time[c]				
Total interactive throughput[d]				
NPT tr/h[e]				
PCS tr/h[f]				
Passthrough tr/h[g]				
DDM target tr/h[h]				
S/36 tr/h[i]				
MRT tr/h[j]				
Total active interactive jobs[k]				
Active workstations (%)[l]				
CPU Utilization @ > = priority 20^m				
Machine pool NDB faults (s)[n]				
Total DB and NDB faults (s)[o]				
Average actuator utilization[p]				
CPU seconds per transaction[q]				
Synchronous disk I/Os per transaction[r]				
Exceptional wait per transaction[s]				

Most of these data items are easily located in the few subdivisions of the System Report; the remainder (l and s) are in the System Summary Data section of the Job Summary Report.

[a]'Right side of the heading of every page (Fig. 8.2).

[b]'Right side of the heading of every page (Fig. 8.2).

[c]'Average Response' column of 'Workload' report (Fig. 8.2). Note: This does not include line time and no distinction need be made between local and remote workload components for our purposes. This is our prime measure of the efficacy of system tuning measures.

[d]'Total of 'Tns/Hour Rate' column of 'Resource Utilization' report (Fig. 8.3).

[e]'Tns/Hour Rate' figure identified as 'Interactive' job type in the 'Resource Utilization' report (Fig. 8.3). Note: NPT = non-programmable terminal.

[f]'Tns/Hour Rate' figure identified as 'PC Support' in the 'Resource Utilization' report (Fig. 8.3). This is the workstation function part of the PC activity.

[g]'Tns/Hour Rate' figure identified as 'Passthru' in the 'Resource Utilization' report (Fig. 8.3). This represents transactions executed on the measured machine by virtual devices, associated with workstations attached to another machine in the network.

[h]'Tns/Hour Rate' figure identified as 'DDM Server' in the 'Resource Utilization' report (Fig. 8.3). This represents the Distributed Data Management requests satisfied by the measured machine for transactions running on other machines in the network.

[i]'Tns/Hour Rate' figure identified as 'S/36' in the 'Resource Utilization' report (Fig. 8.3). All S/36 environment jobs that are not MRT jobs are counted.

[j]'Tns/Hour Rate' figure identified as 'MRT' in the 'Resource Utilization' report (Fig. 8.3). These are a special type of S/36 environment transaction.

[k]'Nbr Jobs' figure for interactive job type in 'System Summary Data' section of 'Job Summary' report (Fig. 8.4). Note that the total 'Active Jobs Per Interval' figure from the 'Resource Utilization' report is likely to be too large, due to the way PC Support jobs are counted.

[l]'Est Of AWS' from right-hand side of 'System Summary Data' section of 'Job Summary' report (Fig. 8.4). Divide this by the total active jobs figure and note the percentage.

[m]'Cum Util' figure against the lowest-priority 20 job type in the 'Resource Utilization Expansion' report (Fig. 8.5).

[n]'Top figure in the 'Non-DB Fault' column of the 'Storage Pool Utilization' report (Fig. 8.6).

[o]'Sum of the two totals under the 'Non-DB Fault' and 'DB Fault' columns of the above report (Fig. 8.6).

[p]'Average figure under the 'Percent Util' column of the 'Disk Utilization' report (Fig. 8.7).

[q]'Average figure under the 'CPU Seconds' column of the 'Resource Utilization' report (Fig. 8.3).

[r]'Average figure under the 'Sync Disk I/O' column of the 'Resource Utilization' report (Fig. 8.3).

[s]'Excp Wait/Tns' figure from 'System Summary Data' section of the 'Job Summary' report (Fig. 8.4).

Pool activity record

System pool no.	Pool size (K)	Activity level	DB faults per second	NDB faults per second	AW trn/min	WI trn/min	AI trn/min
1		N/A					
2							
3							
4							
5							
6							
7							
8							
9							
10							
11							
12							
13							
14							
15							
Totals							

Note. These data items are easily located in the 'Storage Pool Utilization' section of the System Report (Fig. 8.6).

Performance-related system values

System value	Current setting	Default setting	Recommended change	Change date
QMODEL		N/A	N/A	N/A
QSRLNBR		N/A	N/A	N/A
QACTJOB		20		
QTOTJOB		30		
QADLACTJ		10		
QADLTOTJ		10		
QCTLSBSD		QBASE QSYS		
QMCHPOOL		1500		
QBASPOOL		500		
QBASACTLVL		6		
QMAXACTLVL		*NOMAX		
QTSEPOOL		*NONE		
QAUTOCFG		1		
QPFRADJ		2		
QINACTITV		*NONE		
QINACTMSGQ		*ENDJOB		
QDSCJOBITV		240		
QDEVRCYACN		*MSG		
QCMNRCYLMT		0 0		
QDBRCVYWT		0		
QRCLSPLSTG		8		

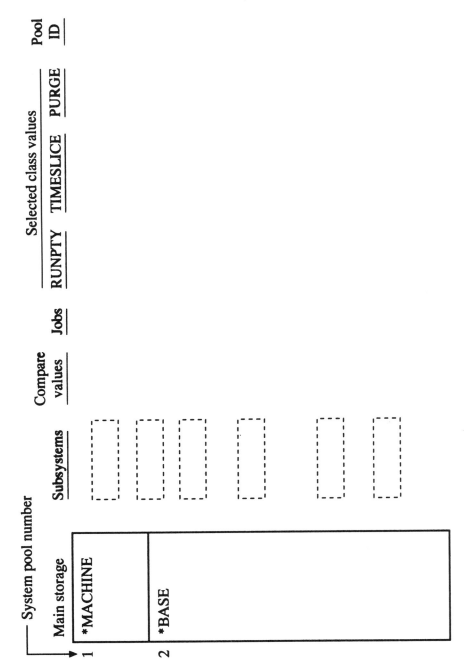

Figure 9.1.   Memory partitioning and usage by subsystems.

Appendix 2
Glossary

access path The part of an AS/400 database file which provides access to records, and the facilities of record sequencing and selection.

adapter A part that electrically or physically connects a device to a computer or to another device.

Advanced Function Printing (AFP) Pertaining to the ability of programs to use the all-points-addressable concept to print text and images on a printer.

APPC (advanced program-to-program communications) Data communications support that allows programs on an AS/400 system to communicate with programs on other systems having compatible communications support. APPC on the AS/400 system provides an application programming interface to the SNA LU type 6.2 and node type 2.1 architectures.

APPN (advanced peer-to-peer networking) Data communications support that routes data in a network between two or more APPC systems that do not need to be adjacent.

ASCII (American National Standard Code for Information Interchange) The code developed by the American National Standards Institute for information exchange among data processing systems, data communications systems, and associated equipment. The ASCII character set consists of 7-bit control characters and symbolic characters, plus one parity bit.

authority lookups Part of the process whereby the licensed internal code determines whether a particular user is authorized to access a specific object.

authorization list A list of two or more user IDs and their authorities for system resources. The system-recognized identifier for the object type is *AUTL.

auxiliary storage All addressable disk storage other than main storage. Contrast with **main storage**.

auxiliary storage pool (ASP) A group of units defined from the disk units that make up auxiliary storage. ASPs provide a means of isolating certain objects on specific disk units to prevent loss of data due to disk media failures on other disk units. See also **system ASP** and **user ASP**.

BSC (binary synchronous communications) A data communications line protocol that uses a standard set of transmission control characters and control character sequences to send binary coded data over a communications line. See also **SDLC (synchronous data link control)**.

buffer (1) A routine or an area of storage that corrects for the different speeds of data flow or timings of events, when transferring data from one device to another. (2) A portion of storage used to hold input or output data temporarily.

bus One or more conductors used for transmitting signals or power.

cache An area of memory from which data can be read or to which data can be written. Cache memory provides faster access than disk for reading data. It also allows faster write operations than to disk. The use of cache memory allows data to be read or written to physical disk asynchronously.

card A plug-in circuit assembly.

CL (control language) The set of commands with which a user requests system functions.

close The function that ends the connection between a file and a program, and ends the processing. Contrast with **open**.

command A statement used to request a function of the system. A command consists of the command name abbreviation, which identifies the requested function, and its parameters.

commitment control A means of grouping database file operations that allows the processing of a group of database changes as a single unit through the Commit command or the removal of a group of database changes as a single unit through the Rollback command.

communications line The physical link (such as a wire or a telephone circuit) that connects one or more workstations to a communications controller, or connects one controller to another.

compaction A function that removes repetitive bits from the data being processed and replaces the repetitive bits with control bits. Compaction reduces the amount of storage space required for the data.

compression A function that removes repetitive characters, spaces, or strings of characters from the data being processed and replaces the repetitive characters with control characters. Compression reduces the amount of storage space required for the data.

configuration The physical and logical arrangement of devices and programs that make up a data processing system.

control block A storage area used by a program to hold control information.

controller A device that coordinates and controls the operation of one or more input/output devices (such as workstations) and synchronizes the operation of such devices with the operation of the system as a whole.

controller description An object that contains a description of the characteristics of a controller that is either directly attached to the system or attached to a communications line. The system-recognized identifier for the object type is *CTLD.

CPU (central processing unit) The central processing unit of the AS/400 supplies the functions for: retrieving and storing data, processing arithmetic and logical data, running instructions in a particular sequence, controlling communications between main storage and the I/O devices.

data integrity (1) The condition that exists as long as accidental or intentional destruction, alteration, or loss of data does not occur. (2) Within the scope of a unit of work, either all changes to the database management systems are completed or none of them are. The set of change operations are considered an integral set.

data management The part of the operating system that controls the storing and accessing of data to or from an application program. The data can be on internal storage (for example, database) on external media (diskette, tape or printer), or on another system.

data queue An object that is used to communicate and briefly store data used by several programs in a job or between jobs. The system-recognized identifier is *DTAQ.

database All the data files stored in the system.

database file One of several types of the system object type *FILE kept in the system that contains descriptions of how input data is to be presented to a program from internal storage and how output data is to be presented to internal storage from a program. See also **physical file** and **logical file**.

database manager The system component which coordinates database activities and provides database functions (such as projection, joining, triggers and referential integrity).

DDM (distributed data management) A function of the operating system that allows an application program or user on one system to use database files stored on a remote system. The systems must be connected by a communications network, and the remote systems must also be using DDM.

device description An object that contains information describing a particular device or logical unit (LU) that is attached to the system. A device description is a description of the logical connection between two LUs (local and remote locations). The system-recognized identifier for the object type is *DEVD.

DOS (disk operating system) An operating system for personal computers that can only perform tasks one at a time.

DSPT (display station pass-through) A communications function that allows a user connected directly to one machine, to sign on to another machine in the network, and use that system's programs and data. Sometimes called pass-through.

DWS (dependent workstation) A workstation that does not have processing capability and does not allow the user to change its functions. Also called non-programmable terminal (NPT) or non-programmable workstation (NWS). Contrast with **programmable workstation (PWS)**.

dynamic Pertaining to events occurring at run time, or during processing.

effective address overflow (EAO) exception A condition in which the Licensed Internal Code must make address adjustments not made above the machine interface.

EHLLAPI Emulator high-level language application program interface.

emulation Imitation of one system or device by another.

file A generic term for the object type that refers to a database file, a device file, or a save file. The system-recognized identifier for the object type is *FILE.

folder (1) A directory for documents. A folder is used to group related documents and to find documents by name. The system-recognized identifier for the object type is *FLR. Compare with **library**. (2) A list used to organize objects.

frame In communications, the unit of transmission sent and received by the data link layer, one of the seven layers defined in the ISO standard.

graphical user interface A type of user interface that takes advantage of high-resolution graphics. A graphical user interface includes a combination of graphics, the object-action relationship, the use of pointing devices, menu bars and other menus, overlapping windows, and icons.

group profile A user profile that provides the same authority to a group of users.

hardware Physical equipment, rather than programs, procedures, rules, and associated information.

history log A summary of the system activities, such as system and job information, device status, system operator messages, and a record of program temporary fix (PTF) activity on the system. The history log is identified by the name QHST, and the system-recognized identifier for the object type is *MSGQ.

HLIC (Horizontal Licensed Internal Code) Programming that implements the internal hardware instruction set.

ICF (inter-system communications function) A function of the operating system that allows a program to communicate interactively with another program or system.

ILE (Integrated Language Environment) Pertaining to a set of constructs and interfaces that provides a common run-time environment and run-time bindable application program interfaces (APIs) for all ILE-conforming high-level languages.

index A table containing the key value and location of each record in an indexed file.

indexed file A file in which the key and the position of each record is recorded in a separate portion of the file called an index.

initial program load (IPL)   The process that loads the system programs from the system auxiliary storage, checks the system hardware, and prepares the system for user operations.

job accounting   A system function that collects information about a job's use of system resources and records that information in a journal.

job log   A printed record of requests submitted to the system by a job, the messages related to the requests, and the actions performed by the system on the job. The job log is produced when the job terminates, by merging and filtering the contents of various temporary message queues.

journal   (1) A system object used to record entries in a journal receiver when a change is made to the database files associated with the journal. (2) To place entries in a journal and its associated receivers.

journal receiver   A system object that contains journal entries recorded when changes are made to the data in database files or the access paths associated with the database files. The object type is *JRNRCV. See also **journal**.

key   The value used to identify a record in a keyed sequence file.

LAN (local area network)   The physical connection that allows the transfer of information among devices located on the same premises.

library   A system object that serves as a directory to other objects. A library groups related objects, and allows the user to find objects by name. The system-recognized identifier for the object type is *LIB.

library list   A list that indicates which libraries are to be searched and the order in which they are to be searched. The system-recognized identifier is *LIBL.

licensed internal code   The layered architecture below the machine interface (MI) and above the machine, consisting of the model-independent and the model-unique licensed internal code. The licensed internal code carries out many functions, including but not limited to storage management, pointers and addressing, program management functions, exception and event management, data functions, I/O managers, security functions, and proprietary system design information.

licensed program   A separately orderable program, supplied by IBM, that performs functions related to processing user data. Examples of licensed programs are PC Support/400, SAA COBOL/400, AS/400 Application Development Tools, SAA OfficeVision/400.

line description   An object that contains information describing a particular communications line that is attached to the system. The system-recognized identifier for the object type is *LIND.

line printer   A device that prints a line of characters as a unit. Contrast with **page printer**.

logical file   A description of how data is to be presented to or received from a program. This type of database file contains no data, but it defines record formats for one or more physical files. See also **database file**. Contrast with **physical file**.

machine interface (MI)   The interface, or boundary, between the operating system and the Licensed Internal Code.

main processor   See **CPU**.

main storage or **main memory**   All addressable storage where programs are run. Contrast with **auxiliary storage**.

member   Different sets of data, each with the same format, within one database file.

menu   A displayed list of items from which an operator can make a selection.

message queue   A list on which messages are placed when they are sent to a user ID or device description. The system-recognized identifier for the object type is *MSGQ.

MI   See **machine interface**.

modification level   A distribution of all temporary fixes to system software issued since the previous modification level. A change in modification level does not add new functions or change the programming support category of the release to which it applies. A new release is shipped with a modification level of 0. When the release is shipped with the service changes incorporated, the modification level is incremented by 1. See also **release** and **version**.

MRT (Multiple Requester Terminal) program   A System/36 Environment program that can process requests from more than one display station or ICF session at the same time using a single copy of the program. Contrast with **SRT program**.

multipoint   In data communications, pertaining to a network that allows two or more stations to communicate with a single system on one line.

NEP (never-ending program)   When a MRT progam is a NEP, it is called a MRT-NEP. A MRT-NEP is not instructed to go to the end of the program when the last device is released. See **MRT program**.

object distribution   A function that allows a user to send source and data files, save files, job streams, spooled files, and messages to another user, either locally or on a SNADS network.

OCL (Operations Control Language)   The set of commands with which a user requests System/36 Environment functions.

open   The function that connects an object of type *FILE to a program for processing.

Operational Assistant   Pertaining to a part of the operating system that provides a set of menus and displays for end users to do commonly performed tasks, such as working with printer output, messages, and batch jobs.

output queue   An object that contains a list of spooled files to be written to an output device, such as a printer.

pacing   In SNA, a technique by which the receiving system controls the rate of transmission of the sending system to prevent overrun.

page printer   In AFP support, any of a class of printers that accepts composed pages, constructed of composed text and images, among other things. Contrast with **line printer**.

paging   To move a page of data between main and auxiliary storage.

panel   A visual presentation of data on the screen.

panel group   An object that contains a collection of any of the following: display formats, print formats, or help information. The system-recognized identifier for the object type is *PNLGRP.

parity   The state of being either even-numbered or odd-numbered. A parity bit is a binary number added to a group of binary numbers to make the sum of that group either always odd (odd parity) or always even (even parity).

PASA (program automatic storage area)   A space allocated within a job's PAG to contain program variables. Each extent is associated with a program subroutine and is initialized when the subroutine is executed. The scope of the variables is limited to the subroutine in which they are defined. Some high-level languages do not allow automatic variables.

pass-through   See **DSPT (display station pass-through)**.

PC (personal computer)   A computer designed primarily for use by one user at a time which can be used for standalone computing and as a workstation to multi-user systems.

physical file   A description of how data is to be presented to or received from a program and how data is actually stored in the database. A physical file contains one record format and one or more members. See also **database file**. Contrast with **logical file**.

point-to-point   Pertaining to data transmission between two locations without the use of any intermediate display station or computer.

poll   To determine if any remote device on a communications line is ready to send data.

polling   (1) The process whereby stations are invited, one at a time, to transmit. (2) The process whereby a controlling station contacts the attached devices to avoid contention, to determine operational status, or to determine readiness to send or receive data.

port   (1) System hardware where the I/O devices are attached. (2) An access point (for example, a logical unit) for data entry or exit. (3) A functional unit of a node through which data can enter or leave a data network. (4) In data communications, that part of a data processor that is dedicated to a single data channel for the purpose of receiving data from or transmitting data to one or more external, remote devices.

print writer   A system program that writes spooled files to a printer.

printer file   A device file that determines what attributes printed output will have. A particular printer may or may not support all of the attributes specified in a printer file.

private authority   The authority specifically given to a user for an object that overrides any other authorities, such as the authority of a user's group profile or an authorization list. Contrast with **public authority**.

program stack   A list of programs linked together as a result of programs calling other programs with the CALL instruction, or implicitly from some other event, within the same job.

programmable workstation (PWS)   A workstation that has some degree of processing capacity and allows the user to change its functions.

PSSA (program static storage area)   A space allocated within a job's PAG to contain program variables. Each active program in the job has its PSSA extent which is initialized when the program is activated, and the scope of the variables is global within the corresponding program.

PTF (program temporary fix)   A temporary solution to, or bypass of, a defect in a current release of a licensed program.

public authority   The authority given to users who do not have any specific (private) authority to an object, who are not on an authorization list (if one is specified for the object), and whose group profile has no specific authority to the object. Contrast with **private authority**.

query   A request to select and copy from a file or files one or more records based on defined conditions. For example, a request for a list of all customers in a customer master file, whose balance is greater than £1000.

queue   A list of messages, jobs, files, or requests waiting to be read, processed, printed or distributed in a predetermined order.

read cache buffering   The function of placing data in cache memory before it is required by a program.

record   A group of related data, words, or fields treated as a unit, such as one name, address, and telephone number.

re-entrant code   A program which does not alter itself or contain data or variables which are altered. Such programs can therefore be executed in more than one job at the same time without the need for multiple copies of the program in main memory.

relational database (RDB)   A data structure perceived by its users as a collection of tables that is organized and accessed according to relationships between data items.

relative record number   A number that specifies the relationship between the location of a record and the beginning of a database file, member, or subfile. For example, the first record in a database file, member, or subfile has a relative record number of 1.

release   A distribution of a new product or new function and authorized program analysis report (APAR) fixes for an existing product. Normally, programming support for the prior release is discontinued after some specified period of time following availability of a new release. The first version of a product is announced as Release 1 Modification Level 0. See also **modification level** and **version**.

remote   Pertaining to a device, system, or file through a communications line.

resident   Remaining in main storage.

RUMBA/400 A feature of PC Support/400, which operates with Microsoft Windows or OS/2, that provides display and printer emulation.

run time The time during which the instructions of a computer program are run by a processing unit.

save file A file allocated in auxiliary storage that can be used to store saved data on disk (without requiring diskettes or tapes), or to receive objects sent through the network. The system-recognized identifier for the object type is *FILE.

SDLC (synchronous data link control) A form of communications line control that uses commands to control the transfer of data over a communications line.

search index An AS/400 object type used to provide access to help modules through key words. The system-recognized identifier for the object type is *SCHIDX.

sector (1) An area on a disk track or a diskette track to record information. (2) The smallest amount of information that can be written to or read from a disk or diskette during a single read or write operation.

server (1) A computer that shares its resources with other computers in a network. (2) In a local area network, a data station that provides services to other data stations.

session (1) The length of time that starts when a user signs on and ends when the user signs off at a display station. (2) The logical connection by which an AS/400 program or device can communicate with a program or device at a remote location.

SNA (Systems Network Architecture) In IBM networks the description of the layered structure, formats, protocols, and operational sequences that are used for transmitting information units through networks, as well as controlling the configuration and operation of networks.

special authority An authority which can be granted to a user to perform types of work appropriate to particular classes of user, such as system operator, or programmer or security administrator. The grantee requires authority to the specific objects (commands, libraries, files, etc.) to be used, in addition to the relevant special authority.

spool The system function of putting files or jobs into disk storage for later printing or processing.

spooled file or spool file A file that holds output data waiting to be processed, such as information waiting to be printed. Also known as spooled output file.

spooling subsystem A part of the system that provides the operating environment for the programs that read jobs onto job queues to wait for processing and write files from an output queue to an output device. IBM supplies one spooling subsystem: QSPL.

SQL (Structured Query Language) A language that can be used within host programming languages or interactively to put information into a database and to get and organize selected information from a database. SQL can also control access to database resources.

SRT program (single requester terminal program) A System/36 Environment program that can process requests from only one display station or ICF session for each copy of the program. Contrast with **MRT program**.

subfile A group of records of the same record format that can be displayed and scrolled at a display station with minimum programming effort. The program sends the entire group of records to the display in a single operation and receives the group from the display in another operation. The system handles the end user roll key interactions.

subprogram A called program. A subprogram is combined with the calling program at run time to produce a run unit and is below the calling program in the program stack.

system ASP The auxiliary storage pool where system programs and data reside. It is the storage pool used if a storage pool is not defined by the user. See also **auxiliary storage pool** and **user ASP**.

System/36 Environment   A part of OS/400 that emulates the System/36 operating system, mapping a subset of System/36 statements to OS/400 CL commands. The System/36 Environment also supports utility programs that perform common service functions.

System/38 environment   A function of the operating system that processes most of the System/38 control language (CL) statements and programs to run System/38 application programs. Contrast with **System/36 Environment**.

token-ring network   A local area network that sends data in one direction throughout a specified number of locations by using the symbol of authority for control of the transmission line, called a token, to allow any sending station in the network (ring) to send data when the token arrives at that location.

trace   A means of tracking the execution of a program. Tracing is primarily used for debugging or investigating the performance of programs.

track   A circular path on the surface of a disk or diskette on which information is magnetically recorded and from which recorded information is read.

TCP (Transmission Control Protocol)   In TCP/IP, a host-to-host protocol that provides transmission in an internet environment. TCP assumes Internet Protocol (IP) as the underlying protocol.

TCP/IP (Transmission Control Protocol/Internet Protocol)   A set of vendor-independent communications protocols that support peer-to-peer connectivity functions for both local and wide area networks.

TRLAN   Abbreviation in the commands, parameters, and options for IBM Token-Ring Network. See also **token-ring network**.

twin axial cable   A cable made of two twisted wires inside a shield that is used on the 5250 family devices.

user ASP   An auxiliary storage pool other than the system ASP. See also **auxiliary storage pool** and **system ASP**.

user interface manager (UIM)   A function of the operating system that provides a consistent user interface by providing comprehensive support for defining and running panels (displays), dialogues, and online help information.

user ID (user identification)   The name of the user profile specified when a user signs on the system.

version   A separate IBM licensed program based on an existing licensed program which usually has significant new code or function. See **release** and **modification level**.

VLIC (Vertical Licensed Internal Code)   Programming that defines logical operations on data. The Vertical Licensed Internal Code translates the machine interface (MI) instructions.

workstation   A device used to transmit information to or receive information from a computer; for example, a display station or printer.

write cache   Cache memory where data can be written faster than to disk. The data is later written to physical disk asynchronously.

WSC (workstation controller)   An I/O controller card in the card enclosure that provides the direct connection of local workstations to the system.

X.25   A CCITT Recommendation that defines the physical level (physical layer), link level (data link layer), and packet level (network layer) of the OSI reference model. An X.25 network is an interface between data terminal equipment (DTE) and data circuit-terminating equipment (DCE) operating in the packet mode, and connected to public data networks by dedicated circuits. X.25 networks use the connection-mode network service.

INDEX

*BASE, *see* shared system pools
*INTERACT, *see* shared system pools
*MACHINE, *see* shared system pools
*SHRPOOL1 – 10, *see* shared system pools
*SPOOL, *see* shared system pools

abbreviations, xv
access arm, 24, *see also* performance
    resources, DASD
access path journalling, 217
active jobs table, 36, 58
active-to-ineligible (AI) transition, 51
active-to-wait (AW) transition, 51
activity level, 41, 47–53
activity level checking, 202–203
activity level estimation, 198–200
actuator, 24, *see also* performance
    resources, DASD
ADDJOBQE (add job queue entry)
    command, 60
ADDPFRCOL (add performance
    collection) command, 249, 251
ADDRTGE (add routing entry) command,
    42
adviser, 191–192
ANZACCGRP (analyze access group)
    command, 47
ANZPFRDTA (analyze performance data)
    command, 191–192
APPC programming, 221–222
AS/400 positioning, 95–97
AS/400 Server series, 96, 110–112, 224
assistance level, 34
authority lookup exception cost, 203–204
automatic performance adjustment,
    189–191
autostart job, 43
autostart job entry (AJE), 41–43
auxiliary storage management (ASM), 63

base pool, *see* shared pools, *BASE
balanced systems, 79
batch jobs, 7, 43, 60–62, 206–208
    attributes from SBMJOB with defaults,
        60
    attributes from tailored job description,
        61
    effect on interactive performance, 62
    implementing separate pools for, 206–208
batch performance
    general, 7–8
    improving, 9–13
    effect of access conflicts on, 14
    effect of CPU speed on, 10
    effect of disk speed on, 10–11
    effect of multiprogramming on, 11
    dependence on synchronous disk I/Os of,
        12–13
benchmarks, 97–110
    effect of DASD failure, 104
    effect of HA options, 103–104
    effect of journalling and commitment
        control, 104–105
    effect of mirroring, 101–103
    F35 restore rates, 109
    F35 save rates, 108
    F80 restore rates, 109
    F80 save rates, 108
    higher end of AS/400 range, 99
    large AS/400 configurations at 70%
        capacity, 100
    lower end of AS/400 range, 99
    RAMP-C, 84–85, 97, 98
    S/36 Environment, 100–101
    TPC-C, 97–98
BEST/1
    acceptability criteria for data input to,
        122–123
    advantages of using, 116–117

BEST/1 (*continued*)
   capacity planning example using, 260–283
      building a model from measured data
         in, 260–269
      validating the model in, 269–277
      modelling asymmetric workload
         growth in, 277–282
   changing workload attributes in, 147
   compared to MDLSYS, 117–118
   concepts, 118–119
   definition of function in, 118–119
   definition of non-interactive transaction
      in, 119
   editing the hardware configuration in,
      147
   menu structure, 119–121
   obtaining input for, 122–124
   overview of, 117–121
   sizing example using, 124–148
      building a model for, 125–133
      input to, 124
      modelling growth and saving results in,
         143–146
      modelling proposed volumes in,
         133–143
      specifying distribution of characters in,
         147–148
   terminology, 118–119
   use of predefined data with, 123–124
blocking data transfers into memory, 12–13,
   45, 56
   see also SETOBJACC, Expert Cache, and
      OVRDBF
business case preparation, 284–288
   detailed case, 284–287
   management summary, 288

capacity planning, 245–288
   collecting data for, 250–253
      use of ADDPFRCOL command in,
         250–251
   compared to sizing, 255–256
   estimating future workload for, 257
   example, *see* BEST/1
   grouping applications for, 257–258
      use of transition detail report in, 258
   identifying workload peaks for, 249–250
   questions answered by, xvi, 247–248
   dealing with new workload components
      when, 258
   objectives, 247
   processes, 248
   selection of data for, 252–253, 256–257
   trend analysis input to, 253–254
   use of BEST/1 for, 260–283

   when to collect data for, 248–250
      using ADDPFRCOL to identify,
         249–250
case notes on system tuning, 235–244
CHGCLS (change class) command, 206
CHGCMD (change command) command,
   214
CHGGRPA (change group attributes)
   command, 59
CHGJOB (change job) command, 214
CHGJOBQE (change job queue entry)
   command, 207
CHGRTGE (change routing entry)
   command, 208
CHGS36A (change S/36 attributes)
   command, 211
CHGS36PRCA (change S/36 procedure
   attributes) command, 211
CHGSBSD (change subsystem description)
   command, 48
CHGSHRPOOL (change shared pool)
   command, 57
class discrimination, 227–228
class object, 36, 37, 43
client/server performance, 14–16, 110–112,
   224
clock rate, 17–18
CLRPOOL (clear pool) command, 231
communications considerations, 105–106,
   217–223
   batch data transfer, 221–222
   CMNRCYLMT parameter, 218
   CNNPOLLTMR parameter, 219
   data compression, 222
   device and session parameters, 220–221
   disclaimer, 223
   frame size, 219, 220
   LANACKFRQ and LANMAXOUT
      parameters, 221
   line utilization, 217–218
   load balancing, 217–218
   MAXFRAME parameter, 218, 219, 221
   MAXLENRU parameter, 218
   MAXOUT parameter, 219
   NDMPOLLTMR parameter, 219
   OUTLIMIT parameter, 219
   pacing, 220–221
   polling inactive controllers, 218–219
   pre-start jobs, 222
   recovery and retries, 218
   remote print throughput, 218
   remote workstation controllers, 219
   token ring LAN throughput, 221
communications subsystem (QCMN), 224
console, 44

controlling subsystem, 44
CPU (central processing unit), *see* performance resources, CPU
CRTCLS (create class) command, 208
CRTDUPOBJ (create duplicate object) command, 207
CRTGPHFMT (create graph format) command, 254
CRTHSTDTA (create historical data) command, 254
cycle time, 17,18

DASD (direct access storage device), *see* performance resources, DASD
database parallel processing, 52
data compression, 222
demand paging, 54–55
disk, 23, *see also* performance resources, DASD
disk activity report, 204–205
disk configuration, sample, 24–26
disk controller, 24, 25
disk housekeeping, 216
disk I/O service time, 24–27
disk I/Os
    physical and logical, 8–9
    synchronous and asynchronous, 9
    database and non database, 9
disk IOP utilization review, 205
disk utilization report, 176
disk utilization review, 204–205
distributed data management (DDM), 221, 222
DMPTRC (dump trace) command, 167
DSCJOB (disconnect job) command, 212
DSPACCGRP (display access group) command, 47
DSPHSTGPH(display historical graph) command, 254
DSPPFRDTA (display performance data) command, 250

EDTS36PRCA (edit S/36 procedure attributes) command, 211, 212
exceptional wait time reduction, 216–217
execution priority, 50
Expert Cache facility, 57–58, 210

favouring selected jobs, 227–234
    batch job considerations, 233–234
        multiple streams, 233
        splitting, 233–234
        dropping or deferring steps, 234
    by blocked data transfers, 231–233
    by enhanced run priority, 228–229
    by exclusive disk unit allocation, 229–230
    by exclusive pool allocation, 229
    by reducing physical disk I/Os, 231–233
    printing considerations, 234
FIFO (first in first out) queuing, 50, 72
file transfer support (FTS), 221–222
forms, 291–296
    memory partitioning and usage by subsystems, 296
    performance related system values, 295
    pool activity record, 294
    workload and performance summary data, 292–293
FSIOP (file server I/O processor), 111–112, 224

glossary, 297–304
group jobs, 58–60
    performance considerations with, 59
    activation groups and, 59–60

HDA (head disk assembly), 23
hierarchy of microprocessors, 62–63

ILE (integrated language environment), 59–60
ineligible queue, 48, 51, 52, 53
initial menu parameter, 43
initial program parameter, 43
integrated operating system, 63
intended reader, xvi-xvii
interactive performance, 13–14
    effect of resource utilization and queuing on, 13–14
    effect of data transmission on, 14
    effect of access conflicts on, 14
interactive pool, *see* shared pools, *INTERACT
interactive pools, size and activity level, 199–200
interactive program statistics, 179
interactive response time components, 53–54
interactive work, use of multiple pools for, 208–210
IOP (I/O processor), 24–26
IPL after abnormal termination, 217
IPL frequency, 215

job, 35–45
    attributes, 36–37
    creation example, 41–43
    definition, 35
job description object, 36, 37, 41, 43
job descriptions in work entries, 39

job descriptions in user profiles, 41
job descriptions and batch jobs, 61
job log production, 215
job queue, 60
job queue entry, 38, 41, 43
job states and transitions, 48–53, 202–203
    active-to-ineligible (AI), 51, 53
    active-to-wait (AW), 51, 53
    ineligible-to-active (IA), 51, 53
    wait-to-active (WA), 51, 53
    wait-to-ineligible (WI), 51, 53
job summary report, 178
job termination, 43, 58
job tracking, 35–36
journalling, *see* benchmarks

LAN Server/400, 111–112
layered machine architecture, 62
lock conflicts, 53
long waits, 51, 53
LRU (least recently used) algorithm, 45, 54,
    55, 56

machine pool, *see* shared pools,
    *MACHINE
main memory, *see* main storage
main storage
    demand for, 45, 46
    documenting usage of, 189
    partitioning of, 44–46, 206–210
    use of, 45–58, 189
megahertz (Mhz), 17, 96
memory, *see* main storage
memory pool, *see* pool
MIPS (millions of instructions per second),
    17, 96
MSDC (magnetic storage device controller),
    25

n-way processors, 21–22
number of jobs in system, 35–36

Object Distribution Facility (ODF),
    221–222
object orientation, 62
ODP (open data path), 46
OptiConnect/400, 97
OVRDBF (override with database file)
    command, 57, 232

PAG (process access group), 46–47, 54–56
PAG swapping, 55–56
page, 45
page fault rate, 185–186
page faulting, 45, 55

page fault guidelines, 201–203
page sharing, 46
paging options, 54–58
PASA (program automatic storage area),
    46
PC attachment considerations, 14, 15,
    223–225
    client/server applications, 14–16, 224
    communications subsystem, 224
    file transfer, 223
    further information, 225
    integrated file system, 225
    overhead relative to NPTs, 223
    shared folders, 223–225
performance
    and workload summary data form, 169
    basic principles of, 3–16
    batch, *see* batch performance
    client/server, 14–16, 110–111
    data from production machines, 112–115
    definitions of, 5–8
    external measures of, 164–185
    factors that control, 8–16
    improving system, 189–226
    in a communications environment,
        105–106
    interactive, *see* interactive performance
    introduction to AS/400, 1–66
    recovery options, 101–105
    relative hardware, table of, 16
    save/restore, 106–110
    secondary indicators of, 185–188
    user perceptions of, 184
performance evaluation, 163–187, 201–203
    acceptance criteria of data for, 168–183
    user input to, 184–185
    using performance tools' reports for,
        166–183
    using WRKACTJOB for, 165
    using WRKDSKSTS for, 188
    using WRKSYSSTS for, 185–187
        page fault rates, 185–186
        ineligible transition rates, 186–187
    versus monitoring, 163
performance examples, 95–115
performance management
    fundamental questions of, xvi-xvii
    in practice, 3–5
    relevance to AS/400 users, 3–4
    the nightmare scenario, 4
performance resources
    CPU, 17–23, 203–204
        packaging, 22–23
        relative RAMP-C throughput of,
            18–19

relative speeds of, 19–21
  effect on transaction character of,
    21–22
  utilization review, 203–204
DASD
  characteristics, 26–28
  components, 23–24
  configuration limits, 28–29
  devices (9332/9335/9336/9337), 24–28
  I/O service times, 26, 27
  IOP service times, 32
  mirroring, 101–103
  rack capacity, 27
  memory, 28–30, 45–58
    control storage, 30
    sizes of, for AS/400 models, 30
    utilization of, 28–30
  communications, 31–32
    local, 31, 32
    remote, 31, 32
    workstation attachment to, 31
performance tools
  advisor, 191–192
  disk activity report, 204–205
  job summary report:
    individual transaction statistics, 181
    interactive program statistics section,
      179
    interactive transactions by 5 minute
      intervals, 180
    job summary section, 178
    longest seize/lock conflicts, 182
    system summary data section, 173
  ENDDSKCOL command, 205
  PRTCPTRPT command, 167, 250
  PRTDSKRPT command, 205
  PRTSYSRPT command, 166, 167
  PRTTNSRPT command, 168, 258
  STRDSKCOL command, 205
  STRPFRMON command, 166
  system report:
    disk utilization section, 176
    resource utilization section, 172
    resource utilization expansion section,
      174
    storage pool utilization section, 175
    workload section, 171
  transition detail report, 259
  use of reports to measure performance,
    166–168
pool activity record, 170
pool page fault guidelines, 202
pool size and activity level estimation, 200,
  202–203, 207
pool utilization report, 175

pool WI transition guidelines, 202
predefined workloads, 83–87
  additional, 87
  batch, 86
  office, 87
  RAMP-C, 84–85
  SPOOL, 85–86
  SQL RTW, 87
printing, reducing the overhead, 215
private pools, 41–43, 49
process control space, 47
programmer functions, reducing the
  overhead, 214–215
PRTCPTRPT (print component report)
  command, 167, 250
PRTSYSRPT (print system report)
  command, 166, 167
PRTTNSRPT (print transaction report)
  command, 168
PSSA (program static storage area), 46
purge attributes, 45–48, 54–56, 206

QACTJOB system value, 36, 192, 193
QADLACTJ system value, 36, 193
QADLTOTJ system value, 36, 193
QAUDLVL system value, 214
QAUTOCFG system value, 193, 195
QBASACTLVL system value, 193, 194,
  198–199
QBASE subsystem, 44
QBASPOOL system value, 41, 193, 194,
  198–199
QBATCH subsystem, 44
QCMD program, 40, 42–43, 61
QCMN subsystem, 44, 224
QCMNRCYLMT system value, 193,
  196–197, 218
QCTL subsystem, 44
QCTLSBSD system value, 44, 93
QDBRCVYWT system value, 193, 197
QDEVRCYACN system value, 193, 196
QDSCJOBITV system value, 193, 195
QINACTITV system value, 193, 195
QINACTMSGQ system value, 193, 195
QINTER subsystem, 38–39, 44–45
QMAXACTLVL system value, 193, 194
QMCHPOOL, 193, 194, 197–198
QMODEL system value, 193
QPFRADJ system value, 48, 189–191, 193,
  194
QPGMR subsystem, 45, 214–215
QRCLSPLSTG system value, 193, 197
QSNADS, 45
QSPL subsystem, 44
QSRLNBR system value, 193

QSTRUPJD job, 41
QSYFIXAUT function, 213
QSYSSBSD, 45
QSYSWRK, 45
QTEMP library, 58
QTOTJOB system value, 36, 192, 193
QTSEPOOL system value, 52, 193, 194,
      205–206
queuing, 72–79
   disk I/O, 75–76
   FIFO, 72
   multi server, 73–75
   multiplier, 73–75
   prioritized, 72
   single server, 72–73
   effect on response time of, 72–73

RAID, 103–104
RAID-5, 103–104
RAMP-C, see benchmarks and pre-defined
      workloads
remote printing, increasing the throughput,
      218
remote users, using separate subsystems,
      216
resource utilization, 172
resource utilization expansion report, 174
response time
   components of, 6, 53–54
   calculation from service time and
      utilization, 74, 75
   versus throughput, 76
RGZPFM (reorganize physical file member)
      command, 232
RIP (relative internal performance), 20, 21
routing, 39–43
   data, 39, 41–43, 60–61
   entries, 39–43
   step, 43
RRTJOB (reroute job) command, 43
RTW, see pre-defined workloads
run priority, see execution priority, 50

SBMJOB (submit job) command, 43, 60–62
seize/lock conflicts, 182
service level agreement (SLA), 149–157
   fulfilling a, 154
   how to establish a, 151–154
   items for inclusion in a, 152–154
   monitoring a, 154–155
   need for a, 149–151, 155
   sample, 155–157
service management, 149
SETOBJACC (set object access) command,
      56, 231

shared pools
   *BASE, 41, 189
      size and activity level estimation,
         198–199
   *INTERACT, 41, 189, 200
   *MACHINE, 41, 189
      size calculation, 197–198, 201–202
      page fault guidelines, 201
   *SHRPOOL1 – 10, 189
   *SPOOL, 189
      size and activity level estimation, 199
short wait extended, 53
short waits, 52–53
SIGNOFF (sign off) command, 43, 58, 212
single level storage, 62–66
sizing, 69–94
   batch, 88–89
   disk space, 90–94
   example, see BEST/1
   factors determining, 69
   manual, 80–83
      CPU, 80–81
      disk, 81
      main storage, 82–83
   measured workloads for, 83–84
   objectives, 79–80
      response time aims as, 80
   predefined workloads for, 83–87
   purpose of, xvi–xvii
   use of BEST/1 for, 116–148
   user-defined workloads for, 88
SMAPP (system managed access path
      protection), 217
spool pool, see shared pools, *SPOOL
STRPFRCOL (start performance
      collection) command, 250
STRPFRMON (start performance
      monitor) command, 166
subsystem description POOLS attribute, 49
subsystem monitor, 34–35, 41
subsystems, 34–35, 41–43
   controlling, 44
   pools in, 40–41
   role in job creation, 37–45
   routing entries in, 39–40
   shipped with OS/400, 44–45
   workstation entries in, 38–39
system overheads, 212–217
   abnormal termination, 217
   authorization checks, 212–214
   disk housekeeping, 216
   IPL frequency, 215
   job and CL logging, 215
   operator and programmer functions,
      214–215

printing, 215
signing off and on, 212
system summary data report, 173
system tuning
action list, 162–163
documenting the process of, 162
expectations, 161–162
for a newly installed AS/400, 225–226
implementation, 189–226
preparing for, 61–188
questions covered by, xvi-xvii
system values, 36
documentation of, 183
recommended changes to, 192–199
used to provide job attributes, 37
System/36 Environment performance,
100–101
System/36 Environment tuning, 210–212
EVKJOBINIT parameter, 211, 212
EVKJOBPOL parameter, 211
EVKJOBPTY parameter, 211
LOG parameter, 212
MRTAUT parameter, 211
MRTDLY parameter, 211
System/36 Migration Aid, 100

task despatching, 49–52
TDE (task despatching element), 49–52
TDQ (task despatcher queue), 49–52
TFRGRPJOB (transfer to group job)
command, 59
TFRJOB (transfer job) command, 39
thrashing, 48
throughput
interactive
from individual user, 5–6
factors which determine total, 6–7
time slice
changing, 205–206
external, 51–52
internal, 49–51
time slice end (TSE), 51–52
TPC, 97–98
TPC-C, *see* benchmarks
transaction
complexity, 69–71
interactive vs. business, 5
report by 5 minute intervals, 180
statistics, 181
volume, 69–70

uneven disk activity, 204–205
user profile object, 36–37
utilization
guidelines, 76–79
thresholds, 76–79

VAT (virtual address translator), 62–66
virtual address, 62–66

WCBT (work control block table), 36, 58
work entries, 38–39, 41–43
work management, 34–66
introduction to, 34
purpose of subsystems in, 34–35
working set, 48, 54, 116
workload
and performance summary data form,
169
characterization, 69–71
monitoring 247–254
report, 171
workstation entries, 38–39, 41–43
WRKACTJOB (work with active jobs)
command
current total active jobs, 35–36
elapsed data, 165
for performance assessment, 165
WRKDSKSTS (work with disk status)
command, 187–188
WRKPFRCOL (work with performance
collection) command, 249, 250
WRKS36A (work with S/36 attributes)
command, 211
WRKS36PRCA (work with S/36 procedure
attributes) command, 211
WRKSBS, 40, 189
WRKSHRPOOL (work with shared pools)
command, 48
WRKSYSACT (work with system activity)
command, 251
WRKSYSSTS (work with system status)
command
changing pool sizes and activity levels
with, 48
for number of jobs in system, 36
for page fault rates, 45, 186
for performance assessment, 186
for pool documentation, 189
transition data display, 49, 53

Further Titles in the IBM McGraw-Hill Series

OS/2 Presentation Manager Programming   Bryan Goodyer
Hints and Tips

PC User's Guide   Peter Turner
Simple Steps to Powerful Personal Computing

The IBM RISC System/6000   Clive Harris

The IBM RISC System/6000 User Guide   Mike Leaver
Hardev Sanghera

MVS Systems Programming   Dave Elder-Vass

CICS Concepts and Uses   Jim Geraghty
A Management Guide

Dynamic Factory Automation   Alastair Ross

Writing OS/2 REXX Programs   Ronny Richardson